Classical Antiquity and the Politics of America

Classical Antiquity and the Politics of America

From George Washington
to George W. Bush

edited by

Michael Meckler

Baylor University Press
Waco, Texas USA

©2006 Baylor University Press
Waco, Texas 76798

Cover Design: Stephanie Blumenthal
Cover Images: Greece: Athens and The Capitol, c. 1880. Used by permission of the
  Granger Collection, New York.
Interior Design: Diane Smith

Library of Congress Cataloging-in-Publication Data

Classical antiquity and the politics of America / Michael Meckler, editor.
   p. cm.
 Includes bibliographical references and index.
 ISBN-13: 978-1-932792-32-4 (pbk. : alk. paper)
 1. United States--Politics and government. 2. Civilization, Classical--Influence. 3.
United States--Civilization--Classical influences I. Meckler, Michael.

 JK31.C53 2006
 320.973--dc22

                                            2006015944

Printed in the United States of America on acid-free paper.

in memoriam

M. R.
et
R. F. M.

Contents

Preface

This volume emerged from a panel organized by the editor at the annual meeting of the American Historical Association held in San Francisco in January 2002. The panel, on "Classical Antiquity and the United States Senate," contained earlier versions of the papers by Carl J. Richard, Caroline Winterer, Michael Meckler, and Robert F. Maddox that have been published in this volume. The panel was sponsored by the Association of Ancient Historians (AAH), and thanks are due to the then-president of the AAH, Richard Talbert, and the former AAH secretary-treasurer, Patricia Dintrone, for their assistance. Special thanks are also due to former AAH president Carol Thomas, who has long championed greater interaction between ancient historians and their Americanist colleagues. The fruits of such interaction include the essay in this volume by John Milton Cooper, Jr., which was originally delivered as a lecture at the annual AAH meeting held in Madison, Wisconsin, in May 2000. The other essays were solicited particularly for this volume.

The editor also wishes to express his gratitude to Frank Coulson and Fritz Graf, the directors of the Center for Epigraphical and Palaeographical Studies at The Ohio State University; to the Center's staff, Philip Forsythe and Wendy Watkins; and to the Chair of Ohio State's Department of Greek and Latin, David Hahm. Personal thanks are also owed to my parents for their sufferance.

This book is dedicated to the memory of Meyer Reinhold and Robert F. Maddox. Both men died within three months of each other in the summer and autumn of 2002, during the early development of this book. Meyer Reinhold passed away on July 2, 2002, at the age of ninety-two. Over the years he kindly offered his advice and assistance to several of this book's contributors. His own research from the 1960s through the 1980s examining American classicism lit the way for further studies, and he eagerly shared his insights with younger scholars. He helped found the International Society for the Classical Tradition, and its journal, *The International Journal of the Classical Tradition*. The circumstances of his own career, which included a decade-long period of involuntary departure from college teaching, would have provided him a prominent place within the history of American academia and its interaction with American politics even without his valuable contributions to scholarship. Yet his perseverance and longevity allowed him to make up for lost time and then some, for he did not retire from his final academic appointment until the age of eighty-five.

Robert F. Maddox did not get to enjoy such a long life. Maddox passed away on September 30, 2002, at the age of fifty-nine. A historian of twentieth-century America, Maddox was most concerned with chronicling the events and personalities of his native state of West Virginia. He spent nearly his entire life in the Mountain State, and had a distinguished career at Marshall University, where he served in several important administrative positions. But he was perhaps proudest of his role as a teacher and preserver of West Virginia history, which he fulfilled as director of Marshall's oral history of Appalachia program and as president of the West Virginia Historical Association.

Maddox was enthusiastic about participating in the AAH-sponsored panel in San Francisco, but deteriorating health prevented him from making the trip. Richard A. Baker, the historian of the United States Senate, kindly agreed to deliver Maddox's paper in addition to serving as the panel respondent. Maddox passed away before plans for the volume were finalized. In preparing Maddox's essay for publication, the editor is grateful for Richard Baker's advice and assistance.

Introduction

—Michael Meckler

Although retired from public office after leaving the presidency in 1809, Thomas Jefferson continued keenly to follow political news that reached his home at Monticello. In December 1819, Jefferson was increasingly troubled by the conflict in Congress over whether Missouri should be admitted to the Union as a state where slavery was permitted. The seventy-six-year-old statesman had long since resumed a regular correspondence with his predecessor and one-time rival, John Adams. Now in the crisis over the Missouri question, Jefferson wrote to Adams of his concerns that the issue of slavery would tear the young nation asunder.

Jefferson's letter also contained musings over the correspondence of the Roman orator Cicero. Cicero, too, had lived in tumultuous times, witnessing the collapse of the Roman Republic, Julius Caesar's rise to absolute power, and the immediate aftermath of Caesar's own assassination. Yet Jefferson was hesitant to draw too many similarities between the Roman and American republics.

"When the enthusiasm however kindled by Cicero's pen and principles," wrote Jefferson, "subsides into cool reflection, I ask myself What was that government which the virtues of Cicero were so zealous to

1

restore, and the ambition of Caesar to subvert? And if Caesar had been as virtuous as he was daring and sagacious, what could he, even in the plenitude of his usurped power have done to lead his fellow citizens into good government? I do not say *restore it*, because they never had it, from the rape of the Sabines to the ravages of the Caesars."[1]

The eighty-four-year-old Adams agreed with Jefferson about the nature of the Roman Republic. Concerning the Romans, Adams wrote in reply, "I never could discover that they possessed much Virtue, or real Liberty there. Patricians were in general griping Usurers and Tyrannical Creditors in all ages. Pride, Strength and Courage were all the Virtues that composed their National Characters. A few of their Nobles, effecting simplicity frugality and Piety, perhaps really possessing them, acquired Popularity amongst the Plebeians and extended the power and Dominions of the Republic and advanced in Glory till Riches and Luxury came in, sat like an incubus on the Republic, victamque ulcissitur orbem."[2]

The Latin phrase with which Adams ended this section of his letter was taken, with not the best memory of grammar and syntax, from a line in the sixth satire of the Roman poet Juvenal, *luxuria incubuit victumque ulciscitur orbem* ("Luxury has rested upon and avenged a conquered world").[3] Throughout this letter Adams expressed a dark concern that the hard work that resulted in prosperity in turn created luxury and moral decay. This pessimism extended even to the American republic's own future.

"I am sometimes Cassandra enough to dream," Adams wrote in the paragraph preceding his above mentioned judgment on the Romans, "that another Hamilton, another Burr might rend this mighty Fabric in twain, or perhaps into a leash, and few more choice Spirits of the same Stamp, might produce as many Nations in North America as there are in Europe."

The joining in a single sentence of Cassandra, the unheeded Trojan prophetess of doom from ancient literature, with the names of Alexander Hamilton and Aaron Burr, demonstrates how integral classical antiquity was to the foundation and interpretation of the governing principles of the United States. The concerns over tensions tearing at the United States in 1819 naturally evoked contemplation of the tensions that destroyed the polities—both real and mythic—of the ancient Mediterranean.[4] Yet the centrality of the Greeks and Romans to early American political thought tended to be discounted by scholars for much of the twentieth century, the extensive allusions by the Founders to ancient literature and history interpreted merely as the ornaments of erudition.[5] During the 1970s and 1980s, a series of articles and essays written by Meyer Reinhold brought greater attention to the influence of antiquity on the political and cultural atmosphere of the colonial period and the early years of the republic.[6] Reinhold's work has laid the foundation for even more extensive studies of the influence of classics on American politics in the eighteenth and nineteenth centuries.[7]

These studies, however, have had only a limited impact among historians and political scientists. Elaine K. Swift, in her study on the creation and development of the United States Senate during its first half century, sees the inspiration for the Senate—despite the legislative body's overtly classical name—as deriving solely from the British House of Lords.[8] Charles A. Kromkowski analyzes how the rules were developed for the apportionment of representatives in Congress in terms of modern game theory, where the expectations were conditioned by colonial patterns of representation.[9]

By framing the creation of United States political institutions solely in terms of adaptations of British and colonial models, these scholars distort the rationale and ideology underlying the workings of American politics. The early years of the republic provided the opportunity for experimentation in how governments should be organized and what governments should do. The Founders and their immediate successors deliberately looked *beyond* their own limited experience to engage alternative understandings of how society should be structured and regulated. In the Bible they found one source for such an alternative understanding; the ancient Greeks and Romans provided another.[10]

Rather than being viewed as a relic of an archaic educational system, references and allusions to classical antiquity display American political thought at its most innovative and idealistic. From slavery to the line-item veto, from freedom of speech to "preemptory first strike," crucial issues of United States policy have often been informed by analysis of the history and literature of the Greeks and Romans. Although the relevance of classical antiquity to American political debate has regularly been questioned from the time of the Founders to the present, the persistent attention paid to the ancients' voice, whether thundering forth or heard only in faint echo, suggests that today's historians and political scientists should pay greater heed both to their own study of ancient Greece and Rome, as well as to those decision makers throughout American history who have been influenced by the world of classical antiquity.

The rationale for the political relevance of the Greeks and Romans has varied among their American supporters. Some have argued that classical antiquity's importance is historically contingent. By this argument, the politics, culture, and society of the United States are viewed as having developed in linear descent from what existed in the British colonial period, back through the Enlightenment, the Renaissance, and the European Middle Ages, to the Roman Empire and before that, to classical Greece. Thus no understanding of contemporary America can be complete without examining the underlying etiology of the entire Western tradition. Classical antiquity's placement at the beginning of that tradition necessarily privileges the Greeks and Romans as a focus of study and attention.

Even those who argue for a fundamental discontinuity between modernity and antiquity may also accept a historically contingent rationale for paying heed to the distant past when making contemporary political decisions. Most of the constitutional principles that today guide the operations of American government were devised in the eighteenth century by individuals who formulated these principles based upon their interpretations of classical antiquity. Regardless of whether the modern world truly represents the continuation and culmination of antiquity, many of the Founders operated as if it were so. Their assumptions about classical antiquity require those of us still living under the rules they fashioned to seek a greater understanding of the ancient Greece and Rome that was important to them within their eighteenth-century context. A similar rationale (with a focus, however, on another century) also underlies the importance of antiquity for fundamentalist Christians who became politically engaged in their attempts to refashion the early Church of the first century A.D. in the United States of the eighteenth, nineteenth, and twentieth centuries, and now in the twenty-first century. That Jesus walked the earth in the time of the Roman emperors Augustus and Tiberius has long been imbued with historical significance. Therefore, to understand the relationship between government and religion, between Caesar and Christ, one must also understand with greater precision the world of the ancient Mediterranean into which the Church emerged.

Others have maintained that the value of classical antiquity to American politics is ahistorical, with no genealogical connection whatsoever to the circumstances surrounding the creation of the United States or to the course of Western civilization. Under this rationale, the ancient Greeks and Romans uncovered universal truths about human behavior and social organization. These truths are not culturally bound but apply to all civilizations, including our own. A variation on this rationale admits that the ideas of the ancients were indeed culturally bound and historically constrained by their own society and existing beliefs, but that the eloquence wherewith they reported those ideas made the Greeks and Romans remarkable witnesses to alternative possibilities for structuring politics and society. The discontinuities between the inhabitants of the ancient Mediterranean and those of the United States of America—the ancients' remoteness in space and time, their remove from current mindsets, and their freedom from contemporary bias—provide them their authority.

Supporters of classical antiquity's relevance have not always been consistent in their choice of rationale, and indeed they may promote both historical and ahistorical rationales simultaneously. One might argue, for example, that the ancients both teach us universal truths about human nature *and* represent the foundation of a Western civilization to which America is an heir. A comment by Jefferson to Adams illustrates the fluidity in trying to rationalize the lessons of classical antiquity to American political debate. In an 1813 letter, Jefferson wrote that the Federalist and Democratic-Republican parties were the descendants of ancient political factions. "The same political parties which now agitate the U.S. have existed thro' all time. . . . Whether the power of the people or that of 'the aristoi' should prevail were questions which kept the states of Greece and Rome in eternal convulsions, as they schismatize every people whose minds and mouths are not shut up by the gag of a despot."[11] Jefferson's recourse to ancient history both demonstrated a universal truth *and* placed American partisan politics within a historical tradition.

The frequent and obvious allusions to antiquity in the eighteenth and early nineteenth centuries may compel some present-day historians and political scientists to concede reluctantly that study of classical antiquity had a formative influence on the Founders, yet these scholars often ignore the subsequent use of the ancients in political debates during the twentieth century and today. Certainly the way in which classical antiquity is invoked has been transformed due to changes that have taken place in American education. From the 1860s through the 1960s, reforms gradually displaced classics from its central role in secondary schools and universities. As a result, for decades many educated Americans have lacked basic knowledge about ancient Greece and Rome and have sometimes failed to recognize or appreciate how modern policy discussions reflect ancient ideas. Gone are the frequent appeals to the ancients that were characteristic of discussions in the early republic. Direct quotations from classical authors fail to convey any meaning to an audience bereft of Latin and Greek. Literary and historical allusions must be limited to only the most commonly recognized names and events.

This diminution in the obvious manifestations of classical allusions in political discourse during the twentieth century is also a product of the increased professionalization of American scholars of antiquity. The American Philological Association was founded in 1869, and the Archaeological Institute of America in 1879. During the twentieth century, as membership in these organizations increasingly came to dominate college and university classics departments, and as academic appointments came to be channeled through a small number of doctoral programs, the professoriate in the United States became increasingly isolated from the educated populace at large, including political decision makers. What the professoriate deemed worthwhile about the ancient Greeks and Romans did not necessarily correspond to the interests and perceptions of the general public. Such isolation within the ivory tower has not, of course, been unique to classics, but the erstwhile closeness between classical antiquity and American political discourse has made this isolation all the more acute.[12]

By the end of the twentieth century, the rare writer on current events who had received professional training in classics (such as Garry Wills, who earned a Ph.D. from Yale; Victor Davis Hanson, with a Ph.D. from Stanford; or Daniel Mendelsohn, with a Ph.D. from Princeton) managed to bridge both worlds. Those without academic credentials in classics, however, who produce writings that directly or indirectly relate classical antiquity to contemporary events, have often found their interests and opinions largely ignored among academic classicists. Even when an author has such widespread prominence in public affairs or in another academic discipline that his or her book necessarily gains popular attention, such as radical journalist I. F. Stone's 1988 book *The Trial of Socrates*, response among academic classicists remains muted.[13] Although Stone's book has been widely adopted in introductory political science courses and remains in print nearly two decades after its initial publication, academic classicists almost never assign the book. Stone's book rarely is cited in articles in professional classics journals, and when it is mentioned, it is usually dismissed for a simplistic understanding of original sources and a failure to acknowledge the importance of religion in Athenian society.[14] Such criticisms are not unfounded, yet more recent accounts of Socrates' trial written by academic classicists have failed to interest the American public to the same degree. Clearly Stone's account, while inadequate for academic classicists, seemed relevant to many politically engaged Americans. The failure of academic classicism to nourish and respond to popular interest in the ancient Greeks and Romans is yet another factor in the apparent decline of classical antiquity from its once central position in fashioning the ideology underlying the role and operations of government in the United States.

Yet allusions to classical antiquity, however infrequent and at times inconspicuous, continue to appear in American political discourse. During debate in the United States Senate in 2001 over the appropriations budget for the Interior Department, Senator John McCain of Arizona introduced an amendment to strike funding for the refurbishment of an iron statue of Vulcan, the Roman god of the forge, that resides in a park in Birmingham, Alabama. McCain's amendment was eventually defeated, but he used the opportunity to bring in playful references to classical mythology in his criticism of what he deemed wasteful government spending.

> At first blush, having the Federal Government give money to a Roman god may appear to violate the constitutional separation of

church and state. Others, with some reason, may believe that this is a rather strange use of limited tax dollars. After all, while the on-budget Federal surplus is rapidly dwindling, why should Federal dollars pay for a face-lift of a statue of a Roman god in Alabama?

But, Mr. President, I worry this appropriation may set a dangerous precedent for others to follow that will only add millions and millions to the billions and billions and billions in pork-barrel spending doled out year after year.

For example, what is to stop a Senator from sunny Arizona or New Mexico from demanding Federal dollars for a statue of Apollo, god of the sun?

Or how do we prevent a Senator from California to beseech money for a statue of Bacchus, god of wine?

Or a Senator from Georgia, home to the great city of Athens, from asking Federal funds to pay tribute to the Goddess Athena?

Or even a Senator from the home of some of the best hunting this side of the Mississippi, West Virginia, from getting Federal funds for Artemis, the ancient Greek goddess of the hunt?

Maybe this is the time to stop this. Not one more Federal dollar should be spent on this kind of foolishness.

I ask my colleagues to extinguish this Roman god of fire and strike a victory for taxpayers—and Metis, the goddess of prudence—by throttling down our insatiable appetite for pork-barrel spending starting today.[15]

McCain's use of mythological references was, of course, occasioned by the particular example of spending he chose to highlight, the statue of Vulcan. Undoubtedly one of McCain's staffers mined a textbook on classical mythology in preparing the senator for his humorous remarks. Nonetheless, how McCain employed these mythological references reveals one way in which, even in the twenty-first century, classical antiquity can still be brought into political debate. McCain tapped into contemporary sensibilities that view study of classical antiquity as a cobwebbed exercise of the ivory tower irrelevant to modern life. His list of gods and goddesses to be honored by the various states provided a delightfully ludicrous juxtaposition between modern America and long-abandoned deities of the ancient Mediterranean. McCain's list of states concluded with West Virginia, a clear nod to one of that state's senators, Robert C. Byrd, who relished peppering his speeches with allusions to the Greeks and Romans as much as he did gaining a disproportionate share of federal funds for projects in West Virginia.[16]

In the end, however, McCain did not present classical mythology solely as an object of ridicule. His final reference is to the goddess Metis. The name Metis was the ancient Greek word for "planning," and the goddess developed from the personification of the qualities of intelligence and foresight. Of the divinities mentioned in McCain's list, only Metis was understood by the ancients solely as an abstract quality. By affording approval to Metis alone, McCain was allowing the ancients some value in twenty-first-century America, but only with regard to their abstract and analytical reasoning. Despite its mocking tone, McCain's soliloquy on the statue of Vulcan reaffirmed that the philosophical ideals of the ancients still had some authority in American political debate.

That authority may emerge in a wide variety of political issues. Less than eight years before McCain's romp through classical mythology, a trial took place in Colorado to evaluate whether an amendment to the state constitution, approved by the voters in 1992, violated the United States Constitution. The Colorado amendment would have prohibited legal status for homosexuals, along with the accompanying protections and preferential treatment. Some of the testimony at the trial dealt with the understandings of the ancient Greeks toward homosexuality, since homosexual relationships were commonly found within ancient Greek society. That classical Greece should provide evidence for how American government deals with homosexuality indicates that the residual authority of antiquity remains very real. Indeed, one of the highlights of the trial was a bitter dispute between two scholars over the proper English translation of the Greek word *tolmema* in Plato, *Laws* 636c.[17]

The debate over gay rights is not the only area of modern political debate where the ancients are regularly invoked. Aspects of classical antiquity remain emblematic of contemporary issues among certain political groups. Libertarians cite the fall of the Roman Empire as an example of the dangers of bureaucracy.[18] Supporters of Afrocentric education for Black Americans claim Pharaonic and Ptolemaic Egypt as sources for Greek and Roman civilization, and thus valorize ancient Egypt as an equivalent, if not superior focus of learning and inspiration.[19] Advocates of a strong military idealize the organization of the armed forces of the ancient Greeks.[20]

The exemplary power of classical antiquity has remained a feature of policy making and political discourse throughout the history of the United States. This volume examines how that power has been employed from the time of the Founders to today. Scholars from classics, history, and political philosophy have prepared essays on topics as diverse as the establishment of the United States Senate; the debate over how best to transform African American society in the aftermath of slavery; and the use of the American military as a means of promoting Western ideals. The individual essays stand alone in portraying the connections between classics and American politics for a particular event at a particular time. Yet taken as a whole, the collection reveals the changes that have occurred in the use, prestige, and influence of the ancient Greeks and Romans.

Furthermore, each of the essays contains points of intersection with other essays in the collection, and the entire volume can be read as a continuous narrative on the history of American classicism, at least with regard to education and public policy. A summary of that history may be useful in discerning trends and understanding the relationship of the individual essays to these larger trends.[21] In colonial America, formal education involved extensive study of the Greek and Latin languages, as well as ancient history and political philosophy. Nearly all of the Founders experienced this form of classical education at some level. There were, however, a few leaders in the early republic who wished to diminish the role of classics in general, and ancient languages in particular, within American education. Their attempts were by and large unsuccessful. In a celebrated response to a resolution introduced in the Connecticut state senate in 1828, the leaders of Yale College affirmed the central position of classics within higher education. During the early decades of the nineteenth century, it remained common for American colleges, whose numbers expanded along with the population and territory of the new nation, to require their students to have a working knowledge of Greek and Latin for admission and graduation.

As the century progressed, the United States witnessed profound changes within society, politics, and education. Immigration and industrialization transformed the nation's white population from one that was overwhelmingly rural, Protestant, and of British descent, into a heavily urbanized mix of European ethnicities that included large numbers of Catholics and a significant number of Jews. The end of slavery brought attention to the question of educational opportunities for African Americans, who as slaves were prohibited from even basic literacy. Rising to social and economic prominence were tycoons who had little or no experience, and even less patience, with classical education. The emergence of Jacksonian democracy before the Civil War, and of political populism after the war, served to taint as elitist the cultural traditions from the colonial period, including classical education. The expanded role of government in the foundation and maintenance of educational institutions—notably in the Morrill Act passed by Congress in 1862 that established the land-grant colleges—gave these social forces the political influence to effect changes to the educational system. Assisting science and industry became a primary goal of both public and private education. The cultivation of virtue that had been at the heart of classical education seemed a quaint notion that failed to ameliorate the nation's immediate and material concerns, and failed to address in any substantial way the chasmic social and economic inequalities that characterized the United States at the dawn of the twentieth century.

By 1917, when Andrew Fleming West, the dean of Princeton University's graduate school, organized a major conference promoting the role of classics in college education, most colleges had already abandoned ancient languages as requirements for admission or graduation. Although the study of Greek withered in American secondary schools as a direct result, high school enrollments in Latin continued to climb into the middle of the twentieth century. Furthermore, colleges began developing large lecture courses on the civilization and literature of classical antiquity in which all of the readings were in English translation. The children of immigrants were important causes for both developments, since these students' families and teachers viewed a basic knowledge of Latin and of Western civilization as keys to successful integration within American society. The level of knowledge about classical antiquity that was common for educated Americans in the mid-twentieth century was not as deep as that which was common among the far fewer who were college educated a century earlier, but in some ways its extent was broader, since a greater proportion of Americans were attending college and taking these Great Books courses.

High school Latin enrollments collapsed in the 1960s. In the public schools, Latin faced post-Sputnik pressure for more classroom time on math and science (and consequently less time on foreign languages). In the parochial schools, the Second Vatican Council's call for the Mass to be delivered in the vernacular removed Latin from its previously essential role in Catholic education. High school Latin enrollments recovered slightly during the 1980s and 1990s, but for nearly half a century, the overwhelming majority of college educated Americans have never studied an ancient language at any time in their lives. At many colleges, Great Books and other classical civilization-in-translation courses—particularly introductory courses on classical mythology—remain popular offerings. Elementary knowledge of the sort imparted by these large lecture courses filtered through American society at the end of the twentieth century, though the resonances of classical antiquity among politicians and policymakers of the time were perhaps the faintest they had ever been throughout American history.

Some of the themes in the history of American classicism connect individuals discussed in separate essays of this volume. For example, Edward Everett in the early nineteenth century, and William Linn Westermann at the beginning of the twentieth, both earned doctoral degrees from German universities. German classicism, as it affected both education and politics, had a profound influence on the United States in the nineteenth century. That influence continued through the twentieth century, as Jewish and leftist intellectuals with extensive training in classics fled Nazi Germany for the United States in the 1930s. These refugees included the sociologist Leo Lowenthal, the political scientist Hans J. Morgenthau, and the philosopher Leo Strauss. Through these refugees, the German tradition of *Altertumswissenschaft* was diffused throughout the social sciences in postwar America, including American politics.

Classicists are particularly fond of academic genealogies. The discipline's compact size in the United States throughout the nation's history ensures that associations and filiations are inevitable among scholars in Greek and Latin philology, ancient history, and ancient philosophy. Among Edward Everett's Greek students at Harvard was Cornelius C. Felton, who later joined the Harvard faculty when Everett was serving in the U.S. House of Representatives. In the course of his career, Everett became president of Harvard, U.S. secretary of state, and a U.S. senator. Felton (who at the end of his career also became Harvard's president) in turn taught Greek to George F. Hoar, who later served in Congress as both a representative and a senator.[22]

Some of the connections are not always as direct. William Linn Westermann, while a professor of ancient history at Columbia University, taught Meyer Reinhold and Naphtali Lewis. Reinhold and Lewis were compelled to resign from the faculty of Brooklyn College during the anti-Communist fervor of the 1950s. One of the students at Brooklyn College at the time was Donald Kagan. A decade and a half later, Kagan was a professor of ancient history at Cornell University during the armed occupation of a campus building by militant black students in 1969. Disgusted by the university administration's capitulation to the militants' demands, Kagan quit Cornell for Yale. Also choosing to leave Cornell were philosopher Allan Bloom and political scientist Walter Berns, both of whom initially moved to the University of Toronto. Bloom and Berns had been students of Leo Strauss at the University of Chicago, where Bloom eventually returned to teach, while Berns moved to Georgetown University. By the late 1980s, Kagan, Bloom, and Berns had become nationally recognized in political and cultural circles as leading conservative thinkers.[23]

By remaining cognizant of the connections among the people and themes of the individual essays, the reader may trace more than two and a quarter centuries of adaptations of and reactions to the use of classical antiquity in American political debate. The selection of topics in these essays can by no means be considered exhaustive of the extensive influence of ancient Greece and Rome, but their variety demonstrates the adaptability and continuing authority of the ancients. Both in domestic and foreign policy, appeals to classical antiquity have had a role in shaping debate and decision making. This volume attempts to give historians and political scientists greater awareness of that role, both as it existed in the past and how it operates today.

In Book 8 of Virgil's *Aeneid*, the Greek refugee Evander gives the Trojan refugee Aeneas a tour of the future site of the city of Rome. In place of the impressive temples, built-up streets, and smart shops of Virgil's own day, the poet described a rustic landscape of forests, hills, and huts. At first glance, the locations must have seemed alien and unrecognizable to Virgil's original audience in the frenetic metropolis of a million souls that was Rome as it existed in the days of the emperor Augustus. Yet throughout Evander's brief tour were hints of the golden city that Rome would become.[24]

The depiction of classical antiquity's influence on American politics may likewise initially seem alien to political scientists and American historians here in the twenty-first century. Yet once the intellectual landscape of American politics is stripped to its basic topography, the importance of the ancient Greeks and Romans becomes readily apparent. The essays in this volume attempt to reveal that importance, and how it has developed and changed from the Founders to the present day.

Chapter 1

Classical Education in Colonial America

—William J. Ziobro

> Tacitus I consider as the first writer in the world without a single exception. His book is a compound of history and morality of which we have no other example.
> —*Thomas Jefferson*[1]

Despite voluminous writings that reveal his polymath interests through essays, speeches, and letters, Thomas Jefferson wrote only one book: his *Notes on the State of Virginia* in 1782.[2] The book outlined a variety of proposals for the organization and operation of the new state government. Among Jefferson's proposals was a system of public education for Virginia, which included a scheme whereby twenty students from across the state would each year be provided free education at state-established grammar (secondary) schools, and ten would have received a free education at the College of William and Mary, then the only degree-granting institution in the state. In discussing the curriculum for his proposed state grammar schools, Jefferson commended the usefulness of studying the ancient languages of Greek and Latin as tools for attaining a deeper knowledge of the wisdom of classical antiquity. He contrasted the prevailing attitudes of Europeans toward ancient languages with those in the

13

nascent United States of America. "The learning of Greek and Latin, I am told, is going into disuse in Europe," Jefferson wrote. "I know not what their manners and occupations may call for: but it would be very ill-judged in us to follow their examples in this instance."[3]

He further discussed the political merit of historical studies, especially ancient history, at all levels of public education. "History," Jefferson wrote, "by apprising them [students] of the past will enable them to judge of the future; it will avail them of the experiences of other times and other nations; it will qualify them as judges of the actions and designs of men; it will enable them to know ambition under every guise it may assume; and knowing it, to defeat its views."[4]

Jefferson was not alone among the Founders in his opinion that study of classical antiquity, through its languages and history, provided salutary protections for the people in the democratic exercise of political power.[5] John Adams also extolled the merits of a classical education. He stated that if in his youth he had studied Greek and Latin more diligently than mathematics and natural sciences, which were his natural inclinations, he would have been better prepared for his career as a politician and states-man—a truly interesting reflection since from the outset of his public life Adams had deliberately imitated Cicero in all his legal and political engagements.[6] At any rate, he was not about to allow his son, John Quincy Adams, to stray in his own educational efforts. In the spring of 1780, with the recently born United States still at war with Britain, the elder Adams was on a diplomatic mission in Paris on behalf of the Con-tinental Congress. The twelve-year-old John Quincy Adams accompanied his father to Europe, where he was enrolled at a school in Passy, roughly sixty miles southeast of Paris. During this time, John Adams wrote sev-eral letters expressing concern that his son was not giving adequate atten-tion to the learning of Greek and Latin, languages the elder Adams described as "useful and necessary."[7]

The utility of classical education did not detract from the refinement it provided to English composition or from the beauty of expression and thought revealed in examining ancient literature in the original—two other common reasons given in the eighteenth century for study of the language and ideas of the Greeks and Romans.[8] Yet the *political* impor-tance attached to classical antiquity ensured its promotion in the public colleges and universities established in the years following the American Revolution. For example, classical education formed the only course of study at the University of North Carolina, which opened in 1795, and at the University of Georgia, which opened in 1801. Very late in his life, Jef-ferson became the creative and motivational force behind the founding of the University of Virginia. He was solely responsible for the design of its classically inspired buildings, the selection of its first faculty, and the format of its earliest curriculum. Needless to say, classical antiquity held a prominent position in the entrance and graduation requirements as well as in the curriculum itself when the university opened in 1825.[9]

Not all of the Founders were as enamored of the Greeks and Romans as were Jefferson and Adams. Prominent critics of classical education included Benjamin Franklin, Thomas Paine, and the physician and signer of the Declaration of Independence, Benjamin Rush. These critics saw the study of classical antiquity as irrelevant to the advance of scientific knowledge, a distraction from the mastery of modern foreign languages, and out of step with the egalitarian spirit of the American Revolution. Some even argued that the paganism and decadence in the tales from classical mythology rendered the ancients baneful to the moral development of the new American republic. In a letter to John Adams in 1789, Rush chose to classify the study of Greek and Latin "with Negro slavery and spiritous liquors, and consider them as, though in a lesser degree, unfriendly to the progress of morals, knowledge, and religion in the United States."[10]

Rush's views, however, remained very much in the minority in the young republic. Neither Benjamin Franklin nor Rush were able to diminish the centrality of Greek and Latin within the early curriculum of the University of Pennsylvania, of which Franklin was the founder and long-time trustee, and Rush a member of the faculty. Nor could Rush displace the study of ancient languages from the curriculum of either Dickinson College or Franklin College (now Franklin and Marshall College), two other Pennsylvania colleges in whose founding Rush had been instrumental. Undoubtedly, part of the allegiance to classical education stemmed from the fact that nearly all of the Founders had themselves begun study of the Greeks and Romans from an early age. In this regard, it is worth noting that Paine never learned Latin, and that Franklin's formal education ended at age ten after only two years of grammar school. Rush, however, experienced a full classical education, which he came to detest later in life.[11]

Although Jefferson left a written record of his educational plans for others and was ever ready to recommend a detailed list of classical authors to young Virginia gentlemen, he was strangely silent about the details of his own education, especially his early training. To be sure, it certainly was classical in content, as all formal education was in the eighteenth century. The only description, however, which Jefferson has provided of his own early study of Latin and Greek is a brief one in his *Auto-Biography*, written at the dusk of his life in 1821:

> He [his father, Peter Jefferson] placed me at the English school at five years of age; and at the Latin at nine, where I continued until his

death [1757]. My teacher, Mr. Douglas, a clergyman from Scotland, with the rudiments of Latin and Greek languages, taught me the French; and on the death of my father, I went to the Reverend Mr. Maury, a correct classical scholar, with whom I continued two years; and then, to wit, in the spring of 1760, went to William and Mary college, where I continued two years.[12]

By the time of his arrival at the College of William and Mary in 1760, Thomas Jefferson was most assuredly an accomplished classicist, but the specific program of study whereby he acquired his language skills in ancient Greek and Latin is only vaguely known. He undoubtedly had previously read the very popular school authors Virgil, Cicero, Ovid, Terence, and Horace, but it is difficult to determine in what sequence he read them.

The pattern of settlement in the Southern colonies made the establishment of preparatory academies difficult. Boys from well-to-do families lived on widely scattered plantations, and their introduction to ancient languages was left mostly to the discretion of the local minister or other college educated men who commonly served as tutors, either in one-on-one learning arrangements, or with just a handful of students. In Jefferson's eighteenth-century South, there simply did not exist a rigidly maintained or universally accepted classical curriculum, such as that which was advertised and followed in the larger, well established Latin grammar schools of the more densely populated seaport communities of New England. And yet, however varied the sequence of study of the classical authors may have been in the different geographical areas of colonial America, there is no evidence to suggest anything other than a remarkable homogeneity in the core list of authors read, whether they were studied in the grammar schools of New England, or on widely scattered plantations in the South. In short, the classical authors with whom Jefferson and his fellow Virginians George Wythe, George Mason, and James Madison were familiar, were virtually identical to those authors whom John Hancock and John Adams of Massachusetts, or John Trumbull of Connecticut, had studied in school.

The uniform familiarity of eighteenth-century educated Americans with a set core of traditional Latin authors is directly attributable to the common British heritage of classical study that formed the basis of colonial American education. Furthermore, the clearly defined objective of the colonial-era Latin grammar school of the North, as well as of the private tutoring prevalent in the South, was to prepare young men to meet the entrance requirements of a college. In colonial America, only nine such colleges were chartered to award degrees: Harvard, William and Mary, Yale, the College of New Jersey (Princeton), King's College (Columbia), the College of Philadelphia (University of Pennsylvania), the College of Rhode Island (Brown), Queen's College (Rutgers), and Dartmouth. All provided an education preoccupied with the study of ancient texts, and all required knowledge of Greek and Latin for admission.

At Harvard College, founded in 1636, these simple admission requirements were described in 1642:

> When any schollar is able to read Tully [Cicero] or such like classicall Latine Authore *ex tempore*, & make and speake true Latin in verse and prose, *suo (ut aiunt) Marte*, and decline perfectly the paradigmes of Nounes and Verbes in the Greeke tongue, then may hee bee admitted into the Colledge, nor shall any claim admission before such qualifications.[13]

Harvard's entrance requirements changed little during the next century. In 1734, for example, very similar requirements needed to be satisfied for admission to Harvard:

> Whoever upon examination by the President, and two at least of the Tutors, shall be found able *ex tempore* to read, construe, and parse Tully, Virgil, or such like common classical Latin authors, and to write true Latin in prose, and to be skilled in making Latin verse, or at least in the rules of Prosodia, and to read, construe, and parse ordinary Greek, as in the New Testament, Isocrates, or such like, and decline the paradigms of Greek nouns and verbs, having withal good testimony of his past blameless behaviour, shall be looked upon as qualified for admission into Harvard College.[14]

The admission procedure for an applicant to Yale College, chartered in 1701, was similar to that of Harvard and consisted of an examination of a few, standard classical authors. The college rector, sometimes assisted by a nearby minister, also a college graduate, administered the test. The Yale entrance examination also aimed at the same objective as that of Harvard, namely, to determine whether the applicant was "duly prepared and expert in Latin and Greek authors, both poetic and oratorical, as also making Good Latin."[15]

The College of New Jersey, chartered in 1746, also required that its applicants be competent in the classical languages. A student would be admitted there in 1748 only if he could "render Virgil and Tully's orations into English and turn English into true & grammatical Latin and translate any part of the four Evangelists from Greek into Latin or English."[16] It can likewise be assumed that the College of William and Mary, chartered in 1693, required all its applicants, Thomas Jefferson included, to satisfy similar classical language entrance requirements, but the exact authors included in its early entrance examinations are unknown since its eighteenth-century records were destroyed by fire.[17]

Every colonial college specifically required knowledge of Cicero and Virgil, and familiarity with elementary Greek for admission.[18] No college, however, was as precise as King's College in listing by title which individual works of the classical authors were needed to satisfy its entrance requirements. In 1785, for example, after King's College had closed during the American Revolution, the now reopened and renamed Columbia College demanded that:

> an applicant must possess the ability to render into English, Caesar's *Commentaries of the Gallic War*, the four orations of Cicero vs. Catiline; the first four Books of Vergil's *Aeneid*; and the Gospels from the Greek.[19]

Understanding the curriculum of the early American Latin grammar school today would be a woefully hopeless task, were it based solely on the scanty information contained in these descriptions of the entrance requirements of the early American colleges. Fortunately, two other documents, which have survived the passage of time, provide detailed information about the classroom pedagogy and, equally important, the sequence in which the classical authors were studied in the Latin grammar school of colonial America. These documents are Cotton Mather's *Corderius Americanus*, a eulogy written in 1708 for Ezekiel Cheever (1615–1708), the famous master of the Boston Latin School; and a letter from Cheever's successor, Nathaniel Williams, sent in 1712 to Nehemiah Hobart, a Senior Fellow at Harvard.[20] Williams's letter, which describes the curriculum pursued by the students at the Boston Latin School as they prepared for admission to Harvard College, reads as follows:

> 1.2.3 The first three years are spent first in Learning by heart & then acc:[ording] to their capacities understanding the Accidence and Nomenclator, in construing & parsing acc:[ording] to the English rules of Syntax *Sententiae Pueriles* Cato & Corderius & Aesops Fables.[21]

> 4. The 4th year, or sooner if their capacities allow it, they are entered upon Erasmus to which they are allou'd no English, but are taught to translate it by the help of the Dictionary and Accidence, which English translation of theirs is written down fair by each of them, after the reciting of the lesson, and then brought to the Master for his observation and the correction both as to the Translatio & orthography: This when corrected is carefully reserved till fryday, and then render'd into Latin of the Author exactly instead of the old way of Repitition, and in the afternoon of that day it is (a part of it) varied for them as to mood tense case number &c and given them to translate into Latin, still keeping to the words of the Author. An example of which you have in the paper marked on the backside A.

These continue to read AEsops Fables with ye English translation, the better to help them in the aforesaid translating. They are also now initiated in the Latin grammar, and begin to give the Latin rules in *Propr: As in pres:* [*Propria: As in praesenti*] & Syntax in their parsing; and at the latter end of the year enter upon Ovid *de Tristibus* (which is recited by heart on the usual time fryday afternoon) & upon translating English into Latin, out of mr Garretson's exercises.[22]

5. The fifth year they are entered upon Tullies Epistles (Still continuing the use of Erasmus, in the morning & Ovid *de Trist*[*ibus*]: afternoon) the Elegancies of which are remark'd and improv'd in the afternoon of the day they learn it, by translating an English which contains the phrase something altered, and besides recited by heart on the repetition day. Ov[id] *Metam*[*orphoses*]: is learn'd by these at the latter end of the year, so also Prosodia Scanning & turning & making of verses, & 2 days in the week they continue to turn mr. Gar[retson's] English Ex[ercises] into Latin, w[hen] the afternoons exerc[ise] is ended, and turn a fable into a verse a distich in a day.

6. The sixth year they are entered upon Tullies *Offices* & Luc[ius] Flor[us]: for the forenoon, continuing the use of Ovid's *Metam-*[*orphoses*]: in the afternoon, & at the end of the Year they read Virgil: The Elegancies of Tull[ius's] *Off*[*ices*]: are improved in the afternoon as is aforesaid of Tull[ius's]: *Epist*[*les*]: & withal given the master in writing when the lesson is recited, & so are the phrases they can discover in Luc[ius] Fl[orus]. All of which they have mett with in that week are comprehended in a dialogue on Fryday forenoon, and afternoon they turn a Fable in Lat[in] Verse. Every week these make a Latin Epistle, the last quarter of the Year, when also they begin to learn Greek, & Rhetorick.[23]

7. The seventh year they read Tullie's *Orations* & Justin for the Latin and Greek Testam[en]t Isocrates *Orat*[*ions*]: Homer & Hesiod for the Greek in the forenoons & Vergil Horace Juvenal & Persius afternoons. As to their exercises after the afternoon lessons are ended they translate Mundays & Tuesdays an Engl[ish] Dialogue containing a Praxis upon the Phrases out of Godwin's *Roman Antiquities*. Wensdays they compose a Praxis on the Elegancies & Pithy sentences in their lesson in Horace in Lat[in] verse. On repetition days, bec[ause] that work is easy, their time is improved in ye Forenoon in makeing Dialogues containing a Praxis upon a Particle out of Mr. Walker, in the afternoon in Turning a Psalm or something Divine into Latin verse. Every fortnight they compose a Theme, & now & then turn a Theme into a Declamation the last quarter of the year.[24]

Williams's letter, perhaps slightly exaggerated to capture the attention of Nehemiah Hobart at Harvard College, adds several other classical authors to Cicero and Virgil, the authors explicitly stated by most of the colonial colleges as requisite for admission. Among the other ancient authors mentioned by Williams are Aesop (i.e., the Latin version of Aesop by the Julio-Claudian era author Phaedrus), Ovid, Florus, Justin, Horace, Juvenal, and Persius in the Latin language; and Isocrates, Homer, Hesiod, and the New Testament in the Greek language. The letter also states that not only were the orations of Cicero ("Tullie," from the name of Cicero's *gens* or clan, Tullius, and a common way of referring to the orator in the eighteenth century) studied, but also Cicero's letters and his essay on moral duties, the *De Officiis*. Finally, Williams's letter indicates that two separate works of Ovid were studied: the *Tristia* and the *Metamorphoses*. Williams's letter fails, however, to mention the second-century B.C. playwright Terence as one of the authors studied at the Boston Latin School, even though orders for multiple copies of this author appear extensively on the eighteenth-century inventories of Boston booksellers, a sure indication that Terence was imported as a school text.[25]

In *Corderius Americanus*, Cotton Mather (1663–1728) did not spell out, as Williams did, the specific sequence of classical authors studied at the Boston Latin School. However, in his tribute to Ezekiel Cheever, who taught for thirty-eight years at the Boston Latin School, Mather confirms virtually the same list of classical authors who were mentioned in Williams's letter:

> All the Eight parts of Speech he taught to them
> They now Employ to Trumpet his Esteem.
> They fill Fames Trumpet, and they spread a Fame
> To last till the Last Trumpet drown the same.
> *Magister* pleas'd them well, because 'twas he;
> They saw that *Bonus* did with it agree.
> While they said, *Amo*, they the Hint improve
> Him for to make the Object of their Love.
> No Concord so Inviolate they knew
> As to pay Honours to their Master due,
> With Interjections they break off at last,
> But, Ah, is all they use, Wo, and Alas!
> We learnt Prosodia, but with that Design
> Our Masters Name should in our Verses shine.
> Our Weeping Ovid but instructed us
> To write upon his Death, *De Tristibus*,
> Tully we read, but still with this Intent,
> That in his praise we might be Eloquent.
> Our Stately Virgil made us but Contrive
> As our Anchises to keep him Alive.
> When Phoenix to Achilles was assign'd
> A Master, then we thought not Homer blind:
> A Phoenix, which Oh! might his Ashes shew!
> So rare a thing we thought our Master too.

And if we made a theme, 'twas with Regret
We might not on his worth show all our Wit
Were Grammar quite Extinct yet at his Brain
The Candle might have well been lit again.
If Rhet'rick had been stript of all her Pride
She from his Wardrobe might have been Supply'd.
Do but name Cheever, and the Echo straight
Upon that Name, Good Latin, will Repeat.
A Christian Terence, Master of the File
That arm the Curious to Reform their Style.
He taught us Lilly, and he Gospel taught;
And us poor Children to our Saviour brought.
Master of Sentences, he gave us more
The[n] we in our *Sententiae* had before.
We Learn't Good Things in Tullies *Offices*;
But we from him Learn't Better things than these.
With Cato he to us the Higher gave
Lessons of Jesus, that our Souls do save.
We construed Ovid's *Metamorphosis*,
But on our selves charg'd, not a Change to miss.
Young Austin wept, when he saw Dido dead,
Tho' not a Tear for a Lost Soul he had:
Our Master would not let us be so vain,
But us from Virgil did to David train.[26]

This brief excerpt from Mather's eulogy readily illustrates that Latin grammar, including construing (i.e., changing the Latin word order to approximate the usual English word order), rhetoric, prosody, and theme writing, were vigorously taught in the grammar schools of seventeenth- and eighteenth-century America. Moreover, the grammar book most frequently used to acquire these grammatical skills was Cheever's own shortened version of William Lily's sixteenth-century *Latin Grammar*, a book long popular in England. Cheever's students were obviously so well drilled in the Cheever-Lily grammar that Mather vividly remembered, long after his own grammar school training, that the adjective *bonus, -a, -um* ("good") served as the example for second declension adjectives, and that the noun *magister* ("teacher") was the sample word for second declension "*-er*" masculine nouns. Furthermore, Mather's recollection of his grammatical lessons was so keen that later in this same poem he even made humorous reference to Cheever's well-advanced old age by employing the seventeenth-century terminology for the pluperfect tense, namely the praeter-perfect:

He Liv'd, and to vast Age no Illness knew;
Till Times Scythe waiting for him Rusty grew,
He Liv'd and Wrought; His Labours were Immense;
But ne'r Declin'd to Praeter-Perfect Tense.[27]

In his poem, Mather was concerned primarily with describing both Cheever's skills as a Latin teacher and the admirable integrity of his character. He was not concerned with listing in their sequential order the classical authors studied in Cheever's classroom. Nevertheless, Mather's poem is so rich in detail that his eulogy contains a working description of the curriculum of the Boston Latin School, and it serves as an informative supplement to Williams's letter. Besides adding Terence, studied for the correctness of his Latin, Mather also confirms the following authors from Williams's list of ancient writers: Ovid (*Tristia* and *Metamorphoses*), Cicero (*De Officiis* and orations), and Virgil (especially Aeneas carrying his father Anchises out of burning Troy in book 2 of the *Aeneid*, and Dido's death in book 4).

It is important to note that most of the classical works read at the Boston Latin School in the late seventeenth and early eighteenth centuries were chosen to impart moral and political lessons. The introductory texts of "Cato" and Aesop's *Fables* were overtly moralistic. The *Dicta Catonis* were not, in fact, written by the early second-century B.C. Roman moralist Cato the Elder, under whose name this collection of brief moral sayings and poems circulated in the Middle Ages. Instead, the text has its origins in late antiquity, a fact already recognized at the end of the sixteenth century (when scholars claimed the author was a "Dionysius Cato").[28] The more advanced Latin texts had clear political messages. Ovid's *Tristia*—poems lamenting the poet's exile to the shores of the Black Sea by order of the Roman emperor Augustus—were interpreted within a political context of how sovereigns and subjects were meant to behave. Cicero's letters, speeches, and the *De Officiis*, all deal, of course, with political issues and events, as does Florus's summary of Roman history to the reign of Augustus, and Justin's epitome of Trogus's summary of Greek history to the collapse of the Hellenistic kingdoms in the time of Pompey the Great. Moral teachings were also reinforced by the Roman satirists Horace, Juvenal, and Persius, as well as by the playwright Terence. Among Greek authors, religious instruction came in the readings from the Gospels, moral teaching from Hesiod, and political lessons in the speeches of Isocrates. Even the section of Homer's *Iliad* expressly mentioned in Mather's poem—the embassy to Achilles in book 9—was understood as an examination of the proper role of a citizen when he believes himself wronged by his political leaders.

When these detailed accounts of the curriculum of the Boston Latin School are compared to the entrance requirements of the colleges of colonial and revolutionary America, the only glaring omission, based upon Columbia's 1785 list, is Caesar's *Gallic Wars*. Caesar does, however, appear on the curriculum of the Latin Academy of Philadelphia in 1756, which provides an even more historically and politically oriented list of

Latin authors. Also included in the 1756 Philadelphia list are Sallust, the highly moralizing Roman historian of the later years of the Roman Republic; Eutropius's late antique summary of Roman history to A.D. 364; and the Augustan-era authors Livy (for his history of the earliest years of ancient Rome), and Cornelius Nepos (for his brief biographies of prominent Greeks and Romans). Missing from the curriculum are the *Dicta Catonis*, Florus, Justin, Juvenal, and Persius. On the Greek side, Isocrates and Hesiod have been replaced by the fourth-century B.C. author Xenophon (undoubtedly for his *Cyropaedia*, or "Education of Cyrus," a discussion of Cyrus the Great that provides a discourse on political leadership) and by the third-century A.D. historian Herodian, whose moralizing work dealt with the Roman Empire during the sixty years after the death of the emperor Marcus Aurelius. The even more detailed 1795 curriculum from the same school (now the preparatory academy of the University of Pennsylvania) lists the very same authors, but with Ovid also included on the Latin side.[29]

More remarkable than the differences between the Boston Latin School curriculum circa 1700 and the Philadelphia Academy's curricula of 1756 and 1795 is the constancy of classical education across regions and over time. Most of the authors studied were the same: Phaedrus's Aesop, Ovid, Cicero, Virgil, Horace, Terence, and Homer. Indeed, a later critic of classical education, Harvard University president Charles W. Eliot, in a speech in 1910 marking the 275th anniversary of the Boston Latin School, noted the continuing legacy of classical education even into the middle of the nineteenth century:

> Sixty-six years ago [1844], when I entered it [the Boston Latin School], the subjects of instruction were Latin, Greek, mathematics, English composition and declamation, and the elements of Greek and Roman history. There was no formal instruction in the English language and literature, no modern language, no science, and no physical training, or military drill. In short, the subjects of instruction were what they had been for two hundred years.[30]

The origins of this curriculum went back even earlier. Ezekiel Cheever, along with other American schoolmasters of the seventeenth and eighteenth centuries, had been born in Britain and trained in British universities. These schoolmasters simply transported across the Atlantic the same grammar school curriculum of their homeland, a curriculum which had already become standardized at the beginning of the seventeenth century.[31] The immediate source of this bi-continental curriculum can be traced to Erasmus (1466–1536), the most famous of the European humanists and educational theorists, who actively promoted his ideas on early classical education in England at the beginning of the sixteenth century. The ultimate source of Erasmus's grammar school curriculum, however, resided in the much earlier educational theory and practice of the late first-century A.D. Roman educator Quintilian.

Classical education would continue, moreover, for those grammar school and privately tutored students whose parents had the means to send them to one of the nine colonial-era American colleges. Of course, not every young man who completed the course of studies at a Latin grammar school or under the tutelage of a local minister attended college in early America. Among those who did, some did not pursue the full course of college study. Nonetheless, those who completed a grammar school education or attended college in colonial America, however briefly, acquired a substantial background in classical antiquity and were reckoned among the most literate segment of the American population. Those who completed their studies through the collegiate level constituted the heart and soul of a truly intellectual and elitist stratification of American society—an especially important consideration in the late eighteenth century when this group of individuals, more so than any other group, was called upon to devise, debate, create, and administer a new government.

College students in colonial America faced a hard and disciplined course of study. The school day began at six o'clock in the morning and concluded at five o'clock in the afternoon. Instruction took place six days a week for nearly ten months out of the year. Lectures were lengthy, often lasting three to four hours. Students were accustomed to extensive memorization and oral recitation. Textbooks were valuable and were required to be purchased. Students could expect to be granted admission to the college's highly prized library only as a matter of privilege.

The "classical atmosphere" on the early American collegiate campus was intense. The college disciplinary code was written in Latin, which at some institutions entering students were required to translate into English either as part of their admission examination or shortly after enrollment as part of a translation exercise.[32] Many faculty lectures were delivered in Latin, and students were expected to speak in the Latin tongue both in and out of the classroom. Any violation of this regulation resulted in a student fine. At those institutions where the practice of mandatory conversation in Latin was not faithfully maintained, the college often resorted to awarding annual cash prizes to promote the use of the Latin tongue in conversation. All students were expected to keep a "commonplace book" of the eloquent expressions and wise maxims they encountered in their reading of the traditional classical authors. These commonplace books were also subject to periodic examination by the faculty.[33] Furthermore, many philosophy, mathematics, astronomy, natural science, and divinity textbooks were written in Latin, and it was assumed that the student had a sufficiently facile reading knowledge of Latin to readily understand these textbooks.

One of the primary goals of a college education in the seventeenth and eighteenth centuries was the attainment of skill in public speaking, useful to both the minister in the pulpit and the politician in the assembly. The American college student honed his oratorical abilities by intensively studying and implementing the principles and techniques of classical rhetoric extensively described in the treatises of Quintilian and Cicero. By engaging in Latin debates (disputations) and by preparing solo orations (declamations) in Latin and English, at least on a monthly basis and some-times as frequently as on a weekly basis, the early American college stu-dent achieved high levels of oratorical skill.[34] Finally, in his senior year the student spent several months preparing Latin disputations and declama-tions which comprised an extensive part of the elaborate and formal com-mencement exercises, which frequently lasted for a whole day and were a much anticipated and extremely well attended community event.[35]

Similar to the development and structure of the Latin grammar school curriculum in the colonies, the curricular format of the early American college was also not an original creation. It was borrowed from the Euro-pean universities, especially Oxford and Cambridge, whose undergrad-uate curriculum during the seventeenth and eighteenth centuries concentrated on training students in the Seven Liberal Arts. This educa-tional tradition, which can be traced through the Middle Ages back to antiquity itself, consisted of the *trivium* (grammar, logic, and rhetoric) and the *quadrivium* (mathematics, astronomy, theology, and music). In the *trivium*, grammar referred to the study of the Three Languages (Greek, Latin, and Hebrew), and logic and rhetoric were defined almost exclusively in the same terms as they had been described by ancient authors.[36]

During his first year of study at a colonial college, a newly arrived stu-dent was called upon to improve his skills in the Greek language and to advance substantially his study of logic and rhetoric, to which he may have been minimally introduced in the late years of his grammar school education. The most frequently read Greek text in college was the New Testament (as befitted one purpose of these colleges: the training of clergy for North American pulpits). In general, classical influence was far more pronounced on the Roman side than on the Greek. The incoming college student was called upon to reread many of the Latin authors whom he had previously encountered in grammar school. Among those Latin authors most commonly read in the first year of college were Virgil, Cicero (ora-tions), Caesar, Horace, Livy, and Sallust. During the second and third years of college, the Latin authors most frequently read were Cicero (philosophical essays), Horace, Juvenal, Ovid, Quintilian, Terence, and Tacitus. Finally, the fourth year was often considered a review year, designed to prepare the student for the final, public examinations. Once again, many of these same classical authors were reread.

Unlike the curricular rigidity demonstrated by the early American grammar schools, the colonial colleges were considerably more flexible in their course offerings and areas of academic concentration. The College of New Jersey, for example, was especially dedicated to the study of the natural sciences, while Yale was committed to Hebrew. As a result of this variety, not all of the Latin authors previously mentioned were studied in each of the early American colleges in the same sequence. However, no matter what the special characteristic was of any of the colonial colleges, there was found in each a universal and unswerving adherence to the study of classical languages and literatures.

The most classical of all of the curricula of early American colleges (and the most definitive description of an eighteenth-century collegiate curriculum) was that of King's College, whose 1763 course of study is outlined below:[37]

> First Year: Sallust, *Historia*;[38] Caesar, *Commentaries*;[39] Ovid, *Metamorphoses et alia*; Virgil, *Eclogues*; Aesop, *Fables*; Lucian, *Dialogues*; New Testament; Grotius, *De Veritate*;[40] Latin Grammar; Greek Grammar; English and Latin Themes; Cornelius Nepos.

> Second Year: Cicero, *De Officiis et alia*; Quintus Curtius; Terence; Ovid, *Epistles*; Virgil, *Georgics*; New Testament; Epictetus; Xenophon, *Institutio Cyri* and *Anabasis*; Farnaby, *Epigrams*;[41] Greek Grammar; Latin Grammar; Wallisius, *Logic*;[42] Sanderson, *Compendium*;[43] Johnson, *Noetica*;[44] Rhetoric; Latin and English Themes and Verse.

> Third Year: Cicero, orations and *De Oratore*; Quintilian; Pliny the Younger; Catullus; Tibullus; Propertius; Horace; Aristotle, *Ethics* and *Poetics*; Plato, *Dialogues*; Xenophon, *Memorabilia*; Theocritus; Homer; *Compendium Ethicae*;[45] Metaphysics; Syllogistic Disputations; Latin and English Themes; Latin and English Verses.

> Fourth Year: Cicero, *Tusculan Disputations*; Livy; Tacitus, *Histories*; Lucan; Juvenal; Persius; Plautus; Homer, *Odyssey*; Sophocles; Euripides; Aeschylus; Thucydides; Herodotus; Longinus; Demosthenes; Dionysius of Halicarnassus; Isocrates; Hebrew Grammar; Biblical Hebrew; Grotius; Pufendorf; Hutcheson;[46]

Moral Philosophy; Latin Themes; Declamations; Latin and English Verses; Disputations.

Whether or not the early American college student appreciated the rigor of the training that he was receiving is a moot question since the results of that educational process speak for themselves. Simply stated, early American collegiate education, with its pronounced classical bias, successfully met the stated goals of preparing young men for service to religious and public life. There is no better testimony of this success than the record of accomplishment of the 469 graduates of the College of New Jersey during the presidency of the Reverend John Witherspoon from 1769 to 1794. They included fifty state legislators, twelve governors, thirty judges, three United States Supreme Court justices, ten cabinet officers, thirty-nine U.S. representatives, twenty-one U.S. senators, one vice president, and one president (James Madison).[47]

Throughout life, most American college graduates of the eighteenth century continued to pursue intellectual interests in classical antiquity that their education had opened to them. On the enjoyment that at least one of the classically educated Founders derived from his lifelong study of the classics, there can be found no more fitting tribute than Sarah N. Randolph's description of the reading habits of her great-grandfather, Thomas Jefferson, long after his retirement from the presidency and more than a half century after he first learned his Latin and Greek grammar:

> In his youth he had loved poetry, but by the time I was old enough to observe, he had lost his taste for it, except for Homer and the great Athenian tragics, which he continued to the last to enjoy. He went over the works of Aeschylus, Sophocles, and Euripides, not very long before I left him (the year before his death). Of history he was very fond, and this he studied in all languages, though always, I think, preferring the ancients. In fact, he derived more pleasure from his acquaintance with Greek and Latin than from any other resource of literature, and I have often heard him express his gratitude to his father for causing him to receive a classical education. I saw him more frequently with a volume of the classics in his hand than with any other book.[48]

Perhaps the man who received a classical education in eighteenth-century America, whether solely in a grammar school or with further college study, did not deserve the reputation for erudition which he enjoyed among his neighbors. By the standards of today's professionalized academic disciplines, the eighteenth-century gentleman-scholar displayed an erudition that was neither deep nor broad. Nonetheless, when tired out with the supervision of the plantation, or weary with the problems and conflicting interests of political life, he might turn again with a sigh of relief to his Homer or his Horace. The omnipresent character of his engagement with classical antiquity—drilled in through years of study and memorization—guaranteed that his understanding of the proper organization and operation of American government was constructed from his understanding of the political thought expressed in the literature he read from ancient Greece and Rome.

Chapter 2

Classical Antiquity and Early Conceptions of the United States Senate

—Carl J. Richard

The decision by the framers of the Constitution to create a bicameral legislature to replace the Continental Congress was not merely a way to appease the smaller states, whose residents feared a more powerful federal government dominated by the larger states. The divided legislature also reflected the Founders' understanding of American society, an understanding conditioned by their study of the ancient Greeks and Romans. The House of Representatives was meant to be a democratic body, a people's assembly intended to reflect the concerns of the overwhelming majority of citizens who lacked extensive property. By contrast, the Senate was initially designed as an aristocratic council deliberative in nature and gathered from those whose wealth afforded them an education equal to their task. To these democratic and aristocratic elements the Founders added a president, the monarchical element in a mixed government in which authority was shared among the three types of polity (monarchy, aristocracy, democracy) recognized in classical Greece. The framers widely shared such a classically inspired understanding of the Constitution they created, and they actively promoted the ideal of mixed government as found in ancient political theory.[1]

In the decade following ratification of the Constitution, Thomas Jefferson and his new Democratic-Republican Party began to recast the Senate from an aristocratic council into a second democratic assembly working alongside the House. Mixed-government theory was abandoned as the justification for the nation's bicameral legislature. Yet its dismissal was not a rejection of political models taken from classical antiquity. In replacing mixed-government theory, Thomas Jefferson turned to the equally ancient and revered tradition of classical pastoralism to explain the workings of the American political system.[2]

The foundation on which the framers constructed the United States Constitution was ancient in origin, inspired by the theories of Plato, Aristotle, and Polybius. In *Politicus* 291d–303c (cf. *Laws* 756e–757a, 832c), Plato suggested that the best form of government would involve the sharing of power among a single ruler ("the one"), an elite ruling class ("the few"), and the rest of the community ("the many"). This theory of a mixed government combining monarchy, aristocracy, and democracy represented a marked departure from the famous model Plato had earlier described in the *Republic* where he had proposed a simple aristocracy of "guardians" led by a philosopher-king. Aristotle seized upon mixed-government theory, making it the centerpiece of his *Politics* (3.7). Polybius (*Histories* 6.5–18) then utilized it to explain the military success of the Roman Republic.[3]

Regardless of whether the Romans ever really had a mixed government, the beguiling clarity and simplicity of Polybius's analysis convinced Romans themselves, such as Cicero (*Republic* 2.23–30), that their complex system of balances was the chief cause of their success. Mixed-government theory dominated Western political thought throughout the Middle Ages and Renaissance until the rise of Absolutism in the seventeenth century. In response to Absolutist ideas, English republicans like Algernon Sidney (1622–1683) reasserted classical arguments against simple systems of government and added Great Britain to their list of successful mixed constitutions. The king, the House of Lords, and the House of Commons joined the Spartan and Roman governments in the pantheon of mixed-government theorists.[4]

James Harrington (1611–1677) contributed the theory of natural aristocracy, a concept essential to any American adaptation of mixed-government theory. Harrington held that even in a new country that lacked a titled aristocracy, like his mythical Oceana, certain men would possess greater talent than others. In any free society this natural difference in talent would produce unequal wealth. Unequal wealth would, in turn, produce class conflict. Mixed government, combined with a few laws limiting the size of landholdings, was the only means of preventing violent struggles between the classes and the tyranny that inevitably followed these civil wars. Mixed-government theory was used to justify both the British system of government and the American colonial governments, which generally consisted of a governor, a few councilors, and an assembly elected by the colonists.[5]

The Founders had access to every level of this western tradition. Hence it was only natural that, when confronted by unprecedented parliamentary taxation during the 1760s and 1770s, they should turn to the most ancient and revered of political theories to explain this perplexing phenomenon. Patriot leaders ascribed the new tyranny to a degeneration of the mixture of the English constitution. Although the form of the British government remained the same, King George III had destroyed its delicate balance by using his patronage powers to buy the House of Commons and to pack the House of Lords. This corruption had then seeped into colonial governments, where royal governors generally possessed the power to appoint the upper branch of the legislature.[6]

The framers of the new state constitutions that emerged from the Revolution never doubted that their governments should be mixed. Rather, their dilemma was how to mix them in a society that no longer possessed a monarch and that had never possessed a titled aristocracy. The framers decided that these essential roles should be played by an elected governor and a senate consisting of Harrington's "natural aristocracy." They decided that since education and talent often accompanied wealth, and since wealth (unlike either talent or virtue) could be easily quantified, property was the most appropriate criterion for identifying the "natural aristocracy" that would provide their governments with the necessary senatorial stability. Although John Adams was the most visible and persistent proponent of mixed government in America, even Thomas Jefferson, the future champion of representative democracy, embraced the theory during the Revolution. Jefferson proposed the indirect election of Virginia senators for nine-year terms, complaining that, under the state constitution of 1776, they had too much "dependence on the people."[7]

The United States Constitution was also a product of mixed-government theory. At the Constitutional Convention, James Madison, the "Father of the Constitution," argued for a nine-year term for senators. "Landholders ought to have a share in the government to support these invaluable interests and to balance and check the other," Madison said. "They ought to be so constituted as to protect the minority of the opulent against the majority. The senate, therefore, ought to be this body; and to answer these purposes, they ought to have permanency and stability. Various have been the propositions; but my opinion is, the longer they continue in office, the better will these views be answered."

Madison claimed that it was useless to deny the existence of an American aristocracy, though there were no "hereditary distinctions," and though inequalities of wealth were minor by comparison with Europe. "There will be debtors and creditors, and an unequal possession of property, and hence arises different views and different objects in government," Madison said. "This, indeed, is the ground work of aristocracy; and we find it blended in every government, both ancient and modern." Madison concluded that even in his own day America could not be regarded as "one homogeneous mass" and that there were recent "symptoms of a leveling spirit" which he feared might lead to "agrarian attempts" (land redistribution measures) if not checked by an aristocratic senate. Four years earlier, when Madison had chaired a committee to recommend books for congressional use, he had placed Aristotle's *Politics* at the top of his list of works concerning political theory. Thus, it is not surprising that the system Madison helped create balanced power between a president selected by the electoral college, a Senate selected by the state legislatures for a lengthy six-year term, and a House of Representatives elected by the majority every two years.[8]

Madison did not consider the Senate a second democratic body that existed only to protect the interests of the small states against legislation that might proceed from the larger democratic assembly, the House of Representatives. Rather, it was obvious from the Senate's different manner of selection and much longer term of office that it would house a natural aristocracy. Many Americans were uneasy at the prospect of developing a new, institutionalized elite on these shores, so Madison took care to assuage fears that the Senate would convert the government into an oligarchy. In *Federalist* No. 63, Madison asserted that "history informs us of no long-lived republic which had not a senate." Madison then related how the Spartan, Roman, and Carthaginian senates, whose members possessed lifetime terms, had acted as an "anchor against popular fluctuations." He further argued that the danger of a republic's being corrupted was "greater where the whole legislative trust is lodged in the hands of one body of men than where the concurrence of separate and dissimilar bodies is required in every public act." In his notes for the essay Madison cited Aristotle, Polybius, and Cicero as his sources.[9]

Alexander Hamilton also advocated mixed government. Hamilton's outline for a speech given at the Constitutional Convention on June 18, 1787, a speech in which he advocated lifetime terms for both the president and the Senate, included these statements: "Society naturally divides itself into two political divisions—the few and the many, who have distinct interests. If a government [is] in the hands of the few, they will tyrannize over the many. If [it is in] the hands of the many, they will tyrannize over the few. It ought to be in the hands of both; and they should be separated."

Eight days later, Hamilton opposed Roger Sherman's measure to reduce the senators' term of office, reminding him that the House of Representatives would act as "the democratic body." Hamilton further noted that the absence of legal distinctions in America between citizens did not mean that American society was homogeneous. Inequality of property still "constituted the great & fundamental distinction in Society." Making an analogy between the United States and the Roman Republic, he asked rhetorically, "When the Tribunitial power had leveled the boundary between the patricians and the plebeians, what followed? The distinction between rich and poor was substituted." He pointedly concluded, "If we incline too much to democracy, we shall shoot into a monarchy. The difference of property is already great among us. Commerce and industry will still increase the disparity." At the New York ratifying convention Hamilton declared, "There are few positions more demonstrable than that there should be, in every republic, some permanent body to correct the prejudices, check the intemperate passions, and regulate the fluctuations, of a popular assembly." Other Federalists, such as Gouverneur Morris and John Dickinson, echoed the view that the Constitution established a mixed government of the type almost universally praised by ancient political theorists.[10]

Recognizing that mixed-government theory provided the theoretical foundation for the Constitution, most Antifederalists vigorously denied either that mixed governments ever really worked or that examples drawn from classical antiquity had any applicability to eighteenth-century America. The Antifederalist essayist "Centinel" believed history proved that the balance between orders was constantly in jeopardy, if not wholly impossible to maintain. Charles Pinckney stated at the Constitutional Convention, "The people of this country are not only very different from the inhabitants of any State we are acquainted with in the modern world; but I assert that their situation is distinct from either the people of Greece, or Rome, or of any State we are acquainted with among the antients." Pinckney later changed his views, but James Monroe agreed with Pinckney's original argument that the United States was fundamentally different from the ancient republics. At the Virginia ratifying convention he claimed that although the Roman and British governments were based on mixed-government theory, the American situation was entirely different, necessitating government "founded on different principles." The Antifederalists argued that the Constitution was intended to produce an oligarchy, and the clearest indicator was the existence of the Senate. They argued that the proponents of the Constitution were merely utilizing mixed-government theory as a respectable cloak for shameless oligarchical schemes.[11]

The arguments made by the Antifederalists against the relevance of classical antiquity were a direct assault upon the underlying rationale of the framers of the Constitution. The framers received both their general political theory and their principal supporting examples for that theory from the Greeks and Romans. It was, however, a theory substantially altered by modern innovations. Representation removed the people from direct participation in government. Based upon a suspicion of government alien to the ancients, Montesquieu's separation of powers balanced government branches rather than social orders. The executive veto injected a greater degree of monarchical power into modern republics than had existed in the ancient republics. Most significant was Harrington's concept of "natural aristocracy," a concept essential to the American adaptation of mixed government. The United States's eventual replacement of England's hereditary king and aristocrats with an elective monarch and an assembly of wealth necessarily increased the nation's distance from the classical polity. But the general unwillingness of the Constitution's framers to recognize the revolutionary nature of modern innovations to mixed-government theory is one of many testaments to their reluctance to stray too far from the classical font of wisdom and authority.

In the 1790s Jefferson, Madison, and other Democratic-Republicans clearly distanced themselves from mixed-government theory. As early as 1788 Madison had begun expressing ambivalence. Though taking a clear mixed-government position at the Constitutional Convention and in other *Federalist* essays, Madison's *Federalist* No. 10 proposed a different solution to the problem of majority tyranny. Madison suggested that, unlike the ancient republics, a modern commercial nation like the United States possessed more factions than "the few" and "the many." For instance, planters and merchants, though both large propertyholders, possessed different interests. Furthermore, Madison recognized that religious and ideological considerations would also create factions. Hence the number of factions in the United States would be so great that majorities must be weak coalitions, incapable of prolonged tyranny. As the years passed, Madison clung ever more fervently to this solution to the problem of majority tyranny, a solution which not only seemed more appropriate to the American situation, but also justified a form of government more popular with the public.[12]

Democratic-Republicans began to conceive of the entire federal government as fundamentally democratic, and to believe that officeholders were chosen to fulfill the will of the majority as manifest under specific electoral rules and within specific electoral districts. But Jefferson and most other Democratic-Republicans did not base their belief in the viability of representative democracy on Madison's theory regarding the advantages of modern commercial republics. They were unwilling to dismiss the relevance of the ancient Greeks and Romans to their understanding of the new government the Constitution had created. Ancient political theory, however, clearly favored mixed governments and warned that democracies inevitably dissolve into tyrannies.

To support their new understanding of the Constitution, Democratic-Republicans turned to the classical pastoral tradition, a heritage as ancient and revered as mixed-government theory. They comforted themselves with the notion that the United States could safely adopt a democracy, however vilified by classical political theorists, partly because it would feature such "modern improvements" as representation and the separation of powers, but largely because the abundance of land in the United States would allow a citizenry of Virgilian farmers to emerge. When cutting the trusty anchor of mixed-government theory, Democratic-Republicans assuaged their anxiety by fastening the anchor of classical pastoralism with even greater firmness. However ingenious they might be, theories concerning the superiority of modern institutions were, by their very nature, untested, and hence lacked the authority required to reassure a generation raised on ancient verities. Just as the old myth of mixed government had proven a necessary catalyst for the new reality of the Constitution, so the ancient legend of classical pastoralism proved essential to creating the new reality of representative democracy.

Aside from its novelty, there was another, equally important, reason why most Democratic-Republicans found it difficult to embrace Madison's hypothesis. Taken to its logical conclusion, the theory encouraged the very neomercantilist policies they were most anxious to avoid. If a republic's level of justice and stability depended upon the number of its interests, the best policy must be to multiply that number. In a nation of farmers like the United States, such a policy would inevitably entail government measures to redistribute wealth from agriculture to infant industries, the very fiscal program that Alexander Hamilton had introduced and that the pro-agricultural Democratic-Republican Party bitterly opposed.

Furthermore, the formation of the Federalist and Democratic-Republican parties transformed the operations of the Senate. By the second half of the 1790s, partisanship had destroyed any pretense that senators shared a sense of social unity as members of a natural aristocracy. During the Fifth through Seventh Congresses (1797–1803), senators voted with their party at a frequency not seen again until the twentieth century. The partisanship of the "aristocratic" Senate mirrored that of the "democratic" House.[13]

To preserve the authority of classical antiquity that was essential to their understanding of political theory, Democratic-Republicans promoted the ideology of the gentleman farmer. No theme was more ubiquitous in classical literature than that of the superiority of the rural, agricultural existence, a lifestyle wedged comfortably between the extremes of savage and sophisticate. The theme began as the motif of such Greek poets as Hesiod and Theocritus, then it became the central theme of Virgil, Horace, and Ovid, the leading poets of Rome's Augustan Age. Convinced that farmers were the backbone of Rome, Virgil (*Georgics* 2.458–74) exhorted his fellow Romans to regenerate the community after a century of civil war by returning to the plow. Virgil claimed that the farmer's lifestyle was the source of republican virtue.[14]

The pastoral theme was as much a staple of classical political theory and history as of Greek and Roman poetry. Aristotle argued that the best republics were predominantly agricultural. The classical historians considered Sparta and republican Rome models not merely because they had possessed mixed governments, but also because they had been agricultural societies. The historians credited the triumph of Sparta and Rome over their vice-ridden, commercial adversaries, Athens and Carthage, as much to their pastoral virtues as to their government forms. Both produced virtue, the agricultural life by fostering frugality, temperance, and independence, and a balanced constitution by requiring moderation, cooperation, and compromise. The plow was both the symbol and the cause of Cincinnatus's "Roman virtue."[15]

As with mixed government, the Founders derived the pastoral tradition both directly from the ancients, who formed the core of their grammar school and college curricula, and through the medium of modern authors. Having spread throughout the Middle Ages and the Renaissance, pastoralism achieved a virtual cult status in seventeenth- and eighteenth-century England and France. James Harrington praised farmers for their love of liberty, moderated by a stability that he found lacking in the city dwellers of Athens. An enthusiastic supporter of agriculture, King George III was fond of his nickname "Farmer George." George Washington actively managed his family's plantations. Both Farmer Georges, the king and the rebel, corresponded with Arthur Young, one of the high priests of the eighteenth-century pastoral movement.[16]

Pastoralism was an important theme in eighteenth-century American literature. Virgilian influences, especially from the *Eclogues*, provided the prism through which Americans of the day viewed their landscape and society. Funereal elegies are populated with characters whose names are classically sounding (such as "Dulcius" and "Fidelio," in Joseph Green's 1766 poem on the death of Boston clergyman Jonathan Mayhew) or even adapted directly from Virgil's works (such as "Lysidas" and "Damaetas" from the *Eclogues*, in Thomas Godfrey's 1759 poem on the death of British general James Wolfe at the Battle of Quebec in the French and Indian War). These connections to classical antiquity acted as a means of imposing a psychological order on the partially tamed North American environment, as well as providing a respectable heritage for a population lacking aristocratic forebears.[17]

Thomas Jefferson cherished the pastoral tradition. His favorite books concerning agriculture were Columella's *De re rustica* and Adam Dickson's *Husbandry of the Ancients*. Like other Virginia plantation owners, Jefferson designed his estate to resemble the Roman villas Pliny and Varro had described. He also planned the inscription of a passage from Horace (*Epodes* 2.1–4, 7–8, 23–34, 39–40, 43–48, 61–66) near a small temple that he hoped to build on his burial ground. The excerpt exulted in the joys of the rural life. As Gilbert Chinard noted, Jefferson removed from the text of Horace's epode those parts which described elements absent from eighteenth-century Virginia life (shrill war clarions and vineyards, for example). By condensing a poem of seventy-two lines into thirty-two, he presented a picture, however idealized, of his own time and place.[18]

Though certainly aware of classical economists' arguments for the greater productivity of agriculture, Jefferson generally emphasized its moral and political benefits. In a famous passage in the *Notes on the State of Virginia,* Jefferson glorified agriculture in a manner reminiscent of the *Georgics*: "Those who labor in the earth are the chosen people of God, if ever he had a chosen people, whose breasts He has made His peculiar deposit for genuine and substantial virtue. . . . It is the manners and spirit of a people which preserve a republic in vigor." The secret of the ancient republics' success was their pastoral virtue.[19]

The praise of rural life promoted by the Roman poets of the Augustan age was always tinged with a longing for an idealized past. The simple lives of the farmer and shepherd contrasted with the tumult, machinations, and hassles of the city of Rome and its million inhabitants. Ironically, the nostalgia expressed by these ancient authors inspired hope and confidence in their American readers eighteen centuries later. In the 1790 census, the most populous city in the United States was New York with 33,000 inhabitants. Philadelphia was the only other city recording more than 20,000 residents. America was an overwhelmingly rural nation, and Americans like Jefferson expected that centuries must pass before the vast lands of the West were fully settled. Unable to foresee how immigration and industrialization would urbanize much of America's citizenry over the course of the nineteenth century, Jefferson imagined a nation populated by yeomen farmers whose virtuous lifestyle would ensure the continued success and stability of an American democracy. Hence the ideology of classical pastoralism became a source of encouragement to an American sitting on the edge of a fertile and lightly settled continent.[20]

It was as if the pure classical republicanism once espoused by the Founders had died in the 1790s, and its heirs divided the intellectual legacy. The Federalists retained custody of mixed-government theory, while the Democratic-Republicans kept classical pastoralism. Each party became half-classical, half-modern: the Federalists remained aristocratic but embraced the new industry; the Democratic-Republicans remained pastoral but embraced the new democracy.

For the Democratic-Republicans, the conception of the Senate's role in the American democracy was reduced to that of a mediator between the House and the president. By the first decade of the nineteenth century, with Democratic-Republicans firmly in control of both the legislative and executive branches of government, the prestige of the Senate, and of mixed-government theory, was in decline. For a Federalist and supporter of mixed-government theory like former president John Adams, the Senate's less prominent role made him pessimistic. Adams had come to the terrifying conclusion that the mixed government established by the Constitution of 1787 was being transformed, in substance if not in form, into a simple democracy. Divisions between political parties were replacing the intended divisions between branches. In 1806 Adams declared, "I once thought our Constitution was quasi or mixed government, but they have now made it, to all intents and purposes, in virtue, in spirit, and effect, a democracy. We are left without resources but in our prayers and tears, and having nothing that we can do or say, but the Lord have mercy upon us." By "they," Adams meant the Democratic-Republicans, and particularly Jefferson, whose administration he considered subversive of the intent of the drafters of the Constitution. It was of little consolation to Adams that his interpretation of the intent of the framers was more accurate than Jefferson's. It was Jefferson's that prevailed.[21]

Bolstered by the belief that democracy was sustainable so long as the majority of citizens possessed the virtue that flowed naturally from a lifestyle connected to farming and the land, Americans turned increasingly from viewing the Senate as an aristocratic body to envisioning it as a second democratic body whose primary purpose was to prevent hasty action by the House of Representatives. Never mind that the very structure of the Senate—its equal representation for less populous states, its lengthy term, and its indirect election—clearly belied such an interpretation.

Indeed, the modern American political system is a hybrid of democracy and mixed government. While the majority possesses most of the power, elements of mixed government remain. The Supreme Court, whose power has grown steadily, is still appointed by the president, who is still elected by the electoral college. The senators' larger districts still foster a more aristocratic representation than the House of Representatives, while the equality of states in the Senate favors the small states. Hence the passage of congressional legislation requires more than simple majority support. Ironically, in their effort to emulate the systems of Sparta, Rome, and Great Britain, whose status as mixed governments was dubious at best, the founders of the United States may have created the first real mixed government in history—though mixed in a modern sense. The modern mixture does not balance economic classes, as originally intended, but rather it balances the urban and the rural. The more rural, less populated "red states" receive far greater representation in the Senate, and slightly greater representation in the electoral college, than a pure democracy would grant them. Thus, in perhaps the greatest of all ironies, Jefferson's rural folk, today's minority, are now protected from majority tyranny not by their own pastoral virtue but by the mixed elements of the Constitution that survived his own expanding democracy.

Territorial expansion, regional rivalry, and political realignment created tensions that provided the Senate with opportunities to play an increasingly important role in American government during the second quarter of the nineteenth century. Neither the model of a natural aristocracy nor the ideal of the yeoman farmer properly defined the Senate's developing character, yet the creation and promotion of these conflicting concepts of how the Senate was to function reveal how fundamental classical antiquity was in inspiring the nation's Founders.

Chapter 3

Classical Oratory and Fears of Demagoguery in the Antebellum Era

—Caroline Winterer

In the first half of the nineteenth century, increasing immigration from abroad and increasing movement of settlers west of the Appalachians brought significant changes to the political landscape of the United States. Assisted by the economic revolution that also brought canals, railroads, factories, and banks, immigration and westward migration served to dissolve the social hierarchies that structured colonial society. Neither the Tidewater and Low Country gentry of the South nor the old Puritan families of New England could continue to expect the aristocratic deference that characterized the political culture of the eighteenth century. Furthermore, the two-party system that emerged in the 1790s between Federalists and Democratic-Republicans, and reemerged with a vengeance in the 1830s between Democrats and Whigs, injected politics with an anger and passion that rankled the traditionally minded, educated elites. This partisan, political jockeying also corroded the ideal of the gentleman statesman, whose grounding in classical history supposedly had enabled him to steer the nation disinterestedly and virtuously. The expansion of the franchise to all adult white male citizens encouraged populist pandering. The political field now opened to a new class of men who were distinguished less by pedigree than by their own accomplishments.[1]

Already by the 1820s, there were debates about the leadership quali-
fications of the classically steeped gentleman of the East versus those of
the practical, self-made man of the West. John Quincy Adams
(1767–1848) and Andrew Jackson (1767–1845), although born in the
same year and serving as president one after the other, embodied this
division. Jackson, a victorious general in the War of 1812, represented
the vigorous, natural frontiersman, unimpaired by a lengthy formal education. Though he was a Freemason who came to own a large plantation
and live in an imposing, Greek-revival mansion (the Hermitage), Jackson
strove to avoid being tainted by these trappings of elitism. "Old Hickory"
promoted instead his own humble beginnings as an orphan in the Carolina backwoods and successfully cultivated an image as a friend of the
common man, praising popular democracy and the possibility of upward
mobility for poor whites. The historian George Bancroft (1800–1891)
reflected on what this natural leader could offer the new republic.

> Behold, then, the unlettered man of the West, the nursling of the
> wilds, the farmer of the Hermitage, little versed in books, uncon-
> nected by science with the tradition of the past, raised by the will of
> the people to the highest pinnacle of honour, to the central post in
> the civilization of republican freedom. . . . What policy will he pur-
> sue? What wisdom will he bring with him from the forest? What
> rules of duty will he evolve from the oracles of his own mind?[2]

Jackson appointed more men of lowly educational background to his
administration than had John Adams or Thomas Jefferson a generation
earlier. Eight men in his cabinet had no more than a secondary education,
compared with two men each in the cabinets of Adams and Jefferson.[3]

By contrast with the rustic Jackson, John Quincy Adams stood last in
the line of classically educated gentlemen-statesmen familiar in the revolutionary era. Born to the political purple, Adams was a Harvard graduate who had been educated as a teenager in Paris, Amsterdam, and
Leiden. He served as president of the American Academy of Arts and Sciences and as Boylston Professor of Rhetoric at Harvard, spoke seven languages, wrote poetry, and tasted fine wines.[4] He was a great admirer of
the classics and the republican virtues with which they could instruct
modern Americans. In 1830, after his presidential term of office ended
and before his election to the U.S. Congress, Adams spent two hours
every day for ten months reading in Latin the complete works of Cicero,
whom he described as "not only the orator, but the moral philosopher of
Rome."[5] Adams's interest in classical antiquity was not just political, but
literary and artistic as well. He judged Virgil's *Georgics* "the most perfect
composition, that ever issued from the mind of man" and adorned his
house with six bronze classical busts, calling them his "Household

Gods."[6] His classicism contributed to his unpopularity as president. Adams gained the White House in a decision of the House of Representatives after the election of 1824 left none of the four candidates with a majority of the electoral college. This selection seemed particularly undemocratic because Andrew Jackson gained the largest number of both popular and electoral votes. Jacksonians eagerly painted Adams as a stuffed shirt, and even Adams's own supporters found him difficult, remote, and awkward. Adams was defeated by Jackson in his reelection bid in 1828, ushering in an era of self-conscious national populism.

The democratic, commercial spirit of the Jacksonian era led to a renewed outpouring of objections to the classical curriculum in American colleges. Anticlassicists reiterated many of the themes first articulated by Benjamin Rush and others in the late eighteenth century—that the classics were elitist, difficult and immoral—but especially emphasized the uselessness of classical learning in a bustling market economy.[7] Banker and former United States Secretary of the Treasury Albert Gallatin (1761–1849) argued in 1830 that the study of Greek and Latin was a hindrance rather than a help: "[I]f before the Reformation the way to the word of God and to his worship was obstructed by the improper use of the Latin language, we now find the same impediment arresting a more general diffusion of human knowledge." Two years later Gallatin resigned from the council that was in the process of creating New York University when he was unable to convince his colleagues to make study of the classics optional.[8] South Carolina legislator Thomas Smith Grimké (1786–1834) published a series of anticlassical addresses in 1831 in which he complained that classical education was "totally useless to the great majority" of Americans, such as the "working classes" and the "man of business."[9] The physician and Transylvania University professor Charles Caldwell (1772–1853) objected in 1836 to the uselessness of classical antiquity to "practical science" and attributed successes in art and literature to faithful observation of nature rather than slavish devotion to past authority.[10] These increasingly prominent criticisms of classical education have led scholars of American society, education, and politics to view the first half of the nineteenth century as a "silver age" of classicism in America, when Greece and Rome began to decline from the peak of their influence in the late eighteenth century.[11]

Yet there is convincing evidence that reports of classicism's demise are not only exaggerated but patently untrue, that in fact, classicism was alive and well in mid-nineteenth-century America. Most visibly, the first half of the nineteenth century was the heyday of Greek revival architecture, but classicism's influence reached beyond the architects, artists, and sculptors who continually invoked ancient models for the edification of the general public.[12] Popular authors both male and female frequently summoned classical examples for their readers. Nathaniel Hawthorne's novel, *The Marble Fawn* (1860); David Paul Brown's play, *Sertorius: Or, the Roman Patriot* (1830); and the short stories of Martha Bayard Smith set in Nero's Rome that appear in the early 1830s in the *Ladies' Magazine*, all assumed the relevance of antiquity for exploring modern moral and political themes. Furthermore, most American colleges and academies continued to locate Greek and Latin at the core of their curriculum. To be educated in mid-nineteenth-century America still meant having a deep familiarity with the ancient Greeks and Romans through their language, literature, history, and thought. Yet the social and political pressures that emerged with the rise of the West and of Jacksonian democracy transformed classical education in the United States, and these pressures also changed the aspects of classical antiquity deemed most relevant to political life in antebellum America.

For classically trained educators and politicians alike, the growing political fervor among immigrants, westerners, and the unschooled brought fears over the rise of demagogues and the rule of the mob. The source for these fears could be found in the ancients themselves. Aristotle, in the fifth book of his *Politics* (1304b–1305a), blamed demagogues for the collapse of democratic governments. Demagogues employed the courts and the popular assemblies to threaten the wealthy, with the result that either the wealthy banded together to overthrow the democracy and set up an oligarchy, or that the demagogue removed any political rivals and established a tyranny. According to Aristotle, tyranny was a particularly prevalent danger when the demagogue was a general.

Polybius (6.4.6–10; 6.57.5–9) used the term *ochlocracy* (from the Greek *ochlos*, "mob") to describe the decay of democratic government into a frenzy of greedy and irrational attacks upon anyone with a modicum of wealth and privilege. Stirred to anger and puffed up by flattery, the people can become easily controlled by those seeking power. Nineteenth-century Americans tended to use the term *mobocracy* to describe the same phenomenon, of which the violence of the French Revolution provided the most immediate example. After a period of chaos, when a general (Napoleon) came to lead the French people and offered them territorial expansion and riches, tyranny emerged.[13]

Trends in the early national period appeared to some commentators to confirm the ancient prophecies about the perils of democracy. Beginning in the 1820s, a number of classically educated Americans began to express concern that an expanding electorate, unschooled in the history of ancient Greece and Rome, would follow those states into inevitable decay. These commentators could point to alarming developments that seemed to forecast mobocracy: the extension of the franchise, the influx of uneducated immigrants, and the constant annexation of new states and territories. Especially unnerving was the rise of contentious party politicians, whose need to oblige the public made them appear very much like Aristotle's dangerous demagogues. Having the authoritarian general Andrew Jackson in the White House only deepened the concerns of the classically educated over the future of American democracy.

Jackson and his Democratic allies were not alone in playing up the conflicts in class and wealth that divided Americans. With equal fervor arose the Antimasonic party, which was launched in western New York State in 1826 and became a major force in New England and the mid-Atlantic states during the early 1830s. The Antimasons championed farmers and evangelical Protestants who felt threatened both by the economic power of the growing cities and by their religious fears over increasing secularism and Catholic immigration. Antimasons proudly declared that they represented the "lower classes," and they decried the political power of the "ultra aristocracy" with their corrupt morals and education.[14]

To connect with this passionate and largely unschooled citizenry attracted by the populism of the Democrats and the Antimasons, a more direct style of public speaking emerged. Political oratory began to deviate sharply from the ornate, highly formal, Ciceronian "periodic" style so prized in the revolutionary era.[15] The new breed of political orator not only spoke in an unadorned, straightforward style, but he might also openly mock the classically imbued styles of an earlier era. "I had rather speak sense in one plain and expressive language, than speak nonsense in fifty," declared the Irish-born New York state representative Mike Walsh in 1854, to much laughter.[16]

In the 1820s, a new generation of young classical scholars at American colleges began to voice concern about what, to them, marked a deterioration in political discourse. These young classicists and their allies looked upon the rise of unpolished rhetoric as a first step towards mobocracy. Modern politicians, they argued, were dumbing down both the content and the style of their speeches, playing to popular passions rather than deploying ethical and classical models to encourage civic virtue. "Our orators and demagogues pamper the pride of that great despot, the sovereign people, with flattery as fulsome as was ever into a tyrant's ear," remarked the twenty-one-year-old Harvard classicist C. C. Felton (1807–1862) in 1828.[17] The anti-intellectualism of the Jacksonian era also encouraged mobocracy because it made the public unable to distinguish the demagogue from the virtuous leader. "An ignorant community may be virtuous in motive, but cannot be so in practice," continued Felton, "and you will see your peaceful ignoramus" become "the blind instrument of outrage in its blackest forms."[18] The most distinguished politicians in the Congress could not compete with the powerful new oratory of the demagogues, since these out-of-touch leaders were prone to indulge in what another proponent of classicism, the Boston lawyer and politician J. C. Gray (1793–1881), called "irrelevant and ostentatious digressions, in cold and trite similes, and a gay confusion of metaphors, in finical circumlocutions, and a studied avoidance of direct and definite language."[19]

This decline in rhetorical standards appeared not just among the unschooled but among the educated as well, and it accompanied a change in how rhetoric was taught in American colleges. In the second half of the eighteenth century, colleges replaced the formerly required composition and delivery of syllogistic disputations in Latin, with regularly scheduled forensic disputations delivered in English. Forensics was a practicum in how to become an effective public speaker. Upperclassmen were required to prepare speeches on assigned topics that dealt with contemporary politics (e.g., "Would a Permanent Navy be beneficial to the United States?") as well as philosophical, literary, or historical topics (e.g., "Was Brutus justifiable in killing Caesar?"). During the first decades of the nineteenth century, colleges reduced or eliminated forensics from the curriculum. Students found the exercises tedious, and faculty believed the time could be better spent covering additional material in the ever expanding body of knowledge considered relevant for a college education. At Harvard in the 1810s, forensics went from a weekly to a monthly exercise. The University of Pennsylvania dropped forensics for juniors in 1836 and for seniors seven years later. Brown removed forensics from the curriculum altogether by 1827, a step Princeton seems to have taken a decade earlier. College students continued to practice public speaking by joining debate societies, but these societies tended to favor extemporaneous debate over the time-consuming preparation of carefully crafted oratory.[20]

Furthermore, the teaching methods for the classical subjects that remained at the heart of American college education failed to prepare students for their lives as citizens engaged in public discourse. American colleges had long been in the business of training orators for politics and pulpit. Their formal curriculum featured study of the speeches of the ancient orators Cicero, Isocrates, and Demosthenes. Yet by the 1820s classicists on college campuses were expressing growing dissatisfaction with the focus upon grammar and syntax at the expense of content and context. They feared that such a narrow focus prevented classical education from fulfilling its role as buttress against the destructive whims of popular agitation and personal avarice.

Among the earliest and most scathing criticisms of collegiate classicism came from the thirty-one-year-old Princeton Greek scholar Robert Patton (1794–1839) in a lecture he delivered in 1825. Patton linked failures in classical education to the political decline of the young republic.

"The preservation of our political health and vigour demands that we provide, from within ourselves, an antidote to the widespreading corruption which darkens our political prospects," Patton said. "Our citizens may be enlightened—may have a smattering of science, and even be able to construe and parse a passage in Homer or Thucydides—and still be destitute of that kind of intelligence which peculiarly adapts them to the form of government under which we live."[21]

The persistent focus in schools and colleges on the grammar of ancient authors failed to teach students to grasp the real importance of antiquity. The writings of the ancient Greeks and Romans—orators included—needed to be approached not as grammar manuals but as literature that would invigorate the spirit and cultivate the soul. The classical world properly approached allowed students to remake their inner selves, to develop an intellect and sensibilities inured to the ephemeral passions and seductions of modernity. Such an approach demanded the wholesale revision of classicism in American higher education and the connection of that learning to politics. The strategy of this new generation of classicists was not to diminish the importance of the ancients in American education and politics, but instead, to remake classicism by forging anew the relationship between antiquity and modernity.

This desire to make classical education more relevant to American democracy dovetailed with the calls for educational reform that became characteristic of Whig political philosophy. The Whigs no less than their Democratic rivals accepted the primacy of the common man in political decision making. Yet many Whig leaders feared that the poorly educated American populace could easily be swayed by the facile sophistry of the demagogue. Preservation of the democracy demanded that schooling, including the rudiments of classical education, become more widely available and more comprehensive.[22]

Arguing in a speech in 1835 that New York State should fund libraries for the public schools, future Whig governor William H. Seward (1801–1872) declared that basic literacy alone was not a sufficient educational goal. Seward told his audience that the ability to read and write was merely a means for acquiring the true knowledge to be gained from the "higher cultivation of the mind," without which citizens were doomed

> . . . to become the sport of demagogues, and the slaves of popular passion, caprice, and excitement. Something more is wanting. It is necessary, if we would be qualified to discharge the duties of electors, that we should understand some of the principles of political economy, of the philosophy of the human mind, and, above all, of moral and religious science.[23]

Educational reform was foremost on the agenda of Massachusetts Whig governor Edward Everett (1794–1865), who had been Felton's predecessor and teacher while Eliot Professor of Greek at Harvard and who had also been a Harvard classmate of J. C. Gray in the Class of 1811.[24] In 1837, Governor Everett prompted the Massachusetts legislature to establish the first state board of education. Another Whig politician, Horace Mann (1796–1859), became the board's first secretary. Through Mann's urging, Massachusetts established teacher-training institutes ("normal schools"), provided money for school-building construction, and increased the length of the school year.[25]

Both in and out of public office, Everett was a well-respected orator who regularly employed his background as a classicist to promote education. Everett later served as president of Harvard and as a U.S. senator. With his artful gestures, melodious tenor, and his habit of memorizing even the longest of his speeches, he was always in great demand as a public speaker. In a speech he delivered as governor to a meeting of public school officials in 1838, Everett directly connected the spread of education to the preservation of democratic government. Under a constitution that "gives as much weight to the vote of the uninformed and ignorant as to that of the well-informed and intelligent citizen, it is plain that the avenues to information should be as wide and numerous as possible," Everett said. Education allows the voter to "make up his mind for himself." The cultivation of an intellect capable of independent decision making prevented citizens from slavishly following the party line or being seduced by demagogues. "The whole energy should be directed to multiply the numbers of those capable of forming an independent and rational judgment of their own, and to diminish as much as possible the numbers of the opposite class, who, being blinded by ignorance, are at the mercy of any one who has an interest and the skill to delude them."[26]

Germany provided the models and inspiration for this new generation of classicists and educational reformers. Several had first-hand knowledge of German education. Mann visited Germany in 1843 to examine institutions of primary and secondary education, particularly Prussia's mandatory public elementary schools with students organized by age.[27] A generation earlier, Everett, Patton, and Joseph Cogswell (1786–1871) all studied at the university in Göttingen. So had George Bancroft, whose political sympathies were with the Democrats. In 1823, Bancroft and Cogswell established a preparatory academy on the model of the German *Gymnasium* at Round Hill near Northampton in western Massachusetts (the school lasted little more than a decade). Another prominent classicist who pursued training in Germany was Theodore Woolsey (1801–1889), who became the first Professor of Greek at Yale in 1831 and president of that university in 1846. In Germany, Woolsey studied in Leipzig, Bonn, and Berlin. Bancroft, too, had spent time studying in the Prussian capital.[28]

For classicists, German scholarship fused the romantic yearning for an idealized, distant past untainted by the corruption of modernity with a scientific determination to understand the Greeks and Romans within their historical context. Not only were students taught to appreciate the unique, historically contingent qualities that made the Greeks Greek and the Romans Roman, but they viewed ancient history, rhetoric, and literature as paths to political consciousness and self-development rather than merely a source for grammatical details and arcane allusions.

Moreover, classicists now turned their attention away from Rome, which had for so long dominated the educational and political scene, and embraced Greece, especially Athens of the fifth century B.C. Far from fearing Athens as the seat of chaos and mob rule (as Americans had done in the eighteenth century), nineteenth-century classical scholars embraced Athens as the cradle of democracy. They coined a new term to describe this new Greece-centered pedagogical agenda: students, they said, would "become Greek," literally remade by their study of the totality of the art, literature, and history of classical Athens. The term *becoming Greek* fused the new infatuation with Greece to the antebellum faith in "self-culture," the ability to form oneself through individual effort. Hellenism thus became a branch of self-culture, one means among many through which Americans could greet this new era of populism and romanticism.

Although German scholarship had a profound influence on American classicists, significant differences existed in the political uses prescribed for classicism in Germany and the United States.[29] In the first half of the nineteenth century, Germany remained divided into several separate political entities that often marked the divisions between Protestants and Catholics. Classicism, and in particular Hellenism, presented a mode in which national aspirations could break through these divisions. Athens, Sparta, Corinth, and Thebes were separate, independent city-states during the classical period, yet all were Greek and shared a literature, art, culture, and sensibility that transcended political boundaries. For many educated Germans, ancient Greece became the model for envisioning a unified German identity that transcended religious and political differences. German Hellenism maintained this strongly nationalistic character. Although sometimes connected with the desire for liberal political reforms, the love for ancient Greece was not necessarily an outgrowth of a love for democracy. National identity was the form of political consciousness these classicists wished to inspire among their fellow Germans.[30]

In the United States, the political rationale for the turn to Greece was quite different. By the second quarter of the nineteenth century, American government was almost universally understood as a democracy in which the farmer, the merchant, the landowner, and the landless each had an equal say in the decision-making process. It was the ancient Athenian democracy that inspired the classically minded of the Jacksonian era. The example of the Roman Republic, with its rigid class distinctions and aristocratic political leadership, no longer seemed relevant, and Rome's Golden Age under the emperor Augustus was downright repellent. "In Roman literature we have sometimes cause to be disgusted with servile adulation," Bancroft complained in 1824. "[W]e could wish that Horace had not employed his genius in celebrating the victories of Augustus; and should cherish Virgil the more, if something of the rustic republicanism of the elder days were discoverable in his verse." On the other hand, the Greeks were to be favored, particularly the Athenians, because, according to Bancroft, "though they sometimes flattered kings, [they] never eulogised the regal form of government."[31]

These two changes—from classical texts as grammar lessons to classicism as self-culture, and from the reverence for Rome to the infatuation with Greece—led to a reappraisal among classicists and classically trained Americans about the value of the ancient orator Demosthenes. American students had studied both Cicero and Demosthenes since the seventeenth century, but until the antebellum era, Rome's cherished orator enjoyed greater popularity with regard to both rhetorical eloquence and civic virtue. Now, however, Demosthenes, who had lived in the fourth century B.C. during the turbulent final years of Athenian greatness, surpassed Cicero among orators who appreciated the democracy of classical Athens and wished to confer its virtues onto the new republic. Northerners and Southerners both christened each of their most cherished antebellum political orators as a modern Demosthenes: South Carolinians Thomas Pinckney (1750–1828) and Hugh Swinton Legaré (1797–1843), and New Englander Daniel Webster (1782–1852) were all called Demosthenes at various times in their careers.[32]

Demosthenes also gained approval for his cleaner, more straightforward style. Of his language, J. C. Gray wrote in 1826, "We perceive in it nothing vague or extravagant, nothing florid or redundant, nothing strained or ostentatious."[33] This plainer, Attic style of oratory had been proven particularly well suited for communicating to the common man, whether to the humble Athenian juror desperate for his three obols pay, or to the unschooled immigrant or frontiersman of antebellum America. The Attic style typified by Demosthenes also seemed more appropriately manly and muscular than Cicero's Asiatic flourishes. One Southern political commentator praised the "rugged strength" of Demosthenes' speaking style.[34] Study of Demosthenes, argued another commentator, "indurates the mental constitution, gives it muscle and energy, makes it like iron, girds the intellect with power, and teaches it to concentrate its energies." Next to Demosthenes, Cicero often appeared "spiritless."[35]

Americans of the first half of the nineteenth century, then, admired Demosthenes both because he represented and understood the workings of democracy, and because he embodied emerging mid-century ideals of muscular manhood. Yet classicists counseled students not to stop with the mere imitation of Demosthenes' supposedly rugged, manly cadences, nor to assume that oratory in American democracy was merely an extension of oratory in classical Athens. Imitation had been the goal of classicism in the eighteenth century: to emulate Ciceronian cadences was to subscribe to the Enlightenment theory of history, which papered over the chronological gap separating the new American republic from the ancient Roman republic in order to fashion a seamless inheritance of political legitimacy and ethical ideals. To classicists in the middle decades of the nineteenth century, this pedagogical program of imitation became unacceptable because it failed to show students how different Greece and Rome were from modern America. It failed, in other words, to transport them to a radically remote and different antiquity that would purge them of their modernity. The utility to be found in the study of the writings of the ancient Greeks and Romans was precisely that their civilizations, just like their languages, were dead, utterly sealed off from the present day.[36]

The purpose of an education in classical oratory was not to enable politicians obtrusively to sprinkle purple passages into otherwise mundane and insipid popular panderings, but to allow these future leaders to envision American society anew, unencumbered by the increasingly materialistic and mercantile character of antebellum democracy. Rather than imitating Cicero, which would bestow only a veneer of classicism, mid-nineteenth-century students should attempt to transform their inner selves. "I become loftier, and am no longer the man I was," proclaimed the classicist C. C. Felton in a speech in 1830. "I seem to myself to be Demosthenes, standing upon the tribunal, pronouncing that same oration, exhorting the assembled Athenians to imitate the valor and win the glory of their ancestors."[37]

The romantic ideals of self-culture echo in this new pedagogical program, and indeed the new popularity of Demosthenes in American colleges formed part of the Whig philosophy of remaking the nation by remaking the self.[38] Even the Democrat George Bancroft praised the speeches of Demosthenes for teaching the doctrine of liberty "not merely because it makes a nation more prosperous, but because it is essential to the moral dignity and intellectual freedom of individuals."[39]

"Becoming" Demosthenes, classicists hoped in the early national era, would make students into better participants in the American democracy. They could on the one hand profit from the social, economic, and political freedoms of the early national era that had encouraged Americans to draw new parallels between their nation and ancient Athens. Yet on the other hand, they would resist the dangers of those same liberties, rebuking the demagogue with the wisdom bestowed by a classical education. Against Jacksonian anti-intellectualism they would offer knowledge of the most politically relevant societies in human history; against the pursuit of material gain they would offer a higher spiritual wisdom; and against the vulgarity of the age of Barnum they would offer the timeless beauties of ancient art and literature. In an era that began to denigrate conspicuously the relevance of classicism to the political scene, classicists in American colleges responded with a wholesale revolution of antiquity's function in the new republic. Abandoning the Enlightenment premise that antiquity offered direct political and ethical parallels to the modern era, they argued instead that a new, historicized classical world better suited the new era and would prevent the democracy from sliding into mobocracy. Students would read Demosthenes in ancient Greek not to imitate him but to become him, to surrender their objectionable modernity in a new program of self-culture that would secure the health of the infant nation for many decades to come.

The Hellenism of the nineteenth century was successful in maintaining the centrality of antiquity within antebellum American education. In the political sphere, however, the focus in the United States upon individual self-improvement rendered study of the ancients far less able to cultivate a transcendent sense of national identity and unity. Classical education proved fundamentally incapable of reconciling Americans over the issue of slavery, an issue that ultimately tore the Whigs, and the nation, apart.

No political leader better represented the hopes and outlook of transcendent classicism than Edward Everett. Bitterly disappointed when the Civil War broke out, he blamed Southern demagogues for misleading the masses by using the slavery issue to cloak their own designs for power. As a staunch Unionist but a tepid abolitionist, Everett had the respect of both moderate Democrats and the remnant of the so-called Cotton Whigs, Northerners who were reluctant to join the antislavery Republican Party. Although in his late sixties and often in poor health, Everett gave speeches in support of the Union cause during the Civil War.[40]

In the autumn of 1863, Everett was asked to give the dedicatory oration for the cemetery at Gettysburg, the final resting place of the soldiers killed in the famous battle that had taken place in July of that year. Although the brief, closing remarks of President Abraham Lincoln have garnered greater subsequent fame, Everett's speech can be seen as the culmination and coda of classically inspired public oratory from the antebellum era. Everett's speech at Gettysburg has been lampooned because it lasted nearly two hours, compared with the paltry three minutes for Lincoln's remarks. But the fact was that Everett had been commissioned specifically to give the main oration of the day, while Lincoln was asked afterward to give what the program described as "dedicatory remarks." Both men, that is, did what they were asked to do by the organizers. Everett's long, exploratory, and instructive oration fulfilled the expectations of nineteenth-century listeners who not only expected lengthy speeches from the pulpit, the stump, and the lecture circuit, but relied on such speeches as a major source of information and education. Knowing this, Everett spent a great deal of time preparing for the speech to make his facts accurate. Lincoln's remarks, delivered after Everett's, could be short because Everett's had been so expansive.[41]

Though it does not suit modern tastes, Everett's speech embodies the nineteenth-century conviction that Attic models—not just of oratory, but of mourning, valor, and honor on and off the battlefield—could do most to lend the appropriate gravity to the cemetery's dedication. He opened the speech by likening the fallen soldiers at Gettysburg to the ancient Greeks who fell at Marathon in 490 B.C., defending their soil from Persian invasion, and he saluted the assembled crowd by equating them with the mourning matrons and daughters of Athens.[42] Stylistically, Everett's language conformed to Attic models of oratory, including the beloved Demosthenes. Everett avoided subordinate clauses and extensive ornamentation. The vocabulary, by nineteenth-century standards, was restrained, more monosyllabic and Anglo-Saxon than polysyllabic and Latinate. Most of the speech was taken up with historical narration of the battle, which was related energetically and crisply. And while painstakingly detailed in recounting the blow-by-blow of the battle of Gettysburg and the South's culpability in the Civil War, Everett's oration barely mentioned modern slavery and blacks (whom he called the "helpless colored population"), alluding to them only a few times in the speech. In fact, he was as interested in pointing out the "Asiatic despotism and slavery" of the Persians in 490 B.C. as he was in the slavery of the South. We Americans are all Greeks, Everett seemed to be saying, and by being Greek we can transcend the immediate tragedy of America's failure to prevent civil war and endow the war with higher historical purpose.[43]

In subsequent generations Everett's speech would become little noted nor long remembered, but the achievement of Everett and other antebellum classicists in establishing classicism as antimodernism and antimaterialism would remain a strain in American political thought to the present day.

Chapter 4

William Sanders Scarborough and the Politics of Classical Education for African Americans

—Michele Valerie Ronnick

The preeminent Southern political leader in antebellum America was John C. Calhoun. The South Carolinian served in Washington as a congressman, senator, secretary of war, secretary of state, and vice president. He was a staunch defender of white Southern interests, in particular, the "peculiar institution" of slavery. During the 1830s, when the abolitionist movement was beginning to gather wider support among Northerners, Calhoun is reported to have told two visiting Boston abolitionists that "if he could find a Negro who knew the Greek syntax, he would then believe that the Negro was a human being and should be treated as a man."[1]

White Southerners did not wish to take any chances that such a situation could arise. Few African Americans in the antebellum South had even the basic literacy skills of reading and writing. Already in colonial times, South Carolina had enacted a statute that prohibited teaching slaves how to read and write, yet it was in reaction to the slave revolt led by Nat Turner in 1831 that most Southern states systematically prevented slaves, and sometimes free blacks as well, from acquiring the ability to read and write. These laws from the 1830s included fines and prison sentences for white teachers, and whippings for free black teachers and slaves alike.[2]

Instruction of individual slaves took place, but such activities were conducted secretly and sporadically in private homes. Occasionally those suspected of teaching slaves were put under police surveillance and arrested. A Norfolk, Virginia, judge sent Margaret Douglas, a white widow who secretly taught free black children in her home, to prison for one month in 1853. It has been estimated that in 1860, fewer than two percent of slaves knew how to read and write. Even including the more highly educated free blacks of the North, still only ten percent of all African American adults on the eve of the Civil War seem to have had basic literacy skills.[3]

Fewer still had experienced advanced, formal education, which was available only in a few institutions in the North, or in Europe. Oberlin College, founded in 1833, was strongly abolitionist in character and welcomed black students. Black Oberlin alumni of the antebellum era included attorney John Mercer Langston, who later served as a U.S. ambassador; and Benjamin F. Randolph, a Methodist minister who was assassinated while serving as a South Carolina legislator in 1868. Like Randolph, nearly all of the African Americans then familiar with Greek and Latin were ordained ministers. Bishop Daniel A. Payne of the African Methodist Episcopal Church studied at the Lutheran Theological Seminary at Gettysburg. Francis L. Cardozo won prizes in Latin and Greek at Glasgow University in Scotland, with additional British education at the United Presbyterian Theological Hall, Edinburgh, and at New College, London, a Congregationalist seminary. Both Payne and Cardozo were freeborn natives of Charleston, which, along with New Orleans, were the only Southern cities with significant numbers of educated, free blacks before the Civil War.[4]

During the Civil War, abolitionists pressed for the establishment of a government program to promote the education of emancipated slaves. Only a month before his assassination, Abraham Lincoln signed into law a bill establishing the Freedmen's Bureau, which, among other tasks, oversaw the operations of new schools set up to educate former slaves. Although the Freedmen's Bureau provided confiscated buildings for use as schools, as well as military protection for teachers and facilities, the schools' salaries, staffing, and supplies were the responsibilities of private organizations.[5]

The most prominent was the American Missionary Association, an evangelical Protestant abolitionist group. The AMA established schools across the South both to prepare former slaves for their lives as free citizens, as well as to inculcate religious teachings that adhered to the theological views of the Congregationalists, Methodists, and Baptists who were the mainstay of the organization. AMA officials were firm believers in racial equality, and they viewed part of their educational mission to provide for the creation of a black intellectual elite that would eventually assume the leadership of the African American community. The new black elite needed the same educational background as the leaders of white America. The goal was to have these former slaves assist their fellow freedmen in forming a society that mirrored white society, promoting the ideals of prosperity, civic mindedness, and Christian ethics as understood by the AMA's white supporters.[6]

AMA leaders were well aware that nearly all college-preparatory schools and universities in the South, and many such institutions in the North, refused admittance to blacks. For this reason, the AMA included college-preparatory work for special students in some of the common schools and normal schools, in addition to establishing seven colleges in the South during the four years after the end of the Civil War. Classical education became available to African Americans on the widest scale theretofore seen.[7]

One of the students who learned Greek and Latin at AMA-sponsored schools was William Sanders Scarborough. Scarborough was born with the official status of a slave in Macon, Georgia, in 1852. Scarborough's mother was also a slave, but for reasons unknown, her owner allowed her to marry a black freedman and raise a family with her husband. The couple had three children, but William was the only child who survived beyond age three. He had been secretly taught how to read and write by a white man who, ironically, was opposed to legal improvements for slaves and free blacks.[8]

After the Civil War, Scarborough attended freedmen's schools in Macon, and at the AMA-sponsored Lewis High School, he was first introduced to Latin and Greek. Scarborough was an excellent student and at the age of seventeen, he continued his studies at Atlanta University, another AMA institution. Two years later, he entered Oberlin, where he graduated four years later in 1875 having successfully completed the classical course of study. Scarborough returned to Macon, teaching in his old high school.[9]

The outcome of the presidential election of 1876 dramatically changed the situation for African Americans in the South. After the Civil War, the Republican-controlled Congress demanded that Southern states "reconstruct" their governments and political systems to allow freedmen to vote. Through constitutional amendments and military force, this system of Reconstruction enabled mixed-race Republican governments to emerge in the states of the former Confederacy. During the Republican administration of Ulysses S. Grant (1869–1877), however, widespread corruption and an economic downturn in 1873 caused many Northern voters to sour on the Republican party. In the South, so-called "Redeemer" governments made up exclusively of white Democrats began to take power at the state level once federal troops were withdrawn from supervising the electoral process. The resulting widespread intimidation of blacks prevented them from voting. In the 1874 elections, Democrats regained control of Congress for the first time since the Civil War. Two years later, Democratic presidential candidate Samuel J. Tilden won the popular vote over his Republican rival, Rutherford B. Hayes, but Republicans refused to accept that Tilden had won in Florida, South Carolina, and Louisiana, the only Southern states still under federal military control.[10]

The conflict was eventually resolved when Democrats agreed to allow Hayes to win the three disputed Southern states and the election, in return for the end of Reconstruction. In the meantime, violence against blacks and black institutions—an ever-present danger since the Civil War—sharply increased. Lewis High School in Macon, where Scarborough worked as a teacher, was destroyed by arson in December 1876.[11] Although classes continued to be taught in the basement of a church, the following year the AMA decided to close the school. Scarborough was out of a job.

Scarborough gained an appointment as principal of a South Carolina school affiliated with the African Methodist Episcopal Church, but afraid for his personal safety, he returned to Oberlin to study Hebrew with a possible view of entering the ministry. Passing the summer in New York, Scarborough received a letter offering an appointment to teach classics at Wilberforce University, another educational institution affiliated with the AME Church. Wilberforce is located near the southwestern Ohio city of Xenia, roughly fifty miles northeast of Cincinnati.[12]

Ohio remained Scarborough's home until his death in 1926. He spent the rest of his career at Wilberforce and affiliated institutions, serving as the university's president from 1908 until his retirement in 1920. Scarborough also enjoyed an active scholarly career. He contributed over twenty pieces to *Transactions of the American Philological Association*, the official publication of the professional organization for classics professors in the United States. These pieces were summaries of papers he had delivered at the organization's annual meeting. He even represented the association at a conference at Cambridge University in England in 1921. His 1881 textbook, *First Lessons in Greek*, was adopted in college-preparatory academies across the country. His academic renown also made Scarborough a prominent African American leader in the late nineteenth and early twentieth centuries. Scarborough frequently gave speeches before black audiences. He also wrote numerous essays for newspapers and periodicals, both in the black press as well as for publications, such as *The New York Times*, having a predominantly white readership.[13]

Scarborough was also a leading figure among African Americans in the Republican party. He became involved in Republican politics not long after his arrival at Wilberforce in 1877. In 1879, he worked on behalf of Alphonso Taft in Taft's unsuccessful bid for the Republican nomination for Ohio governor. Scarborough's closest political connection would be made with an affable and charismatic Cincinnati politician only six years his senior, Joseph B. Foraker.[14]

Foraker was the Republican candidate for Ohio governor in 1883, but he lost in a Democratic landslide due to GOP attempts to regulate alcohol. He was more successful two years later. Foraker's tenure as governor marked a period of improving conditions for Ohio's African Americans. Although the original Ohio constitution prohibited slavery, laws were enacted early on to restrict black immigration, employment, redress through the legal system, and educational opportunities. Blacks also did not have the right to vote. Some of the harshest restrictions of the "Black Laws" were removed before the Civil War, but even after Ohio blacks finally gained the vote through ratification of the Fifteenth Amendment in 1870, the educational provisions requiring segregated schools remained. Foraker used his influence to get the last of the "Black Laws" taken off the books. Although discrimination in housing and redrawn school districts continued to keep most Ohio public schools highly segregated, such segregation was no longer enshrined in official law.[15]

Foraker also pushed for public financing for Wilberforce. In 1887, the legislature approved funds for teacher training and industrial education at the university. Wilberforce's president, Samuel T. Mitchell, sought state money to stabilize the school's shaky finances. Mitchell realized that funds might be available through Ohio's proceeds from the Morrill Act, which was passed by Congress in 1862 giving states title to federal lands to be sold for the establishment of public universities. Ohio, however, already had its "land-grant" university, Ohio State. Working through Benjamin Arnett, the financial secretary of the AME Church who had been elected to a term in the Ohio House of Representatives, Mitchell was able to convince the Republican-controlled legislature to fund an additional small program in agricultural and mechanical training at Wilberforce. The university, in turn, would merge its already existing teacher-training efforts into the state-financed program. The new Combined Normal and Industrial Department at Wilberforce was overseen by a separate board of trustees, with some trustees appointed by the governor and others appointed by the university.[16]

Public funding for the C. N. & I. (as the program was familiarly called) conformed to dominant white views in the late nineteenth century about the types of education that were proper for African Americans. Many whites believed that blacks were best served not by a classical education, but instead by learning a skilled trade that would teach them discipline, occupy their days in hard work, and enable them to find employment in an industrializing America. The organization that did the most to promote industrial education among African Americans was the Slater Fund, established with one million dollars by Connecticut textile manufacturer John Fox Slater in 1882. During its first decade of existence, the fund distributed more than $200,000 to black educational institutions. Leading the fund's board of trustees was former U.S. president Rutherford B. Hayes. Hayes wrote in his diary that Slater money should be used to teach blacks that they "must earn their own living, and that by the labor of their hands as far as that may be. This is the gospel of salvation for the colored man.[17]

The moralizing Hayes had been a strong supporter of African American political rights. During his first campaign for Ohio governor in 1867, Hayes also touted a ballot issue that would have given Ohio blacks the right to vote. Hayes won the election, but the ballot issue on black suffrage was defeated. Although the Ohio legislature initially rejected the Fifteenth Amendment, Governor Hayes was able to get the legislature to ratify the amendment on a second vote. When it came to education, Hayes was consistent in his promotion of industrial training not just for blacks, but for poor whites as well. He was governor at the time of the establishment of what became The Ohio State University, and he wanted the land-grant college to keep its focus on agriculture and manufacturing. Even in retirement, Hayes kept active in Ohio educational politics. The former president objected to plans by Governor Foraker to appoint Scarborough to Ohio State's board of trustees. Hayes insisted that the board needed a representative of agriculture rather than a classics professor, and Foraker felt compelled to accede to Hayes' request.[18]

Foraker, however, shared with Scarborough a universal regard for classical education and disdain for its wholesale replacement by utilitarian training. The first major speech of Foraker's successful 1885 campaign for Ohio governor was the commencement address at Wilberforce University. While much of the speech concerned civil rights, the first third of the address promoted the importance of Greek and Latin. Foraker argued that ancient languages provided insights to the human mind and fostered intellectual curiosity, elements that allowed human beings to live deeper, more meaningful lives. He told the graduates that "instead of neglecting language study, study it—study it in all its length and breadth, in all its wonderful meaning. . . . Let your studies be broad that your minds may be broad, and that your duties in life may be successful in the highest sense.[19]

The Wilberforce commencement address should not be dismissed as merely the conventional words of a campaigning politician. Although Foraker was not the sort of individual whose classical education remained immediate and evergreen, he showed great appreciation for those in whom it did. Foraker requested from Scarborough a copy of

Scarborough's Greek textbook, and upon its arrival sent the professor a letter of thanks in which he stated, "Surely there is nothing more calculated to test the intellect than the preparation of a Greek work." Years later, when the retired Foraker was visiting his son Benson who was dying, father and son spent part of the time discussing the Roman philosopher Lucretius.[20]

Scarborough saw his duty as a teacher and a scholar to impart that wider world opened by the study of classical antiquity, to enable his students "to live on higher planes."[21] He was acutely aware that the opportunity to engage the ancients was not available to many African Americans, and Scarborough constantly promoted Greek and Latin as necessary components within the spectrum of black education. Whites who were opposed or gave only tepid support to classical education for blacks did not just have in mind the practical concerns of finding employment in a segregated society in which blacks were excluded from many professions. There were political concerns as well.

The same reactionary warnings over the dangers of demagogues and mob rule prompted by universal white male suffrage in the antebellum era were repeated in the wake of the Fifteenth Amendment, particularly in the post-Reconstruction South. Atlanta newspaper editor Henry W. Grady told fellow whites in Augusta, Georgia, in 1887 that the black vote "is ignorant, easily deluded or betrayed. It is impulsive, lashed by a word into violence. It is purchasable, having the incentive of poverty and cupidity and the restraints of neither pride nor conviction."[22]

Half a century earlier, similar fears over the growing electoral might of immigrants and poor whites led to calls by Whig reformers for expansion of educational opportunities and instruction in classical antiquity. The response to black suffrage after the Civil War was different. Southern whites used the chimera of mobocracy to support restrictions on African American voting. Whites were especially concerned that their own internal squabbles could allow African American voters to hold the balance of power in elections, as blacks did in some Northern states, particularly Ohio. Legally suppressing the black vote to the point of insignificance prevented that possibility. Underlying the explicit promotion of industrial education for blacks was the implicit understanding that classical education would transform African Americans into an informed and engaged electorate who on their own would be able to guarantee their fair share in the political process.

Whites also had a proprietary fetish over classical antiquity, which they did not want to share with African Americans. Newspaper editor Walter Guild of Tuscaloosa, Alabama, wrote in *The Arena* magazine in 1900, "The civilization of the ancient Greek owes its potent influence upon the enlightenment of the nineteenth century to the purity of that

Caucasian blood that was kept inviolate. The age of Pericles and Alexander, with its grand achievements in molding the destinies of the civilized world, is a striking illustration of the supreme mission of the white race. The South, inspired by the old Roman's reverence for his household gods, claims the right of holding sacred this heritage, and like him to keep pure and undefiled the spirit that worships at the family shrine."[23]

Scarborough recognized the political importance of classical education, and this is one reason why he so strenuously opposed the growing dominance of industrial education in African American colleges. The struggles occurred at his own institution, Wilberforce University. The establishment of the C. N. & I. led to tensions between the state of Ohio and the university over control. In 1896, the Ohio legislature increased the number of C. N. & I. trustees to give the state appointees a majority. Racial politics, however, often dictated the decision-making process on the C. N. & I. board. African Americans lobbied Ohio governors to appoint fellow blacks to the board, especially those connected to the AME Church, under whose control Wilberforce operated. So church leaders generally enjoyed a de facto majority.

Initially, much of the state's dissatisfaction with Wilberforce concerned using state-allocated C. N. & I. funds to pay expenses for other parts of the university. Relations between the state and the university deteriorated further after the retirement of Wilberforce president Samuel T. Mitchell in 1900 and his replacement by Joshua H. Jones. One longtime state C. N. & I. trustee, white newspaper editor Joseph A. Howells (brother of novelist William Dean Howells), publicly criticized Jones for meddling in the affairs of the C. N. & I. and undermining the C. N. & I. superintendent, whose appointment came from the board.[24]

The conflict between classical and industrial education also played out within the larger African American community. In reaction to the greater attention and funding provided to mechanical and industrial training, the Washington, D.C., clergyman Dr. Alexander Crummell organized an all-black learned society, the American Negro Academy, in 1897. Scarborough became one of the founding members, along with the poet Paul Lawrence Dunbar and the sociologist and future civil rights leader W. E. B. DuBois.[25] Although Booker T. Washington also initially agreed to be a founding member of the American Negro Academy, he never paid dues and was dropped from the membership the following year. Washington was the first director of the Tuskegee Normal and Industrial Institute, which was established by the state of Alabama in 1881 to teach skilled labor to African Americans. Washington gained national prominence both for his promotion of industrial education for blacks, and for his accommodationist views on segregation and disenfranchisement.

The 1890s marked a severe reversal in African American legal and political rights. In 1890, Mississippi established a poll tax and a literacy requirement for all voters as a way of effectively skirting the Fifteenth Amendment and preventing nearly all blacks from voting. Other Southern states followed Mississippi's example. In 1896, the United States Supreme Court upheld a Louisiana law requiring separate railway cars for black and white passengers. The decision in *Plessy v. Ferguson* gave constitutional sanction to segregation, which was applied to many aspects of daily life (housing, transportation, accommodation, employment and, of course, education) particularly in the South, but also in other regions of the country.[26]

In this increasingly repressive environment, Washington gave a speech before a predominantly white audience at a commercial exposition in Atlanta in 1895. Employing the phrase "Cast down your bucket where you are" (taken from a story about a ship at the mouth of the Amazon whose crew was seeking fresh water), Washington argued that Southern blacks should "learn to dignify and glorify common labour, and put brains and skill into the common occupations of life. . . . No race can prosper till it learns that there is as much dignity in tilling a field as in writing a poem. It is at the bottom of life we must begin, and not at the top."[27]

The withdrawal from the American Negro Academy of Washington and three other principals of black industrial schools in the South was undoubtedly due to the diametrically opposed views of Crummell, DuBois, Scarborough, and others concerning the need for classical education among African Americans.[28] Crummell attacked the exclusive promotion of industrial education in the Academy's first annual address in 1897. Crummell ridiculed whites such as the Southern Methodist minister Samuel August Steel and the Northern Baptist clergyman H. Lincoln Wayland for trying to limit African American achievement. In the speech, Crummell quoted Steel's comment on teaching Latin to blacks: "*Hic, haec, hoc* is going to prove the ruin of the Negro." Crummell also extensively cited Wayland's essay the previous year in the *Journal of Social Science* on African American higher education in the South, an article in which Wayland stated that the proper instruction for blacks "will do away with pupils being taught Latin and Greek, while they do not know the rudiments of English." Both Steel and Wayland were supporters of black industrial education, but Crummell pointed out that by denying blacks access to a classical education, even these sympathetic whites displayed a paternalism whose result would be to prevent African Americans from ever escaping a life of manual labor and exploitation, and to keep blacks in a form of servitude under the guise of freedom.[29]

Scarborough made similar comments in his own address to the American Negro Academy meeting two years later in 1899.[30] He further developed these ideas in an essay he wrote in 1902 for the predominantly white readership of the general interest periodical *Forum*. Under the title "The Negro and Higher Learning," Scarborough openly addressed the fears of many whites that encouraging African Americans to receive a classical education would lead to black discontent and political upheaval. He countered those fears with two main arguments. First he pointed out that the existence of a permanent black underclass of poorly educated manual laborers would be far more dangerous to political stability. "Two systems of civilization would but create an *imperium in imperio*; for in the lower there would be leaders, and there would grow up a power and system of life which in the end would produce a revolution," he wrote. He further argued that political discontent is not necessarily a bad thing and often leads to important reforms that improve society: "A noble discontent is not harmful to either individual or race. It is the harbinger of better things. It is often truly said that satisfaction with the present is the beginning of decline."[31]

Most of the article, however, was taken up with what African American society could achieve with a numerous and highly educated intellectual leadership. Scarborough found a moral efficacy in classical education, and he believed that those exposed to "higher learning" displayed an ethical behavior that would be passed down and emulated by others. Yet nearly four decades after slavery, no critical mass of the classically educated existed in black society. "Too long already has the race been compelled to content itself with ignorant leaders," Scarborough complained. To indicate the kind of leaders African Americans needed, Scarborough cited the famous beginning of Henry Wadsworth Longfellow's 1849 novel *Kavanaugh* ("Great men stand like solitary towers in the city of God . . ."). Scarborough explained, "Such men are not the product of mere mechanical training, of the industrial idea solely. They are rather the products of the broadest culture. We need them for leaders."[32]

Booker T. Washington, however, remained a far more popular and influential figure among white political leaders during the first decade of the twentieth century. Washington regularly met with President Theodore Roosevelt, was consulted on political appointments, and distributed funds to black industrial schools from John D. Rockefeller's General Education Board. Along with other black critics of industrial education, Scarborough found himself increasingly ignored by white political leaders on the national stage. He met Roosevelt only once, during a reception in the White House for members of the American Philological Association during their meeting in Washington in 1907.[33]

Scarborough's lack of influence was compounded by his association with Foraker, who since 1897 had been one of Ohio's U.S. senators. Foraker, who had presidential ambitions of his own, did not get along with Roosevelt. In the summer of 1906, white residents of Brownsville, Texas, blamed soldiers from a black regiment stationed nearby for a shooting spree that left one white man dead and another injured. Despite unreliable evidence, white military officers believed the townsmen, but none of the soldiers in the three companies of the regiment would admit to shooting anyone. Roosevelt then dishonorably discharged all 167 soldiers in three companies, some of whom had lengthy, distinguished careers and lost their pensions as a result. Foraker publicly challenged Roosevelt's action and demanded a Senate investigation.[34]

Foraker's agitation on the part of the Brownsville soldiers would, in part, bring about the end of the senator's own political career. The enmity with Roosevelt extended to Roosevelt's hand-picked successor in the 1908 presidential election, Secretary of War William Howard Taft. Taft, the son of Alphonso Taft, was an Ohioan who, like Foraker, hailed from Cincinnati. Not only did Taft's Ohio supporters prevent Foraker from gaining the Republican presidential nomination, but even after Taft's successful nomination and subsequent victory in the November election, they worked to deny Foraker his own reelection to the Senate.

In 1908, senators were still chosen by the state legislatures, and Republicans happened to control the Ohio legislature. President-elect Taft and his associates set to work trying to persuade Ohio's GOP legislators to replace Foraker with Taft's brother, Charles P. Taft. Public controversy generated in the press over Foraker's legal work for the Standard Oil Company provided additional ammunition for Foraker's opponents. Although not enough legislators could be found to support Charles P. Taft against Foraker, at the end of December a compromise was reached to replace Foraker with Congressman Theodore E. Burton. Foraker would never again hold public office.[35]

Although President Taft was friendly to Scarborough and had known him for thirty years, the relationship was not as close as Scarborough's connection to Foraker. Booker T. Washington remained the White House's chief advisor on African American interests and continued to direct the attention of white philanthropists toward industrial education for blacks.[36]

Despite the increasing difficulties in gaining both financial and public support for classical education, Scarborough was given the opportunity to counter prevailing notions of industrial education for blacks when he became president of Wilberforce University in 1908. The appointment did not represent an orderly transition and was the result of the seemingly sempiternal machinations and infighting of the university's sponsor and owner, the AME Church. Scarborough was well familiar with how church and university politics were intertwined. In 1891, he was removed from his faculty position at the university due to some dispute involving then-president Samuel T. Mitchell and possibly also Benjamin Arnett, who was now an AME bishop. Scarborough was then transferred to the neighboring AME-affiliated Payne Theological Seminary, where he had to make fundraising tours to pay his own salary. Scarborough was not restored to his faculty position in the university proper until six years later, when he was also made the university's vice president.[37]

Joshua H. Jones, Mitchell's successor as Wilberforce's president, was an ordained AME clergyman. Jones's ambitions within the church—coupled with his mingling of personal and university business interests through purchases of nearby farmland, ostensibly to supply the college dining hall—earned him the enmity of several church leaders. Furthermore, his meddling in the C. N. & I. department soured relations with the state government. In 1908, Jones was forced out. Scarborough was named as the replacement in large part because his academic credibility, fundraising experience, and extensive connections to white politicians offered the possibility of improving the university's finances and curriculum.[38]

Under Scarborough's tenure as Wilberforce's president, relations with the state improved, and the appointment of Scarborough's onetime student William A. Joiner as C. N. & I. superintendent helped. Joiner had himself been a high school Latin teacher before directing Howard University's teacher-training program. At the C. N. & I., Joiner emphasized academic coursework and diminished programs in industrial education. Joiner's goal, a goal generally shared by Scarborough and the state appointees, was to transform the C. N. & I. into a full-fledged teachers' college.

Scarborough generally met with success as a fundraiser and in his attempts to increase enrollments and toughen the curriculum. The transformation of the C. N. & I. was even more dramatic. In 1917 a plan was developed to have temporary faculty appointments in the C. N. & I. teach courses in Wilberforce's liberal arts college. This would have allowed state funds to be used to offset the salary needs and helped stabilize the finances of the private college. The plan gained approval of both the university and C. N. & I. boards, but the plan angered some AME officials who did not want the C. N. & I. to have any authority over faculty teaching in the liberal arts college. The Ohio legislature subsequently refused to approve the plan.[39]

The plan's failure led the state appointees on the C. N. & I. board to consider a separation of the C. N. & I. from the rest of Wilberforce, and the department's establishment as an independent teacher-training college operated entirely by the state. Scarborough was opposed to this separation, but Joiner saw it as perhaps the only way to continue the department's improvements in the face of increasing hostility by church officials. In 1919, former university president Joshua H. Jones was selected as the AME bishop overseeing Wilberforce. Jones, who still nursed resentment over his own dismissal a decade earlier, wanted the C. N. & I. curriculum pared down and both Scarborough and Joiner replaced. Intense lobbying allowed Jones to gain control over the C. N. & I. board, and Joiner was forced to resign. Scarborough understood that Jones was attempting to remove him as well, so the following year the sixty-eight-year-old president announced his retirement.[40]

Scarborough's presidential duties at Wilberforce left him little time for his own scholarship or for the promotion of classical education among African Americans. Opportunities for black students to gain exposure to ancient languages continued to diminish. Writing in his autobiography in 1925, Scarborough complained that few black students pursued the classics. "I see now, as the controversy grows concerning the classics, no young colored men of the immediate present who are even meditating on special classical study. It is a great mistake, as the race will find out, to leave this field to others with the breadth and culture obtainable in it."[41]

Scarborough's own institution, Wilberforce University, would entirely abandon classical education during the course of the twentieth century. Of this country's historically black universities, only Howard University has maintained a continuous tradition of instruction in ancient languages.[42] The promise initially seen in the 1870s and 1880s for black colleges to mold generations of classically educated African Americans to become equal partners in American society never saw fulfillment. The educational response to the Fifteenth Amendment ended up limiting black options as well as black suffrage. The discontent among African Americans that white leaders sought to suppress through industrial education, eventually boiled over in the second half of the twentieth century, just as Scarborough had predicted.

Chapter 5

The Rise of Populism, the Decline of Classical Education, and the Seventeenth Amendment

—Michael Meckler

The rapid economic and social changes that transformed the United States in the half century following the Civil War spawned demands for greater public participation in government and for greater government oversight of business and society. These demands united southern and western farmers angered over railroad monopolies that controlled the transportation of their produce, immigrant laborers upset over working conditions in northern factories, women who found themselves excluded from political decision making, small businessmen brought to ruin by insecure banks, and social reformers disenchanted with the poverty and despair in which many Americans lived. The solutions called for by these groups often shared an underlying concept of populism, a term that can be used to encompass ideas from both the Populist political movement of the 1890s and the Progressive movement of the 1910s.[1]

Several amendments to the United States Constitution grew out of this populist fervor: the Sixteenth Amendment (ratified in 1913), which legalized federal income tax; the Eighteenth Amendment (ratified in 1919), which established Prohibition; the Nineteenth Amendment (ratified in 1920), which provided universal women's suffrage; and the focus of this essay, the Seventeenth Amendment (ratified in 1913), which established the direct election of United States senators.

The rise in populist politics occurred as the traditional education in Greek and Latin came increasingly under criticism and marginalization. The young men of modest means who fought the Civil War and settled the West resented the social distinction classical education seemed to bestow upon their wealthier coevals from the East Coast. The increasing disparity between rich and poor in the second half of the nineteenth century tainted the perception of why the ancients were studied. Classical education was increasingly viewed as a luxury of the well-to-do, a luxury employed primarily to demarcate the leisure class. The farmer and the laborer had no need or desire for such an education.[2]

Social critics were not the only ones to dismiss the study of classical antiquity in late nineteenth-century America. Business leaders also deemed it irrelevant to the demands of an increasingly scientific and industrial age, and they failed to see any connection between the classics and a successful career. Many of those who amassed fortunes from steel, railroads, and oil enjoyed only the slightest contact with the ancient Greeks and Romans in what little formal education they received. These tycoons viewed their ascent in business and society as stemming solely from experience in employment and native talent. Andrew Carnegie, whose formal education ended at the age of twelve, argued against the usefulness of the traditional course of study in colleges and universities, writing in the *New York Tribune* in 1890, "The prizetakers [in American business] have too many years the start of the [college] graduate; they have entered for the race invariably in their teens—in the most valuable of all the years for learning anything—from fourteen to twenty; while the college student has been learning a little about the barbarous and petty squabbles of a far-distant past, or trying to master languages which are dead, such knowledge as seems adapted for life on another planet."[3]

New areas of study seemed more appropriate for America's youth, especially in the applied and social sciences. Engineering and psychology were gaining respect as academic disciplines in their own right. Advances in the natural and physical sciences expanded the amount of study necessary for competence in these fields. Academic disciplines were also becoming professionalized, and a plethora of specialized learned societies appeared, including the American Chemical Society (founded in 1876), the American Society of Mechanical Engineers (1880), the Modern Language Association (1883), the American Historical Association (1884), the Geological Society of America (1889), the American Psychological Association (1892), the American Mathematical Society (1894), and the American Physical Society (1899). With academic professionalization came the establishment of separate canons of knowledge specific to each discipline. This growth in fields of study appropriate to college education made it less tenable for colleges to maintain that all students take a required set of courses in classical studies.[4]

Moreover, the increasing engagement of the United States in the late nineteenth century with the rest of the world made crucial the study of modern foreign languages, especially German. Knowledge of German was necessary in dealing with the powerful, unified German state established after the Franco-Prussian War of 1871, a state viewed by many Americans as both partner and rival. German universities were understood to be at the forefront of scientific advancement, and graduate study in Germany became common among American scientists and academics. By 1890 a full twenty percent of the foreign students at German universities were Americans. The time needed for acquiring modern languages like German necessarily diminished the efforts spent on ancient ones.[5]

The opportunity to reform American college education was embraced by the new land-grant universities, funded as a result of President Lincoln's signing into law in 1862 of the Morrill Act, named for its sponsor, Congressman, later Senator Justin S. Morrill of Vermont. Under the Morrill Act, landholdings of the federal government were transferred to the states for the establishment and maintenance of institutions of higher learning. Although the Morrill Act specifically mentions that classical studies should not be excluded from the curricula of the land-grant universities, the primary fields of study were intended to be "such branches of learning as are related to agriculture and the mechanical arts, in such manner as the legislatures of the states may respectively prescribe, in order to promote the liberal and practical education of the industrial classes in the several pursuits and professions in life."[6]

As public institutions with public sources of funding, the land-grant universities often found themselves at the center of political controversy during their establishment and early years. In many states, public officials often showed great antipathy towards the funding of classical education at what were meant to be the people's universities. In 1869, the Illinois legislature passed a resolution censuring the recently established Illinois Industrial University (now the University of Illinois) for its promotion of classical studies, which legislators deemed irrelevant to the university's primary purpose of training farmers and mechanics.[7] A motion was defeated by only one vote at an 1873 meeting of the board of trustees of the newly founded Ohio Agricultural and Mechanical College, which shortly became The Ohio State University, that would have prevented the school from hiring its first professor of ancient languages. Those opposed to the teaching of classical studies gained some measure of revenge through the Ohio legislature, which for several years refused to allocate funds to pay the trustees' expenses.[8] The curriculum of the Pennsylvania

State University became a campaign issue in the Pennsylvania governor's race in 1882. After his victory in the election, Governor Robert E. Pattison tried to force the university's trustees to eliminate the faculty position in ancient languages. The attempt was unsuccessful, but the institution redirected its focus towards engineering and agriculture.[9]

One of the important changes coming from these new universities was to allow college students greater freedom in deciding their course of study. By the middle of the nineteenth century, many American colleges already allowed upperclassmen, who had already completed requirements in ancient languages, a limited choice in coursework. Cornell University, which opened in 1868 as a land-grant institution, allowed students to choose which group of courses, from among a fixed set of options, would form their curriculum.

David Starr Jordan, who was in the first graduating class at Cornell, refined this system during his tenure as president of Indiana University (from 1885 to 1891) and then for the next twenty-two years as the first president of Stanford University (founded in 1891). Under Jordan's curriculum, students were allowed to choose a major subject with the requirements for the degree to be set by the faculty department supervising the subject. Only minimal college-wide course requirements were imposed, and beyond the course requirements for the major, all other courses were up to the student.[10] With minor variations, the major-subject curriculum has become the standard form of undergraduate education in colleges and universities throughout the United States.

The promotion of elective courses was taken to its extreme at Harvard University under Charles W. Eliot, president from 1869 until 1909. In 1872, seniors at Harvard were freed from required courses. Eight years later, Harvard removed nearly all requirements (including those in classical studies) and allowed even incoming freshmen the opportunity to choose most of their classes. In 1886, the study of Greek in secondary school was no longer required for admission to Harvard.[11]

Harvard's promotion of the elective system and the university's abandonment of classical education provoked controversy, especially from other long-established Eastern colleges and universities. A scathing condemnation of Eliot's curricular reforms appeared in May 1885 in an article in the Yale University magazine, *The New Englander*. The article argued for the continued prominence of ancient languages in college education, ascribing calls for more modern programs of study to a failure of civic leadership by America's elite. In referring to the United States, the article complained, "No country is so little controlled by the opinions of the learned class, and has a learned class that is so fickle and eager for novelty, and at times so loud and voluble in its appeals to popular feeling."[12] Classical education was perceived by its supporters as necessary for those leaders who would safeguard the American republic.

The controversy over the role of classical education in the college curriculum had been highlighted by a debate organized three months earlier between Eliot and James McCosh, the president of the College of New Jersey, now Princeton University. The debate took place in the Manhattan residence of Courtlandt Palmer, Jr., and held under the auspices of the Nineteenth Century Club, a group of prominent New York socialites with progressive and intellectual interests. Eliot's conception of the university as a place where students are given freedom to develop the qualities of self-discipline and curiosity was ridiculed by McCosh, who doubted that most teenagers had the maturity to benefit from an unstructured course of study. Furthermore, the centrality of classical studies to all disciplines, whether in mathematics, philosophy, or the sciences, demanded that requirements in ancient languages be maintained. German was not a valid substitute for Greek. "There should be Modern Languages," McCosh said, "but there should also be Classics. A taste and a style are produced by the study of the Greek and Latin with their literatures, which are expressively called *Classic*. It may be difficult to define, but we all feel the charm of it. If we lose this there is nothing in what is called our Modern Education to make up for the loss."[13]

Princeton would remain a bastion of classical education under the influence of Andrew Fleming West, whom McCosh appointed in 1883 as the first occupant of the Giger Chair in Latin. West would spend forty-five years on the Princeton faculty, and he used his stature within the university and in the nation at large to rally opposition against attempts to end required coursework in ancient languages in secondary schools and colleges.[14]

Opposition to Eliot's changes in the Harvard curriculum was not limited to fellow academics at rival institutions. Harvard alumni who fondly remembered their own classical education were equally distraught. One of the most disheartened Harvard alumni was George Frisbie Hoar, Class of 1846, who served as a United States senator from Massachusetts from 1877 until his death in 1904. Hoar prized his classical education. He regularly told young men that the best training for a life in politics was to read Demosthenes and the other Athenian orators in the original Greek. He even spent time during his years in the Senate preparing his own English translation of Thucydides, a translation meant not for publication but for self-erudition.[15]

On January 16, 1893, during the height of Populist political strength, the House passed a resolution calling for a constitutional amendment for the direct election of senators. Under Section 3 of Article 1 of the Constitution, senators were originally chosen by the state legislatures. After the

Civil War, some western states began using primaries to determine the candidates for United States senator whose names would be submitted to the state legislature. This was a populist means of creating a form of direct election, but true direct election was not possible unless Article 1 of the Constitution was amended.[16]

Beginning on April 6, 1893, and continuing the following day, Hoar gave an oration on the Senate floor against direct election.[17] Hoar's speech, which gained legendary status in his day, squelched for more than a decade attempts to have the Senate seriously consider the issue of direct elections. The speech abounds in classical allusions. Hoar discussed the problems of democratic governments with the standard arguments from classical political thought dealing with ochlocracy, or mob rule. Fears over the short-sighted and short-fused actions of the crowd weighed heavily upon the Founding Fathers, and Hoar quoted James Madison's famous words from *Federalist* No. 55, that even if every Athenian citizen had been a Socrates, every Athenian assembly would still have been a mob.

Hoar also mentioned Cicero's speech on behalf of Flaccus. The senator from Massachusetts noted that Cicero "attributes the decay of Roman and the destruction of Grecian liberty to the substitution of the turbulent popular assembly for the deliberative chamber in wielding the political power of the State. He has left his terrible picture of the popular assemblies of his time as a pregnant lesson for all mankind."[18]

The complaints of the Populists that the spectacular wealth of the industrial tycoons was corrupting the political system was a danger Hoar believed Americans could dismiss with a direct quotation (in Latin) from the end of Cicero's *Second Philippic*: *contempsi Catilinae gladios, non pertimescam tuos* ("I defied Catiline's swords, I won't fear yours").[19] To Hoar, the corruption of senators seduced by the wealth of industrialists could be rooted out without recourse to the drastic step of destroying the contemplative environment engendered by the Senate's slight remove from the people. Indeed, Hoar believed that the people understood the wisdom of the Founders in fashioning the Senate as an appointed body.

Hoar's trust in the people was connected to the knowledge of Greek and Roman antiquity that formed the basis of classical education. "The American youth knows something of the annals of other lands," Hoar said in his speech. "He can tell you something about Solon and Lycurgus, about Romulus and the she wolf, of Numa in his cavern. . . ."

Such a statement about the knowledge of America's youth might have seemed reasonable to those men who sat in the Senate in 1893 and, like Hoar, received their education before the Civil War. Of the eighty-five men serving in the Senate at the beginning of the Fifty-third Congress in 1893,[20] thirty were graduates of liberal arts college and all but three graduated before or during the Civil War. Twenty-one other senators had attended classes either at a college, law school, or medical school, where at least the rudiments of a classical education were required. By this measure, fully sixty percent of senators must have received some level of education on ancient Greece and Rome. Even those senators who never attended college probably had some classical education in secondary school because ancient languages and history were standard subjects in preparatory academies in the pre-Civil War era (see Table 1 below).

Outside of graying college graduates and antebellum alumni of the preparatory academies, the depth of knowledge about classical antiquity among the population at large was quite shallow. The percentage of Americans able to identify the nymph Egeria or to recognize a citation from Cicero was extremely small in 1893, as it is today. Senators must have been aware of the true extent of classical education among the general population. Indeed, the text printed in the *Congressional Record* of Hoar's quotation from Cicero's *Second Philippic* contains two words with glaring spelling errors that would have been caught even by an introductory Latin student.[21]

Hoar's imagined "American youth" is a projection from earlier in the nineteenth century of the young men, primarily those in the Northeast, who were fortunate enough to receive an education based on the study of classical antiquity. Hoar and those Senate colleagues who shared in that past were being invited to recognize the distinction that classical education provided them. The subtle message underlying Hoar's classical allusions was that those lacking education in classical antiquity would not be able to understand the dangers of the mob rule they promoted. Hoar's display of his classical education creates a vivid contrast between those whose erudition enabled them to fulfill the deliberative function required of the Senate, and the rough-hewn Populists who could not even comprehend the Senate's proper role.

The House continued to promote changing the Constitution to allow for direct election of senators, approving resolutions in 1894, 1898, 1900, and 1902. Such resolutions were futile without similar support in the Senate. That support grew during the first decade of the twentieth century, and by the opening of the Sixty-first Congress in 1909, a constitutional amendment for direct elections had a realistic chance of passing in both chambers of Congress.

The membership of the Senate had undergone significant changes in the sixteen years between Hoar's speech at the start of the Fifty-third Congress in 1893, and the start of the Sixty-first Congress in 1909. Senators from western states that had only recently been admitted to the Union at the time of Hoar's speech (six states were admitted in 1889 and 1890) were beginning to take a more assertive role in the chamber. Two more states had since joined the Union: Utah in 1896, and Oklahoma in 1907.

It was a senator from Oklahoma, Robert L. Owen, who championed direct election and introduced the resolution that brought the issue to the fore.

Most of the senators in the Sixty-first Congress had faced voters in a primary election. Only the six New England states, New York, Delaware, and West Virginia did not have some form of senatorial primary. Twenty-seven states had passed resolutions of one form or another calling for a constitutional convention to establish direct election of senators if Congress failed to send the states such an amendment. Direct election of senators had been part of the Democratic Party platform since 1900. A clear majority of senators now favored the idea.[22]

Owen's resolution was initially bottled up in committee. In a speech on the Senate floor at the end of May 1910, Owen blamed six senators for trying to thwart the majority's will: Nelson Aldrich of Rhode Island, Henry Cabot Lodge of Massachusetts, John Kean of New Jersey, Eugene Hale of Maine, Boies Penrose of Pennsylvania, and Chauncey Depew of New York.[23] All of these senators were from the Northeast, and all had received a form of classical education. Indeed Depew, who was an 1856 graduate of Yale, had defended classical education in a published reply to Andrew Carnegie's complaints in 1890.[24] Lodge and Penrose were Harvard graduates in the years before Eliot's major reforms of the curriculum, and Lodge himself had taught history at Harvard in the 1870s. Kean had attended Yale. Although neither Hale nor Aldrich had gone to college, both studied ancient languages in secondary school as part of the standard curriculum of college-preparatory academies in New England before the Civil War.

Their classical education, however, placed these senators in an ever-shrinking group. Although the percentages of senators from the Sixty-first Congress who were college graduates or had attended college were comparable to the numbers from the Fifty-third Congress (38 percent were college graduates in 1910, compared to 35 percent in 1893; 62 percent had college experience in 1910, compared to 60 percent in 1893), the changes that had swept through higher education in the late nineteenth century meant that having a college degree no longer guaranteed having an extensive classical education (see Table 2 below).

A case in point comes from the comparison of two senators from Wisconsin, William F. Vilas (from the Fifty-third Congress) and Robert M. La Follette (from the Sixty-first Congress). Both men were graduates of the University of Wisconsin, Vilas in 1858 and La Follette in 1879. When Vilas attended the school, study in both Greek and Latin were required. Even as an adult, Vilas continued to enjoy reading Virgil's poetry in Latin. By the time La Follette enrolled at the school, he along with most other Wisconsin students chose the "scientific" course of study, which required no coursework in ancient languages, only one course in ancient history, and two courses in philosophy. La Follette paid little attention to his ancient history course, which he barely passed, and he seems never to have developed any lasting interest in classical antiquity.[25]

The attempts in the Sixty-first Congress by senators from the Northeast to block discussion of an amendment for direct elections were increasingly hindered by the growing national furor over Republican Senator William Lorimer of Illinois. Although Illinois Republicans, who controlled the state legislature, had conducted a primary election to determine their candidate for the Senate term beginning March 4, 1909, no candidate in the crowded primary had won a majority. Stalemate ensued for months until Lorimer, with significant Democratic support, was finally chosen by the Illinois legislature. The following year, the *Chicago Tribune* reported that four legislators had been bribed to vote for Lorimer. The scandal, which would lead to Lorimer's expulsion from the Senate in 1912, increased public pressure for a vote on Owen's resolution.[26]

By this time, however, classical education's influence on the American public, and especially on their leaders, had waned. Furthermore, higher education itself was not reckoned a sign of fitness for leadership. Between Owen's speech in the Senate in May 1910 and the final debates leading to a vote in February 1911, four senators died in office: Jonathan Dolliver of Iowa, Alexander Clay of Georgia, Stephen B. Elkins of West Virginia, and Charles J. Hughes, Jr., of Colorado. Dolliver and Clay were college graduates, and Elkins and Hughes were law school graduates. Colorado did not immediately fill Hughes's seat and none of the men chosen to fill the other three seats (Lafayette Young of Iowa, Joseph Terrell of Georgia, and Isaac Stephenson of West Virginia) were college graduates or had even attended college.[27]

The vote on Owen's resolution came at the end of the Sixty-first Congress, on February 28, 1911. In the month leading up to the vote, the resolution was debated on the Senate floor. Henry Cabot Lodge delivered a speech on February 6 that affirmed both his opposition to direct election and his agreement with Hoar's speech eighteen years earlier. Lodge provided examples from history about the dangers of democracy, including an interpretation of the fall of the Roman Republic. "In Rome the elections were annual and offices were multiplied, to the end that one elected officer might watch another," the professorial Lodge instructed his Senate colleagues, "and yet despite this precaution it was the democracy of Rome which, after many trials, with Caesar at its head, finally overthrew the old government, an intolerable oligarchy controlled by violence and money, and then under a thin veil of the ancient forms established the empire."[28]

Two days later, Elihu Root, senator from New York, in his speech on the Senate floor opposing the amendment, compared the allure of direct election to the song of the Sirens in book 12 of the *Odyssey*.

> As Ulysses required his followers to bind him to the mast that he
> might not yield to the song of the siren as he sailed by, so the Amer-
> ican democracy has bound itself to the great rules of right conduct
> which are essential to the protection of liberty and justice and prop-
> erty and order, and made it practically impossible that the impulse,
> the prejudice, the excitement, the frenzy of the moment, shall carry
> our democracy into those excesses which have wrecked all our pro-
> totypes in history.[29]

The patterns of Senate debate and the educational background of senators had changed dramatically over the previous two decades. In 1911,
appeals to classical antiquity did not have the weight they had a generation earlier. The vote for Owen's resolution was fifty-four in favor, thirty-
three opposed, with four senators not voting. Although approval fell
seven votes short of the necessary two-thirds majority, it was already clear
that a direct-election resolution would pass in the next Congress. Aldrich,
Hale, and Kean were retiring, and the seventy-six-year-old Depew had
failed in his attempt for a third term. Nine incoming senators planned to
support direct election in contrast with their predecessors. In the Sixty-
second Congress, debate was passionless and short. The resolution
passed on June 12, 1911, with sixty-four in favor, twenty-four opposed,
and three senators not voting.

The decline in classical education in nineteenth-century America
sapped antiquity of its exemplary power in American political debate.
Although a classical education did not, in and of itself, taint its recipients
as implacable opponents to populist ideas and agitation, recourse to the
ancient Greeks and Romans came to be seen by many Americans in the
early years of the twentieth century as a relic of an obsolete, antidemocra-
tic, and antimodern mentality. Those who cherished the classical tradition
also tended to be sympathetic to traditional understandings of how American government and society were supposed to function. The social privilege and distance provided by the study of Greek and Latin remained
strongest in the Northeast, the region of the country with the oldest and
most firmly rooted educational institutions. Yet the rise of populism and
the growing political power of the West relegated classical studies from the
center of political thought to a dusty corner in the ivory tower. This transformation is clearly paralleled in the Senate's own transformation from an
indirectly to a directly elected legislative body.

Table 1

Educational Background of Senators at the Start of the Fifty-third Congress

A. Senators Who Were College Graduates

WHITE (California)	Santa Clara, Class of 1871
HAWLEY (Connecticut)	Hamilton, 1847
HIGGINS (Delaware)	Yale, 1861
GRAY (Delaware)	Princeton, 1859
PASCO (Florida)	Harvard, 1858
COLQUITT (Georgia)	Princeton, 1844
DUBOIS (Idaho)	Yale, 1872
VORHEES (Indiana)	Indiana Asbury [now DePauw], 1849
TURPIE (Indiana)	Kenyon, 1848
ALLISON (Iowa)	Western Reserve, 1849
BLACKBURN (Kentucky)	Centre (Kentucky), 1857
FRYE (Maine)	Bowdoin, 1850
GIBSON (Maryland)	Washington (Maryland), 1863
HOAR (Massachusetts)	Harvard, 1846
LODGE (Massachusetts)	Harvard, 1871
DAVIS (Minnesota)	Michigan, 1857
WASHBURN (Minnesota)	Bowdoin, 1854
COCKRELL (Missouri)	Chapel Hill (Missouri), 1853
VEST (Missouri)	Centre (Kentucky), 1848
MURPHY (New York)	St. John's [now Fordham], 1857
RANSOM (North Carolina)	North Carolina, 1847
BRICE (Ohio)	Miami, 1863
CAMERON (Pennsylvania)	Princeton, 1852
QUAY (Pennsylvania)	Jefferson [now Washington & Jefferson], 1850
DIXON (Rhode Island)	Brown, 1869
KYLE (South Dakota)	Oberlin, 1878
COKE (Texas)	William & Mary, 1849
PROCTOR (Vermont)	Dartmouth, 1851
SQUIRE (Washington)	Wesleyan, 1859
VILAS (Wisconsin)	Wisconsin, 1858

B. Senators Who Attended College, Law School, or Medical School (Graduation Year of Professional School Given)

WOLCOTT (Colorado)	Yale; Harvard Law, 1875
GORDON (Georgia)	Georgia
PALMER (Illinois)	Alton Seminary (Illinois)

WHITE (Louisiana)	Mount St. Mary's; Loyola (New Orleans); Georgetown
CAFFERY (Louisiana)	St. Mary's (Baltimore); Louisiana University [now Tulane]
ALLEN (Nebraska)	Upper Iowa
STEWART (Nevada)	Yale
CHANDLER (New Hampshire)	Harvard Law, 1854
GALLINGER (New Hampshire)	Eclectic Medical Institute (Cincinnati), 1858
SMITH (New Jersey)	St. Mary's College
VANCE (North Carolina)	Washington College (Tennessee); North Carolina Law
ROACH (North Dakota)	Georgetown
DOLPH (Oregon)	Genesee Wesleyan Seminary
BUTLER (South Carolina)	South Carolina College
IRBY (South Carolina)	Princeton; Virginia
PETTIGREW (South Dakota)	Beloit; Wisconsin Law
BATE (Tennessee)	Cumberland Law, 1852
DANIEL (Virginia)	Lynchburg College; Virginia Law
CAMDEN (West Virginia)	West Point
FAULKNER (West Virginia)	Virginia Military Institute; Virginia Law, 1868
CAREY (Wyoming)	Union (New York); Pennsylvania Law, 1864

Number of Senators at the Start of the Fifty-third Congess	85
Number of Senators Who Were College Graduates	30
Percentage of Senators Who Were College Graduates	35%
Number of Senators With College, Law, or Medical School Experience	21
Percentage of Senators With College, Law, or Medical School Experience	25%
Percentage of Senators Exposed to Post-Secondary Academic Education	60%

Source: Biographical Directory of the United States Congress, http://bioguide.congress.gov
[accessed May 19, 2004]

Table 2

Educational Background of Senators in May 1910 During the Sixty-first Congress

A. Senators Who Were College Graduates

DAVIS (Arkansas)	Vanderbilt, Class of 1884
BRANDEGEE (Connecticut)	Yale, 1885
DU PONT (Delaware)	West Point, 1861
FLETCHER (Florida)	Vanderbilt, 1880
BACON (Georgia)	Georgia, 1859

CLAY (Georgia)	Hiwassee (Tennessee), 1875
BEVERIDGE (Indiana)	Indiana Asbury [now DePauw], 1885
CUMMINS (Iowa)	Waynesburg, 1869
DOLLIVER (Iowa)	West Virginia, 1876
BRISTOW (Kansas)	Baker, 1886
FOSTER (Louisiana)	Cumberland, 1870
FRYE (Maine)	Bowdoin, 1850
PERCY (Mississippi)	Sewanee, 1879
STONE (Missouri)	Missouri, 1867
DIXON (Montana)	Guilford (North Carolina), 1889
BURKETT (Nebraska)	Tabor (Iowa), 1890
BURNHAM (New Hampshire)	Dartmouth, 1865
DEPEW (New York)	Yale, 1856
ROOT (New York)	Hamilton, 1864
SIMMONS (North Carolina)	Trinity [now Duke], 1873
OVERMAN (North Carolina)	Trinity [now Duke], 1874
BURTON (Ohio)	Oberlin, 1872
OWEN (Oklahoma)	Washington & Lee, 1872
CHAMBERLAIN (Oregon)	Washington & Lee, 1876
PENROSE (Pennsylvania)	Harvard, 1881
OLIVER (Pennsylvania)	Bethany, 1868
WETMORE (Rhode Island)	Yale, 1867
SMITH (South Carolina)	Wofford, 1889
GAMBLE (South Dakota)	Lawrence, 1874
FRAZIER (Tennessee)	Tennessee, 1878
CULBERSON (Texas)	Virginia Military Institute, 1874
SMOOT (Utah)	Brigham Young, 1879
SWANSON (Virginia)	Randolph-Macon, 1885
JONES (Washington)	Southern Illinois, 1885
LA FOLLETTE (Wisconsin)	Wisconsin, 1879

B. Senators Who Attended College, Law School, or Medical School (Graduation Year of Professional School Given)

HUGHES (Colorado)	Missouri Law, 1873
HEYBURN (Idaho)	Pennsylvania
BORAH (Idaho)	Kansas
SHIVELY (Indiana)	Valparaiso
PAYNTER (Kentucky)	Centre (Kentucky)
THORNTON (Louisiana)	Louisiana Seminary
RAYNOR (Maryland)	Maryland; Virginia
CLAPP (Minnesota)	Wisconsin Law, 1873

MONEY (Mississippi)	Mississippi Law, 1860
WARNER (Missouri)	Lawrence Law; Michigan Law
BROWN (Nebraska)	Iowa Law, 1883
NEWLANDS (Nevada)	Yale; Columbian [now George Washington] Law
GALLINGER (New Hampshire)	Eclectic Medical Institute (Cincinnati), 1858
KEAN (New Jersey)	Yale; Columbia Law, 1875
MCCUMBER (North Dakota)	Michigan Law, 1880
GORE (Oklahoma)	Cumberland Law, 1892
BOURNE (Oregon)	Harvard
CRAWFORD (South Dakota)	Iowa Law, 1882
TAYLOR (Tennesee)	Pennington Seminary
MARTIN (Virginia)	Virginia Military Institute; Virginia
ELKINS (West Virginia)	Missouri Law, 1860
CLARK (Wyoming)	Iowa

Number of Senators in May 1910 During Sixty-First Congress	92
Number of Senators Who Were College Graduates	35
Percentage of Senators Who Were College Graduates	38%
Number of Senators With College, Law or Medical School Experience	22
Percentage of Senators With College, Law or Medical School Experience	24%
Percentage of Senators Exposed to Post-Secondary Academic Education	62%

Source: Biographical Directory of the United States Congress, http://bioguide.congress.gov [accessed May 19, 2004]

Chapter 6

William Linn Westermann at the Paris Peace Conference of 1919

—John Milton Cooper, Jr.

History, in many circles, is a derisive, even pejorative word. In movies, the killers often dispatch their victims with the sneer, "You're history!" More generally, all kinds of people dismiss something as irrelevant by saying, "That's history." Professional historians dislike this use of the word, but in their heart of hearts they often feel the sting of truth.

Every historian has occasionally sighed with regret that he or she was not there to witness or participate in an event that he or she was studying. Many historians, even those working in recent political history, believe that they take a vow of renunciation from public affairs when they decide to pursue their discipline. Journalists and political scientists often regard historians of the recent past as quaint or archaeological. *History*, in the pejorative sense, has a way of beginning very recently, and think how much worse this stigma is for those who study more remote times in the past.

Yet there have been instances when a historian has been able to participate in history as it was unfolding. A few historians have been able to do this, without setting aside their professional credentials, by, for example, serving in the military or going into politics. Still others have participated in a great event because of something they brought to the enterprise from their scholarship. Occasionally, historians have been enlisted to witness what they would later record. World War II saw Samuel Eliot Morison's assignment to write the history of the United States Navy, with a set of orders that allowed him to go wherever he wanted to see the action. The U.S. Army in that war had "combat historians" who witnessed specific battles and campaigns.

One historian was able to do even more. He was commissioned to be part of a great event more or less in his professional capacity. William Linn Westermann (1873–1954), then professor of ancient history at the University of Wisconsin, served as a member of the American delegation to the Paris Peace Conference in 1919. On November 30, 1918, he received an appointment to what was called a "Specialist in Western Asia," at a salary of $400 a month with an allowance for transportation and "subsistence" expenses.[1]

The United States entered World War I in April 1917, more than two and a half years after hostilities broke out. It shortly became clear to President Woodrow Wilson that the other Allies had already made extensive plans for the postwar settlement, plans that were not in accord with American interests or ideals. By the autumn of 1917, Wilson decided to entrust his political right-hand man, Colonel Edward M. House, with the task of collecting a group of experts to conduct research and draft policy papers. The experts initially assigned to study disposition of the Ottoman Empire were primarily scholars of antiquity. This subgroup was under the supervision of Dana C. Munro, a professor of medieval history at Princeton University, the university Wilson had previously led before entering politics.[2]

At the time of World War I, modern history had existed as a distinct subject within the academic discipline of history for only a generation or so, and the contemporary Middle East had yet to become a focus of university appointments and scholarly research. In the United States at the end of the nineteenth and the beginning of the twentieth centuries, biblical scholars, scholars of antiquity, and Jews were those consulted as the experts for policy decisions involving the Ottoman Empire. Of the nine men who served as the United States ambassador to the Sultan in the four decades leading up to America's entry into World War I, four were Jews and two others were scholars of academic repute with interests in antiquity: James B. Angell, the president of the University of Michigan and William McKinley's first ambassador to Constantinople in 1897 and 1898; and the diplomat and scholar of East Asian antiquities, W. W. Rockhill, who represented the United States from 1911 to 1913 under William Howard Taft.[3]

Westermann, who had earned his Ph.D. in Germany at the University of Berlin, was a rising star among historians of classical antiquity. When he agreed to serve in the delegation to the Paris Peace Conference, he was in his mid forties and was being recruited by both Cornell University and the University of Nebraska. Nebraska was offering him an annual salary of $4,000, a big sum in those days, negotiable up to $4,500, while Cornell promised to make him the highest paid nonadministrator on the faculty. With a show of modesty, Westermann commented from Paris to his friend and dean at Wisconsin, George Sellery, "I am deriving a good deal of undeserved merit by my presence here." Being a participant in history evidently carried cachet with other professors of history. In Paris, Westermann was quartered with the rest of the American delegation at the Hôtel de Crillon, that elegant establishment on the Place de la Concorde. His room was down the hall from Colonel House's suite. During his seven months in Paris, Westermann went to a number of operas, ate fine meals, and took a few trips outside the city to see famous sites and the damage left by the just-ended war.[4]

The prestige allotted to those involved in the writing of history who also have experience in the making of history is longstanding. Such prestige has regularly flavored interpretations of the founders of Western historiography, the ancient Greek authors Herodotus and Thucydides. Thucydides had been a prominent Athenian leader until the failure of a military operation under his command forced him into exile during the middle of the Peloponnesian War, whose history he later composed. Herodotus, however, does not seem to have held any position of significant political leadership. Their differing backgrounds have been adduced as key to understanding their differing analytical techniques and literary styles. Herodotus has received criticism for his gossipy digressions on social customs, while Thucydides has reaped praise for seeking to understand the underlying causes of events.

Westermann himself reflected these opinions in an essay he wrote on Greek civilization a decade after the Peace Conference. Although Herodotus displayed a "peculiar charm in narration," Westermann remarked, "Herodotus was unable to discern the political, economic and social forces which determine historical events." Thucydides, on the other hand, "eliminated from his narrative everything of a purely episodical character which seemed to him unimportant, consciously sacrificing historiographic interest to historical importance."[5]

During his time as a member of the American delegation at the Paris Conference, Westermann was deeply conscious of his role in making history. For probably the only time in his life, Westermann kept a diary. Nearly every day he wrote a detailed account of what he saw, heard, did, and thought. Westermann was in good company. It seems as if everybody who was at the conference kept a diary. For example, Colonel House continued his diary, as did the president's physician, Admiral Cary T. Grayson, and the chief press officer of the delegation, Ray Stannard Baker.

If Westermann the historian aspired to be a Thucydides, Westermann the diarist comes across as more of a Herodotus. Westermann described the physical characteristics and personality traits of the conference participants. He chronicled their conversations and opinions, but he rarely discussed his own duties. His diary conveys a fine feel for the atmosphere of the conference, especially the rumor mills that ground constantly as a consequence of the leaders' reluctance to share hard information. The diaries of Baker, Grayson, and Colonel House reveal far more of the doings at the highest level, but Westermann was able to convey an excellent account of the second level of the conference—what was going on among the myriad of so-called "experts" and among the various nationalities and ethnic groups that were lobbying to get what they considered a fair shake out of the peace settlement. Westermann's diary is in the same league with similar diaries and detailed letters written home by such men as Charles Seymour, the Yale historian and future president of that university, and the British diplomat and future writer and politician, Harold Nicolson.

The adventure in making contemporary history for this scholar of the ancient world began with his departure from the United States on December 4, 1918. Westermann traveled to France with the rest of the American delegation on the U.S.S. George Washington. The voyage offered him a chance to observe and describe the leaders of the delegation. Secretary of State Robert Lansing was "a small man, with grey or blue eyes pouched in flesh rolls." Henry White, another of the four commissioners, was "a very large man with a kindly appearance, either lame or so bow-legged as to be lame." Westermann almost missed his first chance to see President Wilson up close. He belatedly learned that Wilson had called a meeting with the entire delegation and heard only the last fifteen minutes of the president's talk to the young men. Like other witnesses who described this meeting, Westermann was struck by a famous utterance of Wilson's, which he set down this way: "One of his phrases, characteristic of his style of expression which was often of picturesque literary quality, was: 'Tell me what is right and I will fight for it. Give me a guaranteed position!'" Like others on the staff, Westermann took that declaration to mean that he and his colleagues would play an important role in shaping the peace settlement.[6]

These experts assigned to the delegation would later discover that their efforts had little influence, but in the meantime, Westermann was a witness to the cast of characters who gathered in Paris in early 1919. He did not meet all of the present and future notables, but he encountered a large number of them. For example, Arnold Toynbee struck Westermann as "an extremely nice fellow but ready to accept ideas very quickly; that is, I don't think he tests them out critically before accepting them." Harold

Nicolson looked to him to be "curly-haired, confident, cocky, and self-serious. He is a poor but stubborn mind, ill-informed." Westermann described the Zionist leader Chaim Weizman as "a bitter prophet. He told me his history and of his plans for Palestine. His tone was threatening. 'If the Jews do not get what they want, this Peace Conference will be a failure. We will break their treaties to bits. We Jews broke Russia.'" Westermann met a number of Zionists, including one who became a friend. This was Felix Frankfurter, the future U.S. Supreme Court justice, who had served in and advised the Wilson administration and was representing American Zionists in Paris. Westermann found Frankfurter "very interesting, a bright chap. His [Frankfurter's] estimate of president Wilson was one of great love and adulation and the assumption of mental capacity which does not permit him to delegate authority or work. He says that he [Wilson] has not a great amount of 'horse power,' meaning the ability to carry on successfully a great amount of work, such as Th[eodore] Roosevelt had."[7]

Of all the players in the international game whom Westermann met in Paris, the two who made the greatest impression on him were deeply involved in his own area of expertise, the Middle East. They were T. E. Lawrence and Prince Faisal. Westermann met "Lawrence of Arabia" during his first month in Paris at a party given for several Americans by Lord Robert Cecil. Evidently Lawrence dominated the evening with tales of his exploits and expressions of his opinions because these are all that Westermann records from the encounter. He describes Lawrence as "a quite clean-minded little fellow of 29." Later Westermann also remarked on Lawrence's "gentle voice and girlish eyes." Among other things that Westermann noted from that evening was that "Lawrence follows the Muslim law, apparently, of drinking no wine. He hates the 'townee' Syrians and believed in the Arabs of the desert. 'They are real. We Occidentals can't spoil the desert Arabs. The desert is too big for us.'"[8]

Faisal made an even bigger impression on Westermann. Just over a week after meeting Lawrence, Westermann wrote in his diary, "Tonight I have a great experience, that of dining with Emir Faisal and Colonel Lawrence here at the hotel." Both men were in Arab dress, and after the meal Faisal gave his version of Arab relations with Europeans and the Turks. "His story was a dramatic one and wonderfully told, all in Arabic, a musical language, with gesticulations few but graceful. His fingers were long and the nails spotlessly clean. His nose comes almost straight down from the brow, in the Greek line. Colonel Lawrence translated." Faisal, whose army had taken Damascus, was most concerned about French designs on Syria and Lebanon, and was seeking American aid to counteract those designs. At the end of the evening Westermann concluded, "This is a remarkable man really. Lawrence is not his brains as I thought.

Lawrence says that he can help him on details, but when he starts on principles Faisal goes off like a 60 power car." Westermann also had the opportunity to see Faisal present his case before the Council of Ten, the body of presidents and premiers that functioned as an executive committee for the peace conference.[9]

Westermann had extensive contacts with Zionists and Arabs. He does not seem to have liked the Zionists much—there are whiffs of that mild and unconscious anti-Semitism that infected most white Americans and Europeans of that era. For example, after a dinner with Henry Morgenthau, who had been one of Wilson's ambassadors to Turkey, Westermann commented in his diary, "Talk of the power of the Jews in American politics today! This is my first real knowledge of it, and of its cool realization of power." After recounting an expression of views about Armenia by Morgenthau, he wrote, "So works the real estate mind in international politics."[10]

As his fascination with Faisal suggests, Westermann sympathized with the Arabs, but not totally. He also recounted remarks by people who disparaged the Arabs, such as a judgment by the president of the American University in Beirut "that these people are like children, pleased at notice, vain, and superificial." Westermann noted, "I judge that he is right. But they are very gentlemanly and attractive, though all noisy eaters." He likewise represented the views of the Middle East hand Gertrude Bell, that "no Oriental ever told what he actually thought about matters, openly and in a public way". To which Westermann commented, "She is quite sure of this and I think she is right."[11]

One of Westermann's few accounts of his own work involves his contributing to and trying to revise a report early in the conference on what he calls "Western Asia." Evidently, the overall chief of the experts, Sidney Mezes, who was president of the City College of New York and Colonel House's brother-in-law, "so badly altered [the report] that a statement entirely unfavorable to the 'Jewish State' idea, though granting an independent Palestine, had become entirely favorable to the idea. . . . I must therefore reject the report when it comes up for consideration and then have a talk with Dr. Mezes, because this sort of thing is impossible. Many of the ideas are not mine and it reads like a valedictorian High School address."[12]

Beyond revising this report and attending the meetings of the Council of Ten when Faisal and others presented their arguments, Westermann does not seem to have had much to do with the Middle East settlement. He does appear to have helped in lobbying to send a joint commission to observe the situation in Syria. "I cannot see that I can be of much more use here," he wrote to his wife at the end of April, "and certainly do not expect to be connected with the work after the first of July, although this will mean that the decisions in the Near East will not be taken by me, except as through my office work, I have been able to affect them." About two weeks later, he commented on the provisions of the newly disclosed draft of the peace treaty that divided the Ottoman Empire into "a Greek section in Asia Minor, the Italians in the Adalia section, the Americans in Armenia, French in Syria, the Zionists in Palestine." He concluded, "If this is the case the Turkish Empire is the loot of war."[13]

Actually, interested as he was in the Middle East, Westermann devoted most of his work not to that region but rather, he concerned himself with, and tried to exert what influence he could, on the settlement of Asia Minor, what is present-day Turkey. Even before the conference opened, he was discussing what would happen to the various nationalities there. In December 1918, he met the Greek premier Eleutherios Venizelos, who impressed Westermann with his frankness. Later in the month, one of the American Peace Commissioners, General Tasker Bliss, called Westermann in for a talk. Bliss expressed his reservations about creating independent Greek and Armenian states in Asia Minor, and he seemed to Westermann "troubled by the consideration that we specialists were carving up the world arbitarily, we believing that states with lines drawn on abstract considerations, would be workable." Bliss also impressed Westermann with his knowledge of the parts played by Greece and Turkey in the war and with his way of thinking "on definite lines drawn by a belief in honesty and in the principles laid down by President Wilson. I judge that he will be a hard man for the diplomats to handle in the Peace negotiations."[14]

Westermann and his colleagues spent the first month of the conference working on various plans for the disposition of Asia Minor. He encountered considerable lobbying by representatives of the involved nationalities, particularly the Armenians. At one point, an Armenian leader asked Westermann's advice about what form of government an independent Armenia should have. "Think of it! . . . And I am a mere Professor." Even headier moments followed. On February 3, as he recorded in his diary, "I was called in . . . among the Olympians in the Foreign Office at the Quai d'Orsay. It was the great committee of the Peace Conference, the Committee of Ten," which included President Wilson, British Prime Minister David Lloyd George, French Premier Georges Clemenceau, and Italian Prime Minister Vittorio Orlando. "I suppose that this was the great occasion of my life. I go again tomorrow at 11 o'clock when Venizelos takes up the claims in Asia Minor."[15]

Westermann was there to supply information if he was called on, but he does not record that anyone asked him to speak. Five days later, he was also present when Faisal presented his case to the Council of Ten. Westermann served on a committee that the council appointed to review the Greek claims in both Europe and Asia Minor. "There was a lot of talk back and forth," Westermann noted in his diary, "much as at a faculty committee meeting, which did not get anywhere. Finally it was agreed that each delegation should make a proposal as to what it deemed to be a just line between Greece and Albania and bring it in Sat[urday] morning at the next meeting." What happened at that next meeting evidently did not strike Westermann as worth noting in his diary.[16]

More than the Greeks—who he thought were greedy in their claims to portions of coastal Asia Minor—it was the Armenians who absorbed Westermann's attention and elicited his greatest sympathy. In the middle of April, he secured a meeting with Secretary Lansing, General Bliss, and Henry White, at which he unrolled a map to show how the Allies wanted to carve up Turkey along the lines of their secret treaties. "I took up the question of sending American officers first to Armenia to occupy the harbors on the gulf of Alexandretta and work inward to the country and to come in from the north." Lansing raised the objection that this "would mean a declaration of war on Turkey as, he said, we were not at war with Turkey and could not send troops there." Perhaps there could be a military mission, Westermann suggested, and the four men talked about details. "The suggestion came up in the course of our conversation that the only way to get any action in the matter would be through the Armenians creating a propaganda for an American mandate in the United States which would force action in Congress and I asked if that would not meet with criticism from the members of the Commission. Mr. Lansing said that it was very dangerous and I should have nothing to do with it as long as I was working in Government employ. After some more conversations of this character, I withdrew."[17]

As that diary entry notes, proposals were afloat at the Peace Conference for the United States to occupy parts of Turkey under the mandate system that was to be set up under the new League of Nations. Besides being used as a cover for dividing up former German colonies among the Allied powers, the mandate system was extended to the Middle East in the form of a British mandate in Palestine and a French mandate in Lebanon and Syria. Additionally there were proposals for mandates in Turkey under Greece, France, Italy, and the United States. The plan involved having the United States serve as the "honest broker" among the powers by occupying Constantinople and the Straits and by serving as the mandatory power in Armenia. Much as he disliked some of the proposed mandates, Westermann was heart and soul for having his country involved in Constantinople and Armenia.

Westermann's efforts to promote this policy led to his most impressive occasion at the Peace Conference. On May 22, 1919, Westermann and David Magie, a professor of classics at Princeton who had also been serving as an advisor on "Western Asia," met with President Wilson to discuss

Turkey. Wilson told them he was prepared to propose the Armenian mandate to Congress and he thought it might go through. Constantinople was "doubtful," Wilson believed, even though he thought the United States "would be the best mandatory for Constantinople because it would be the least likely to foment trouble there." Wilson showed an intimate knowledge of the area and the various proposals for intervention there. "Returning to the question of the best mandatory for Turkey," Westermann recorded, "the President said that the United States, if it held mandates over Armenia and Constantinople, would be in a strategic position to control that portion of the world, and that, under the Covenant of the League of Nations, it would be the duty of the United States to report to the League any dereliction of duty on the part of the nations in control of Turkey. . . . Throughout the interview, the President declared himself as strongly opposed to the secret agreements. We think that he will still fight them."[18]

This was Westermann's closest brush with participation in the work of the Peace Conference and his best chance to make history. Yet the circumstances of the meeting displayed how little influence Westermann had on the negotiations. The meeting with Wilson was occasioned by a bitter letter Westermann and Magie sent the president on the day before. Westermann and Magie complained in their letter that, although the peace commissioners were negotiating the disposition of the Ottoman Empire, "we have no knowledge, except from the daily papers and vague rumor, as to what is being done. The only technical advice which is being heard, so far as we know, is apparently that of British Foreign Office experts and of Mr. Venizelos, all of whom are interested parties." The letter concluded with a request that Westermann and Magie be granted a personal meeting with Wilson, a request that was granted the following day.[19]

Magie's name on the letter ensured that it would be read by the president. Magie came from an illustrious Princeton family. His grandfather, James McCosh, had been president of the College of New Jersey (as Princeton was then known) when Wilson was a student. Magie himself had been a student at Princeton when Wilson was on the faculty, and Magie was appointed to the faculty while Wilson was Princeton's president. Furthermore, Magie's uncle, William Francis Magie, was one of Wilson's Princeton classmates.

Westermann must have been well aware that Wilson agreed to the meeting more as a favor to Magie than in appreciation of Westermann's own work. A week and a half before the meeting, Westermann wrote to his Wisconsin dean, George Sellery, of his profound disillusionment with the conference and with his own prospects for doing anything useful in Paris. "There is a great disappointment about the Peace Treaty," Westermann told Sellery. "Everything has been sacrificed for the League of Nations."[20]

As for himself, Westermann had long since told his wife that he was not accomplishing much. He also told Sellery in a later letter, "The fact is that my work is of no value here, and the chances are very great that the United States, which has no policy in the Near East, will only sit in on the discussion of the Turkish treaty, without power to act, since we are not at war with Turkey." Westermann was expressing more than a policy disagreement. He was personally sick of what he called "this damned three ring circus. . . . [T]he tawdriness of the circus is much more apparent to one who is a peg driver in the big tent than to the audience. The absolute incompetence of the administration diplomatic organization is something that would sadden the American heart."[21]

By June, Westermann was pulling all the strings he could find to get home. Getting off the peace conference staff seems to have been like getting out of military service. People concocted reasons to be released early. In Westermann's case, he asked Sellery. "Please write me a rather peremptory letter which will make it perfectly clear to me that I shall be needed at the University of Wisconsin by August 1st. . . . A slight intimation that the consequences will be serious for me if I do not get back, may help me in my situation here." Sellery obliged with just such a peremptory letter, although it proved unnecessary. Through his own and other experts' exertions, Westermann was among those who wrangled a berth for himself on the USS George Washington to return with the presidential party immediately after the signing of the peace treaty.[22]

Westermann also obtained a ticket to the signing ceremony on June 28 in the Hall of Mirrors at the Palace of Versailles. "This was the great day," he recorded later in the diary. "It had singularly little of grandeur. Except for the one thrill when the five Germans entered it left me cold.

"I cannot believe that this treaty is a great document. It is certainly, possibly rightly, based upon the theory of punishment. Many of the territorial settlements will soon be unmade, and it will cost human blood to do it."[23]

With that prescient comment, Westermann ended his diary, but this was not quite the end of his brush with history making. In an entry that was written on the voyage back, he had a conversation with a future president that also forecasted how public policy would be made, and by whom. Aboard ship, Westermann talked about Armenia with Herbert Hoover, who "said that he was against our taking Armenia, because everybody was willing to let us have it because there was nothing worth while there. . . . The attitude is very interesting and sensible as a business proposition. Unfortunately the whole thing is *not* a business matter, and the commercial standpoint is not applicable."[24]

Hoover, who was roughly the same age as Westermann, represented the future of American policymaking and leadership. Hoover's presidential predecessors, Wilson, Taft, and Theodore Roosevelt, were men of intellectual ambition and scholarly interests who had studied classical antiquity from childhood through college. Hoover, an orphan from Iowa raised by his uncle in small-town Oregon, received interrupted and irregular schooling as a child. His only education on the ancient world consisted of a few weeks of ineffective tutoring in Latin at age fifteen.[25] Hoover was in the first graduating class at Stanford University where he earned a degree in geology. He went on to make a fortune as a mining engineer working throughout Asia and Australia. Hoover brought a businessman's approach to public policy, an approach that found little practical value in the history and literature of the ancient Greeks and Romans.

The failure of Westermann's work in the American delegation to the Paris Peace Conference was connected to the seeming irrelevance of his background in relation to the task at hand. Westermann, the ancient historian, could not appreciate how much American commercial interests and domestic politics influenced the decisions to be made.[26] He may have remained oblivious to the concerns of business and industry, but others in the Wilson administration could not. Both the State and War Departments requested advice independent of Westermann and his staff on the disposition of the Ottoman Empire.[27]

Westermann's recommendations for Asia Minor and the Middle East were by and large ignored. The United States never did assume the mandate over Armenia or even join the League of Nations. In view of his comments on the treaty and his part in it, it is clear that Westermann had had enough of observing and making history. Whether he would have echoed Edward Gibbon's famous remark, "The captain of the Hampshire militia was not useless to the historian of the Roman Empire," is debatable. Still, it must have been exciting to have been in the cockpit of world affairs. Westermann kept his historian's head about him and kept a record of what he saw and did. In that way, he really did make *history*—that is, as professionals use the term. His diary has become a primary source for scholars studying the aftermath of World War I, and for this, at least, later historians are deeply grateful to him.

Chapter 7

The World of Moses Finkelstein
The Year 1939 in M. I. Finley's Development as a Historian

—Daniel P. Tompkins

Sir Moses Finley's involvement with American politics consumed a brief but fateful period in his life.[1] Finley (1912–1986) is famous both as one of the most influential ancient historians of the twentieth century and as one of the most prominent academic victims of the anti-Communist furor in the early years of the Cold War. Dismissed from his faculty position at Rutgers University in December 1952 after refusing to answer questions from the Internal Security Subcommittee of the U.S. Senate (under the chairmanship of Senator Pat McCarran of Nevada), Finley left the United States in 1954, returning rarely. He gained international eminence for his analyses of slavery and the ancient economy while a professor of ancient history at Cambridge University, became a British citizen in 1962, and was knighted in 1979. After moving to England he said little in public about American politics, although his occasional remarks were poignant and forceful. Cold War historian Ellen Schrecker has documented the period of his life from 1951 to 1954, including the twenty months when his Rutgers dismissal left him without a teaching position.[2] But the following passages, written by friends and colleagues, illustrate how hazy his early years remain:

From the galaxy of stars in the Institute [of Social Research, then located at Columbia University, where Finley attended graduate school] he clearly acquired his Marxism. . . . But theirs was the liberal Marxist dialogue of the Gründrisse against the deadening effect of Stalinist orthodoxy.[3]

About 1936 he took the surname Finley.[4]

Of humble upbringing, he had been made by academe. . . . Born Moses Finkelstein in 1912, he changed his name to Finley in 1941, having published a solitary article on ancient Greek commerce under his born name. His upbringing, since he was named Moses, is likely to have been orthodox. A prodigy, he was graduated with the highest honors from Syracuse University at the age of 17 and received a rabbinical training.[5]

The war years are something of a blank in Finley's career. . . . His attention was diverted to what he called "war relief agencies."[6]

[H]aving come under attack . . . in the notorious committee run by Joseph McCarthy, he emigrated to Britain.[7]

Here we find a series of errors, minor but significant. Karl Marx's *Gründrisse*—the notes Marx used in preparation for writing *Das Kapital*—were first published in Moscow only in 1939 and not widely known in the West until the Berlin edition of 1953. Finley, as a Columbia graduate student in the 1930s, was completely unaware of the *Gründrisse*, though he did read and make use of them after he had emigrated to England.[8] The adoption of the surname Finley did not take place until 1946, and under the name M. I. Finkelstein he published two articles and several reviews from 1934 to 1941.[9] Finley's father, Nathan Finkelstein, designed gears for Buick and was never without a job during the Depression. Moses and his three siblings grew up in a successful middle-class family and succeeded in business, the law, and medicine. Family photographs reveal long summer vacations to a cottage. Moses's bachelor's degree from Syracuse came less than a month after his fifteenth birthday, not at age seventeen. He never trained for the rabbinate, though he was descended from a long line of rabbis and delivered a well-received bar mitzvah speech.[10] During World War II, his *curriculum vitae* was not at all "blank," for he held prominent positions in Russian War Relief, ending up as the organization's national campaign director. He never appeared before Senator Joseph McCarthy's Permanent Subcommittee on Investigations, which did not hold hearings until after Finley had left Rutgers; Finley came "under attack" by the McCarran Committee.

These statements illustrate both how remote the details of Finley's American experience were to his British friends, and how little effort

Finley devoted to being his own Boswell. Sir Moses neither concealed nor advertised his earlier life as Moe Finkelstein, as this essay will refer to him when discussing events before 1946.[11] Sometimes he could appear almost offhand, as in this description of a fateful moment: "Early in 1952 I had a minor brush with the Senate Committee."[12] The scholar who reports most knowledgably and sympathetically about Finley's life in the 1930s is Pierre Vidal-Naquet, a leftist who shared Finley's antipathy to the historian Karl August Wittfogel.[13] When Moses and Mary Finley sailed for England in 1954, leaving their Ford automobile with Max and Sylvia Goldfrank and packing nearly everything else, Mary told Sylvia that no return was likely.[14] They left behind no diaries, memoirs, caches of letters, or closets of rough and rejected drafts.[15]

Interviews, archives, and careful reading of his published work, however, do enable us to begin to recover Moe Finkelstein. Occasionally, even anonymous hints lead to a fuller picture, as in this reminiscence in 1955 by New Dealer and labor activist Gardner (Pat) Jackson:

> [O]ne of the things that engaged me [in 1939] . . . was a committee set up to have an influence, presumably on Hollywood so as to get films produced to serve the interests of democracy. I wish I could remember the name of the fellow who persuaded me on that: he was one of the most beguiling guys, a young professor up at Columbia University. Films for Democracy was what we called ourselves, I think. . . . A fellow from Warner Brothers came to me secretly and said he was working with this beguiling young professor—I wish I could remember his name.[16]

Cross-checking with the Boas Professional Papers at the American Philosophical Society, we find that the seductive young man was Moses Finkelstein.[17]

Although a full picture of his life in America will require further inquiry, Moe Finkelstein emerges as a remarkably effective political organizer and activist on the Left, an intellectual with a wide and exciting group of friends and colleagues, and a devoted and successful teacher. His success as an organizer and activist won not only allies but enemies, particularly in the twelve months that began in August 1938, a "year of living dangerously" for himself and many others. By the autumn of 1939, he was squarely in the crosshairs of some prominent and remorseless foes.

Finkelstein's numerous associations in this period include the eminent anthropologist Franz Boas; the philosophers John Dewey and Sidney Hook (who were opponents of Boas on the anti-Stalinist Left); Finkelstein's dissertation advisor at Columbia University, the ancient historian William Linn Westermann; the faculty and graduate fellows of the Institute of Social Research, including Max Horkheimer, Leo Lowenthal, and

Karl August Wittfogel; fellow Columbia University graduate students
Meyer Reinhold, Naphtali Lewis, Theodore Geiger, Daniel Thorner, and
others; fellow lecturers in the history department at City College, such as
William M. Canning and twins Phil and Jack Foner; and City College student Daniel Bell. Other individuals appear at the fringes: the controversial City College English instructor Morris Schappes; the Marxist
sociologist Bernhard Stern, founder of the journal *Science and Society*; and
Lawrence Rosinger, one of the China scholars ruined in the McCarran
hearings.[18] Many of these individuals figured significantly in postwar
debates about Communism.

Finkelstein's most important and consequential relationship from this
period has received remarkably little attention. In the spring of 1938, the
graduate student began working as an organizer and activist on behalf of
the octogenarian anthropologist Franz Boas (1858–1942). The following
letter from Finkelstein to Boas was written while Finkelstein was spending time in a cottage on Cape Cod.

> 4 Conant Street
> Provincetown, Massachusetts
> August 3, 1938
>
> Dear Professor Boas,
>
> I am terribly sorry to have been so remiss in my correspondence, but
> I can only plead the confusion involved in trying to get away from
> New York. . . .[19]

These bland words are the earliest surviving evidence of a collaboration
that would shape American public opinion about race and anti-Semitism,
and would lead to accusations that Finkelstein/Finley was engaged in
Communist activities. Finley's later reticence regarding his intellectual
and political background included his association with Boas. Colleagues
at Cambridge were surprised in 1977 when a query about the "most
underrated" thinkers of the preceding seventy-five years elicited this
response from Finley:

> Franz Boas. The giant among the founders of modern anthropology,
> swept aside in this country by two successive waves of fashion, func-
> tionalism and then structuralism, so that he is not merely under-
> rated, he is unread.[20]

This praise was a bolt from the blue, hinted at nowhere in Finley's pub-
lications, letters, or testimony before the McCarran Committee.[21] After
Boas's death in 1942, Boas and Finley were linked only in their FBI files.
But they had worked intensely on causes they cared about, and—in ret-

rospect—an intellectual affiliation is also evident: Boas, the physical anthropologist, regularly condemned overreliance on physical evidence. Finley, the ancient historian, regularly doubted the stories artifacts alone could tell. Both men distrusted narrators, both recommended employing multiple methodologies to capture a culture, and both were capable of trenchant methodological critiques. Neither developed "laws"; both insisted on studying the "mental life" or cultural predilections of their subjects.[22] Boas's insistence in 1899 that "the tendency of developing a cast-iron system of measurements . . . is a movement in the wrong direction," would certainly have appealed to Finley, who nearly three-quarters of a century later, decried the utility of trying to fashion modern economic measurements to gauge commercial activity and social organization in the ancient world.[23]

In 1938 Moe Finkelstein was a twenty-six-year-old graduate student writing a dissertation in ancient history at Columbia University. He first came to Columbia in 1927 having just graduated *cum laude* with a degree in psychology from Syracuse University. Finkelstein initially intended to pursue a legal career and therefore earned a master's degree in public law two years later. At Columbia's law school, Finkelstein became acquainted with A. Arthur Schiller (1902–1977), who recently arrived from Berkeley to teach Coptic and Roman law.[24] Finkelstein, however, left academia in 1929 to work in the legal department of a large corporation.

After six months on the job, the seventeen-year-old decided that a career in law was not to his liking. Finkelstein quit, choosing to work as a fact checker on (and ultimately contributor to) the *Encyclopedia of the Social Sciences* under the editorship of retired Columbia economics professor Edwin R. A. Seligman (1861–1939) and Seligman's onetime student, economist Alvin S. Johnson (1874–1971), who was director of the New School for Social Research. Finkelstein also renewed contact with Schiller, and the teenager decided to enroll in Columbia's doctoral program in history. He finished his coursework in 1932 at the age of twenty. That autumn, he had already decided to write his dissertation on trade in classical Athens. He served as Schiller's research assistant for the 1933–1934 academic year, and the following year Finkelstein held a university fellowship.[25]

Finkelstein's dissertation advisor was the ancient historian William Linn Westermann. Westermann was a papyrologist with interests in the economic aspects of classical antiquity in general, and of Greco-Roman Egypt in particular. He tended to prefer the minute examination of detailed evidence to the grand sweep of theoretical models. He was held in the highest esteem by academic historians, and in 1944 he would serve as president of the American Historical Association. Westermann heightened the perception of his formidable intellect by maintaining a formal and chilly relationship with his students. One former student who later became a history department colleague wrote of Westermann, "He inspired more admiring wonder for his expertise than affection for his person, because his attitude toward students (and some colleagues) was on the German model. Rigorous scholarship requires frigorous human relations."[26]

Finkelstein's mind was far more expansive and theoretically engaged than that of his advisor. In 1936, Finkelstein wrote a brief review of his advisor's magisterial essay on slavery in antiquity that Westermann composed for the massive German classical encyclopedia commonly referred to as "Pauly-Wissowa." Couched in the short review is a sentence that noted how Westermann's essay lacked "a real theoretical discussion and synthesis of many fundamental questions." More than forty years later, Finley would write in his own book on ancient slavery that he believed Westermann's "Pauly-Wissowa" essay was a scholarly disaster and that the review was a desperate and ultimately vain attempt "to flash signals" to his eminent advisor.[27] Disappointed in what Finkelstein regarded as the antiquarian nature of Westermann's scholarship, the young man instead found intellectual inspiration from other researchers and graduate students.

At Columbia, Moe Finkelstein was among a circle of intellectually precocious young scholars, many of whom were, like Finkelstein, the children of Jewish immigrants. Other Westermann students at that time included Meyer Reinhold (1909–2002) and Naphtali Lewis (1911–2005). Reinhold, whose appreciation of theoretical approaches to antiquity more closely matched those of his graduate school colleague Finkelstein, ended up writing his dissertation (a biography of Augustus' right-hand man and son-in-law Agrippa) under Latin professor Charles Knapp. Nonetheless, Reinhold retained a more charitable view of Westermann's scholarship than did Finkelstein.[28] Lewis, a friend of both Finkelstein and Reinhold, became a papyrologist whose work owed far more both in substance and in methodology to that of his advisor, Westermann.

The backgrounds of Finkelstein, Reinhold, and Lewis were not atypical for Jewish intellectuals in the New York of the 1930s. The children of eastern European immigrants, most studied Latin in the city's public high schools, and many continued to examine one or more aspects of classical antiquity while in college. Even though in the half century between 1870 and 1920, nearly all American universities had removed the study of ancient languages as requirements for admission and graduation (and high school enrollments in Greek plummeted), high school enrollments in Latin continued to grow in the first four decades of the twentieth century. Much of that growth occurred in public schools and was fueled by the children of immigrants, particularly Jews, who saw knowledge of classical antiquity as the key to gaining entry to full participation—intellectual, social, and political—in American life. Enrollments in Latin classes at public high schools in the United States peaked in the mid 1930s, when nearly 900,000 students were learning the language. This high mark, which has not been surpassed in the seven decades since, came a little more than a dozen years after the Immigration Act of 1921 sharply curtailed Jewish immigration into the United States.[29]

Although the study of Latin was widespread among these children of immigrants, expertise in the language was not always particularly deep. One former student at Boys High School in Brooklyn at the end of the 1910s later claimed that "although we learned to read Cicero, we could hardly say 'Please give me a glass of milk' in Latin."[30] Furthermore, collegiate exposure to classical antiquity came primarily in the form of English translations of Greek and Roman authors. In 1912 appeared the first twenty volumes in a series of pocket-sized books of ancient literature in which the original text appeared on the left-hand page and a facing English translation on the right. Publication was funded by the American philanthropist James Loeb, who wanted to ensure a wider readership for Greek and Roman authors in an era of diminishing attention paid to ancient languages. With roughly a dozen or so additional volumes published every year up until World War II, the Loeb Classical Library— whose volumes continue to be printed and revised to this day—became a familiar resource to American college students.[31]

Colleges in the late 1910s began establishing required or recommended courses that surveyed (in English translation) major works in world literature, including a heavy dose of the ancients, from Homer's *Iliad* to Augustine's *Confessions*. These "Great Books" courses were primarily designed to promote the moral virtues to be gained from exposure to long-cherished exempla of humanistic expression, as against the hardheaded commercial practicality that some businessmen wished to impose on higher education. Even so, John Erskine (1896–1954), the Columbia University English professor credited with starting the "Great Books" movement, argued at his own school that study of the masterworks of world literature would aid in the acculturation and intellectual development of the children of Russian and central European immigrants.[32]

To this interest in classical antiquity, the children of immigrants often brought a familiarity with socialist ideas gained from associations with socialist labor and political groups. Some of their parents had been involved in similar groups in Europe, yet the impetus for the flourishing of socialist ideas among Jewish immigrants and their children primarily developed from their experiences in America. Most immigrants in New York at the beginning of the twentieth century faced an abrupt transformation from their former lives in Europe as village craftsmen and agricultural laborers, to factory workers crammed into tenements in what was quickly becoming the most populous city in the world. They viewed the solidarity of labor organizations as the only effective means of demanding improved working conditions and providing financial support for the family after a worker's injury or death.[33]

Immigrants, and especially their children, also sought to fashion in America a new Jewish identity freed from the strictures of traditional religious culture and its domineering rabbis. Socialism provided a cosmopolitan identity whose intellectual rigor was appealing precisely because it could compete so well against the Talmudism of the past. Sociologist Daniel Bell (born 1919), who grew up in New York's famed Lower East Side, recalled studying Marx as a teenager in the same way he had learned Torah and Talmud in Hebrew school. Bell confronted his rabbi shortly after his bar mitzvah to proclaim himself an atheist and that he was abandoning religious practice to join the Young Socialists League.[34]

Finkelstein had a similar distance from his religious upbringing. Born to immigrant parents in New York City, Finkelstein was descended on his mother's side from one of the great rabbinic dynasties of Central Europe, and his grandfather had been chief rabbi of St. Petersburg. After Moses's birth, the family moved to Syracuse, New York. As a child, Finkelstein received substantial religious education, but by the time he reached his twenties, his secularism was evident to all.[35]

Exactly when Finkelstein became interested in Marx and Lenin remains unclear. He arrived at Columbia just weeks after the execution of Sacco and Vanzetti had brought rioting in cities around the world.[36] The case of these anarchists was skillfully manipulated by Comintern agent Willy Münzenberg for maximum gain.[37] The Crash and the Great Depression may also have influenced Finkelstein, as may have collaboration with older leftists such as Bernhard Stern on the *Encyclopedia of the Social Sciences*. For Moe Finkelstein as for many other young Jewish Americans at the time, a move to the Left was overdetermined but underdocumented. The rise of Hitler and his virulent anti-Semitism added urgency to the embrace by these intellectuals of communist and leftist ideas.[38]

Marx seemed particularly relevant to understanding the connections between past and present. Although, as Finley himself pointed out decades later, Marx wrote very little that directly discussed classical antiquity,[39] he provided a theoretical framework for understanding the totality of human history. For Marx, economic production was the defining characteristic of a society. The earliest human societies shared the responsibility of providing food for the entire tribe, a primitive form of communism. But already in prehistoric times, the concept of private property led to divisions between rich and poor, free and slave. In Marxist thought, Greek and Roman civilizations were fashioned through having slave labor serve as the primary mode of production. Slavery-based economies necessarily collapse, and the Middle Ages ushered in a new European civilization based upon feudalism. Feudalism was in turn replaced by capitalism, whose own economic collapse would one day enable workers in a revolution to seize control over the means of production and to establish common ownership and common goals for agriculture and industry.[40]

The arrival of modern communism was always conceived by Marx as a global phenomenon. World War I seemed to mark the beginning of capitalism's collapse, yet despite revolutions taking place in several European nations, only in Russia did communism take root. Why this was so became a matter of intense debate among Marxist thinkers in the following two decades. Many believed that workers' revolutions would soon spread around the world, and they saw the Great Depression as additional evidence for the imminent arrival of communism even in the United States. Others were not so sure, arguing that the American economy was different or at an earlier stage of development than the European economy. Another vexing problem concerned the rise of fascism and its spread throughout Europe in opposition to communism. Furthermore, some Marxists even questioned the validity and viability of the Russian form of communism, since the Soviet Union was an economically isolated and only partially industrialized country that did not seem to fulfill all of the characteristics for a proper revolution.[41]

Varying interpretations of Marxism sharply split the radical Left in New York in the late 1930s, but the primary division was between those who saw Stalin and the Soviet Union as Marxism's culmination, and those who believed that Stalin had betrayed the revolution. Many of the Stalinists took the additional step of joining the Communist Party of the United States of America, which provided them with a sense of direction and a social circle. The party followed directives from the Comintern in Moscow, which was under Stalin's control and was preparing for global revolution. Party members often assumed new or secret names, and membership lists were kept hidden from both rank-and-file members and even party officials. These elements added a flavor of adventure and intrigue to party membership, as well as preventing anti-Communist employers and associations from discovering party members and dismissing them.

Other individuals of a more independent streak were content to remain outside the official apparatus of the party even though they were sympathetic to the Soviet Union and Stalin's regime. These individuals, to use the argot of the day, were called "fellow travelers." They often assisted in programs and operations promoted by the party, and they were welcomed within the social networks of American Communists.[42]

Those opposed to Stalin were a far more heterogeneous lot. Some followed the ideas of Stalin's exiled rival Trotsky. Others supported the home-grown Socialist Party under the leadership of Norman Thomas (1884–1968). Still others were loyal to expelled former Communist Party USA leader Jay Lovestone (1897–1990). Many were not tied to any one particular anti-Stalinist group but shared in the ideals of revolutionary socialism developed from Marx's writings.[43]

On the Columbia University campus, Marxist theory infused the writings, seminars, and public lectures coming out of the Institute of Social Research. Although loosely affiliated with Columbia, the institute was an independent center that had been established in Frankfurt, Germany, in 1923. The institute's original purpose was to examine the totality of historical and cultural experience within a Marxist theoretical framework, with an ultimate goal of revealing how best to implement socialism in the modern world. A decade later when Hitler came to power, the institute and most of its primarily Jewish faculty fled to Geneva, Switzerland. In 1934, institute director Max Horkheimer (1895–1973) accepted an offer from Columbia University's president, Nicholas Murray Butler (1862–1947), to relocate the center to New York.

Although the institute's influence at Columbia was limited by the German researchers' difficulties with English, as well as their fierce sense of independence from the university's regular faculty and departments, and a deliberate lack of extensive lecture and seminar offerings, Moe Finkelstein gained a deep, personal acquaintance with the institute's teachings and operations. He seems to have become aware of the institute not long after its arrival at Columbia.[44] In 1937, Finkelstein started working as an editorial assistant at the institute, where he helped edit and provide English translations for the institute's German scholars.

The extraordinary richness of Finkelstein's involvement with the institute included the opportunity not only to write book reviews, as Finkelstein did from 1935 through 1941, but to collaborate actively with the institute's scholars as he fashioned English translations for publication. The institute never listed translators or editors, so the task of determining which of the several Americans who worked there assisted on any given text is difficult. Finley himself revealed that he worked on Otto Kirchheimer's contributions to the 1939 book *Punishment and Social Structure*, and on Max Horkheimer's 1941 essay, "Art and Mass Culture."[45] He contributed to institute publications on a contract basis until the mid 1940s.

When Finley sought academic work in the later 1940s, Paul Lazarsfeld and Max Horkheimer were to write his longest and strongest recommendations. Lazarsfeld, the Viennese empiricist who worked closely with the institute, was impressed with Finkelstein's leadership of a research group. Horkheimer credits Finley with working

> . . . in close consultation with the authors [at the institute], to help
> revise the texts in order to render them as clear and intelligible as
> possible for American readers. Anyone familiar with German philo-
> sophical terminology will appreciate the problems of such an assign-
> ment.

Horkheimer adds that Finley played a major role as the institute was
"making the transition from the German to the American scene" because
he was expert in history, sociology, and philosophy and had "the knack
of lucid presentation. . . . It is worth mentioning, finally, that reviewers of
the volumes he prepared for publication invariably commented on the
skill of the translation."[46]

Clearly, Finkelstein's editing activity and attendance at seminars and
lectures contributed to his own understanding of Marx, Weber, and others, although we are only beginning to probe these relationships. In one
sense, there is no comparing Finley's essay, "Was Greek Civilization Based
on Slave Labor," with Max Horkheimer's famously elliptical "Authoritarian
State," a piece that appeared in German between 1941 and 1942 but was
not translated into English until 1972.[47] On the other hand, the essays
share some features. They range easily, for instance, among the authors of
the Western intellectual tradition: Finley invokes Kant, Durkheim, Marx,
and—a Frankfurt School favorite—Nietzsche: this was not common fare
in articles about ancient history in 1959. Finley invokes Marx's claim that
"the history of all hitherto existing society is the history of class struggles"
to illustrate the political challenge to discussions of slavery; he cites Kant
to counter "sterile" attributions of cause and effect, Durkheim to dismiss
any role of slaves' "volition," and Nietzsche to stress the "ambiguity" or
"conflict" that governed Greek and Roman attitudes toward slavery.[48] He
had already used Weber (without naming him) in suggesting that slavery
spanned a "spectrum of statuses."[49]

Both Finley and Horkheimer favor dialectical approaches, both could
frankly admit that ambiguity clouded understanding, and both used the
essay form to raise as well as answer questions: the final paragraph of
"The Authoritarian State" is founded on contingency in a way perhaps
unmatched in any essay of similar stature. Littered with conditionals,
awash in paradox, it leaves the reader gazing into a horrid abyss:

> It would be sentimental to remain opposed to state capitalism
> merely because of those who have been slain. One could say that the
> Jews were for the most part capitalists, and that the small nations
> have no justification for their existence. . . . This much is true, that
> with the return to the old free enterprise system, the entire horror
> would start again from the beginning under new management. But
> the historical outlook of such reasoning recognizes only the dimen-
> sion of the cycle of progress and regression: it ignores the active

intervention of men. It values men only for what they are under capitalism: as social quantities, as things. As long as world history follows its logical course, it fails to fulfill its human destiny.

I have mentioned tendencies that the later Finley shared with Horkheimer, but differences stand out as well: the prose here is far more ser-
monic, elliptical, abstract, and embittered than Finley's own at any point
in his career.

Reading a paragraph like this, we are forced to wonder, what did
Finkelstein think of such thinking? The answer is, frankly, that we do not
yet know what Finley thought of Horkheimer. He seems never to have
said, even to Martin Jay when they met in 1972 (although he did note
that Horkheimer manipulated and terrorized his colleagues).[50] One reason to cite this paragraph then, is to make the point that biographers may
be too eager to "domesticate" the Frankfurt Institute thinkers. They were,
after all, serious Marxists, although increasingly doubtful from 1927
about the prospects for the Soviet economy. Two among them, Paul Massing and Franz Neumann, may have engaged in espionage for the Soviet
Union.[51] Fierce critics of fascism and subtler critics of Stalin, they also
kept their distance from American democracy. The claim that Finley was
not a Stalinist but a participant in the "liberal Marxist dialogue" of the
Frankfurt School may rest not on analysis of Horkheimer's hard words
but on a sort of anxiety: what if Finkelstein's Marxism should make
him—to use a phrase he made famous—"desperately foreign"?[52]

Finkelstein discussed the ideas he acquired from his exposure to the
institute with his fellow graduate students. His best friends were the
future sociologist Benjamin Nelson (1911–1977), who, like Finkelstein,
worked as an editorial assistant at the institute; the Renaissance historian
Charles Trinkaus (1911–1999); and the economic historians Daniel
Thorner (1915–1974) and Theodore Geiger (1914–2004). Competition
between Geiger and Finkelstein over a teaching position at Columbia
may have cooled the relationship. A memorandum from Westermann
reported that Finkelstein displayed a flash of anger to his advisor after
learning that Geiger got the position.[53]

Finkelstein, his fellow graduate students, and the émigré scholars at
the Institute of Social Research were certainly not alone on the Columbia
University campus in their interest in Marx and Lenin. Despite the conservative administration of the autocratic, septuagenarian president
Nicholas Murray Butler, Columbia University in the 1930s was popularly
perceived as a center of leftist ideology and activism. Derided as "The Big
Red University," Columbia claimed many prominent liberal activists
among its faculty, particularly in positions connected to teaching in the
Core Curriculum, Columbia's undergraduate "Great Books" program. The

art historian Meyer Schapiro (1904–1996) was active in Marxist organizations and publications, though his scholarly pursuits and Trotskyist outlook prevented him from joining the Communist Party. Well after it ceased to be fashionable, Schapiro remained philosophically opposed to the "imperialism" of World War II.[54] Philosophy professor Irwin Edman (1896–1954), who regularly wrote newspaper and magazine essays and spoke on the radio, prominently supported leftist causes and at times associated himself with Norman Thomas's Socialist Party. Lionel Trilling (1905–1975) of the English Department was a frequent contributor to the Marxist literary journal, the *Partisan Review*.[55]

"The Big Red University" was merely a paler shade of pink compared to the political activism on the campuses of the municipal colleges of the City of New York. In the 1930s, the city's Board of Higher Education oversaw four public colleges: City College, whose main campus is located in Manhattan roughly twenty blocks north of Columbia, with a branch campus downtown containing the business school (now Baruch College); Hunter College, a women's school on the Upper East Side with a branch campus at that time in the Bronx; and in the outer boroughs, the newer institutions of Brooklyn College (opened in 1930) and Queens College (opened in 1937). The municipal colleges provided free instruction to city residents, and their students overwhelmingly came from the children of Jewish immigrants. In 1938, only about one in five parents of incoming freshmen at City College had been born in the United States and more than eighty percent of the student population was Jewish.[56] These students were deeply involved in leftist politics. Demonstrations and protests were a regular occurrence at City College during the 1930s. The student cafeteria at City College was the center of debates and organizing activities. The cafeteria contained several alcoves where student groups met. Alcove one was the home of the Trotskyists and other radical socialists opposed to Stalin's control of the Soviet Union. Alcove two was the gathering place of the Communists, who defended Stalin and the Soviet "workers' paradise."[57]

Some of the teachers at City College were just as radical as the students. The municipal colleges handled the tremendous enrollment growth after World War I by appointing large numbers of temporary instructors whose annual contracts were regularly renewed. Many of these instructors were graduate students or recent Ph.D.'s who shared the same social, economic, and cultural background as their students. Finkelstein was just such an instructor, and since 1934 he had taught history courses at City College. His Columbia graduate school colleagues, Benjamin Nelson and Theodore Geiger, also taught at City College, as did another Westermann advisee, Benjamin Paskoff. Through his teaching, Finkelstein met and became friends with other history department instructors, including Jack and Phil

Foner, twins interested in labor history; as well as the English department tutor Morris Schappes (1907–2004). Schappes was a prominent Communist Party activist, and in 1936, the City College administration chose not to renew his contract. The ensuing campus uproar—involving sit-ins and marches—got Schappes his job back and made him a celebrity among Marxist intellectuals.[58]

Another history department instructor was William M. Canning. Canning began teaching at City College in 1934. Although raised a Catholic, his social circle was predominantly Jewish. He had been befriended by the Foner twins, who regularly invited him to their parents' home for meals.[59] He also knew Morris Schappes, and his wife was the former Edna Moskowitz.

Canning's relationship to Finkelstein is harder to determine. They certainly knew each other through the City College history department and had the Foner twins as mutual friends. Canning claimed before the McCarran Committee in 1951 that he was part of a Communist study group that met weekly for several months at Finkelstein's home, presumably during the 1937–1938 academic year.[60] Interestingly enough, in Finley's testimony before the same committee the following year, Canning's name never came up. By all accounts, Canning was not the sort of clever and imaginative conversationalist whose company Finkelstein preferred. And, as subsequent events would reveal, Canning's understanding of Marxism was juvenile and crude.

In March 1941, during an investigation by the Rapp-Coudert Committee of New York state legislators into Communist Party activities in New York City's municipal colleges, Canning testified that he joined the party in 1936; had worked with Schappes in trying to recruit members among the faculty, staff, and students; and identified fifty-four other Party members at City College. Among those named was Moe Finkelstein. A decade later, Canning would repeat his testimony before the McCarran Committee while his wife worked for the committee as a researcher.[61]

But to return to 1938, Canning's social interactions with Finkelstein appear not to have been extensive. Finkelstein himself was already married. He met Mary Moscowitz (no relation to Canning's future wife) at Columbia, where Mary was, like Moe, pursuing graduate work in history. The couple wed in 1932 and would remain deeply devoted to each other for the rest of their lives. Indeed, their attachment even extended to the timing of their deaths. Decades later in Cambridge, England, Mary became increasingly frail and was lovingly cared for by her husband. When she finally succumbed in June of 1986, Moses Finley returned to the home they shared. Within four hours, he suffered a massive cerebral hemorrage. He never regained consciousness and died the very next day.[62]

In their graduate student days, Moe and Mary Finkelstein shared intellectual, political, and recreational interests, though Mary was remembered as being even more politically and socially engaged than her husband. On Sunday evenings, the couple regularly invited other graduate students to their apartment for socializing. Both Finley and Daniel Thorner would later testify before the McCarran Committee that these get-togethers primarily consisted of listening to music from the couple's substantial record collection.[63] The Finleys' records would migrate with them to Cambridge, where graduate students report being impressed by them.[64]

Finkelstein had been hired by the eighty-year-old Boas in the spring of 1938 to assist in his campaign against the scientific propaganda of the Nazis. The two seem to have initially met through their shared support of the Loyalists in the Spanish Civil War. In April of that year, the prestigious British journal *Nature* published an article by the rabidly anti-Semitic German physicist Johannes Stark. Stark, a 1919 winner of the Nobel Prize, had long harbored two hostilities: one against theoretical physicists, and another against Jews. He was so outspoken that he lost his university position in Germany in 1922. Eight years later, he joined the National Socialists, gaining the patronage of Alfred Rosenberg and using German scientific journals to promote "Aryan physics." Stark blamed Jews and "White Jews" (gentiles who believed in relativity and quantum theory) for corrupting the academic discipline of physics. While a Bertoldt Brecht play from this era mentions only the Nazis' hostility to Albert Einstein, Stark indicted a universe: Max Born, Werner Heisenberg, Erwin Schrödinger, Max Planck, and others.[65] What was required, Stark said, was "to exterminate the Jewish spirit" in science. Stark's obsessions did not in the end help him with the Nazis, who chose the "White Jew" Heisenberg over him to direct the German atomic project.[66]

Boas, who had long argued against the concept of race and had been active in promoting liberal causes, decided to form an association of scholars to refute Nazi attempts to cloak their propaganda in the guise of disinterested science. Upon reading Stark's article in the spring of 1938, Boas consulted the geneticist Leslie Dunn and the physicist Harold Urey, prominent scientists with whom he had worked on other causes. In preparing their response to Stark's essay, Boas and his associates received financial support from the American Jewish Committee and named their group the University Federation for Democracy and Intellectual Freedom. Boas hired Finkelstein to organize the group's activities, prepare public statements, develop mailing lists, and approach professional organizations for support.[67] Finkelstein's August 3, 1938, letter from Provincetown, mentioned earlier in this essay, concerned the problems in using the membership mailing list of the American Association for the Advancement of Science.

Finkelstein might well have been enjoying a relaxing day gazing out on the Atlantic Ocean when he wrote this letter to Boas. The vacation house in Provincetown where he was staying—4 Conant Street—is a charming, Victorian structure, with a view of the ferry slip and harbor, and located only a block from the beach. (It is now a bed and breakfast called The Grand View Inn.) Yet Finkelstein seems to have gained little serenity during this vacation with Mary and another couple. As the letter reveals, he was hard at work, instructing Boas on how to build a useful mailing list, and recruiting supporters for a *Manifesto on Freedom of Science* that opposed Nazi racism. But as he later remarked about this month on Cape Cod, "[I]t did not turn out to be a very happy arrangement."[68] The spoiler, he said, was one of his vacation housemates, Karl August Wittfogel.

In the preceding year, the Finkelsteins had met Wittfogel and his second wife, Olga Lang, who was the daughter of an eminent Soviet physicist. Karl Wittfogel had a tall and imposing physical presence, and he was sixteen years older than Finkelstein: in 1938, he would have been forty-one to Finkelstein's twenty-six. Lenin's *Thesis on the Agrarian Question* had won Wittfogel over to Communist Party membership as a young instructor in Germany immediately after World War I. Wittfogel became fascinated by one of the crucial problems in Marxist historiography: why did the economies underlying Asian civilizations not pass through the same slavery-feudalism-capitalism series that marked the history of Western civilizations? Marx tried to define an "Asiatic mode" of production involving self-sufficient villages under political despots who prevented any significant accumulation of private property. The difficulties in the widespread application of such a model formed the inspiration for Wittfogel's research into Chinese history. He became associated with the Frankfurt Institute of Social Research and published a landmark study on *Economy and Society in China* in 1931. Wittfogel argued that the despotism characteristic of Asian civilizations was a result of their reliance upon irrigation agriculture, a feature which allowed Wittfogel to dub these societies as "hydraulic."[69] Wittfogel argued that only a massive governmental bureaucracy could manage a large-scale irrigation system, and that this bureaucracy led to absolutism, a "state stronger than society," that utilized forced labor. Egypt, Mesopotamia, India, China, and pre-Columbian Mexico and Peru would later be adduced as examples for Wittfogel's model.[70]

Wittfogel remained in Germany after Hitler came to power, but his arrest as a Communist and brief imprisonment in a concentration camp convinced him to flee. After spending time in London and New York (where he renewed his ties to the Institute of Social Research, now relocated on Columbia's campus), he decided to travel to China in 1935. The outbreak of the Second Sino-Japanese War in 1937 caused Wittfogel to flee yet again, this time back to New York and the institute.[71]

It was most likely at the institute where Wittfogel met Finkelstein. They agreed to share an apartment with their wives in Provincetown in August. Was the Finkelstein-Wittfogel relationship sponsored by some outside party, or Party? Could Finkelstein have been designated to "handle" Wittfogel on his return from China? So it appeared to some at the time.[72] Chronology seems to stand in the way. By 1938, Wittfogel may already have been moving away from the Communist Party. Around this time he had given a seminar on "Conditions under Which Democracy is Possible," suggesting that the Soviet bureaucracy was "opaque" and calling for a second revolution. Such language suggests Wittfogel's political views were already anti-Stalinist.[73] In the second place, if his contact with Finkelstein had been party-sponsored, Wittfogel would almost certainly have mentioned it when he accused Finley of being a Communist in 1951 before the McCarran Committee. Such an accuser, ready even to tell grand juries details he had not mentioned to the FBI, would surely have mentioned a party-sponsored relationship with Finkelstein.[74]

Wittfogel claimed that Finkelstein organized Marxist study sessions in his home, a claim supported before the McCarran Committee by William M. Canning.[75] Finley, in his own testimony before the same committee, suggested that Wittfogel confused the Sunday evening graduate student get-togethers—to which Wittfogel was not invited—with the luncheon lecture series of the Graduate History Society at Columbia University, whose president in the 1937–1938 academic year was Daniel Thorner. Thorner, in his testimony, described a public luncheon at Columbia during which Wittfogel spoke on the Chinese economy. The event was very ill-attended, and Wittfogel ended up lecturing to several rows of plates with grapefruit on them.[76]

Though Finkelstein and Wittfogel apparently met at the Institute of Social Research, it was hardly a "Stalinist" location. Horkheimer and other institute members had long been cognizant of problems in the Soviet Union and were busy rethinking Marxism.[77] Exactly what Finkelstein, Wittfogel, and their wives were discussing or doing together in July 1938 remains tantalizingly unclear: none of the participants provided any detail, nor have their friends from the period. Wittfogel was open about his growing alienation from Communism. His own difficult personality and his creaky marriage to Olga Lang could not have made life in Provincetown any easier. Back in New York, they would divorce, and he may later have denounced her.[78]

What did all this mean to Finkelstein? We do not know. Fascinatingly, when Wittfogel accused Finley in 1951 of being a member of the Communist Party, he offered few details about that summer in Provincetown thirteen years earlier. We are left imagining these four people from three countries, two beginning a long marriage, the other two dissolving a shorter one. We know that their month together was "not happy," but we do not know if the unhappiness concerned "hydraulic despotism" or who would do the dishes.[79] Whatever happened, it certainly left Wittfogel ready to testify against Finley and all his friends in 1951.

Finkelstein's August 3, 1938, letter to Boas was tellingly mundane: it concerned mailing lists. We would savor a correspondence on racial phenotype or social evolution, but instead the letters detail the daily work of 1930s activism: how to run a committee, recruit members, raise funds, work with the media, and hold rallies. Finkelstein proved himself adept at these tasks. During the autumn of 1938, Finkelstein sent American scientists 12,000 copies of the *Manifesto on Freedom of Science* seeking their public support. By the time of the manifesto's publication on December 10, the document gained 1,284 signatures, a 10 percent response rate that was considered impressive. Furthermore, press attention was both positive and plentiful, despite the fact that the manifesto dealt with the politically divisive topic of race. Singling out Stark, it also attacked the German regime, noting that at least 1,600 scientists had lost their positions in Germany.[80]

Shortly after the appearance of the manifesto, Boas took the largely symbolic step of officially joining local 537 of the College Teachers Union, the union to which Finkelstein belonged as a lecturer at City College.[81] The CTU and its parent, local 5 of the Teachers Union (to which Mary Finkelstein belonged as a teacher in the New York City schools), were at the center of controversy over whether they were under the direct control of the Communist Party. Former union leaders forced out in 1935 had established a rival union, the Teachers Guild. The Guild was lobbying the American Federation of Labor to have the Teachers Union locals expelled and replaced by the Guild. This action eventually took place in 1941.[82] In response to resignations of anti-Stalinists from the CTU, Boas chose to join the union in December 1938 as a show of solidarity, even though he was not himself a Communist. Boas frequently criticized the Soviet Union for its authoritarian methods and suppression of free speech,[83] but he believed that Communist Party members should not be prevented from employment in the schools or from union leadership. The correspondence that survives between Boas and Finkelstein fails to show any connection between Finkelstein's existing union membership and Boas's decision to join. The correspondence does, however, reveal that Finkelstein was familiar with the CTU's organization.[84]

That members of a union widely suspected of being under Communist control were also supervising a nationwide educational program against Nazi science rankled in some quarters, but popular momentum was still on Boas's side. After the success of the manifesto, Boas set Finkelstein immediately to work with the preparations and arrangements for Lincoln's Birthday events in twenty-six cities across the country. Attentive to the marketability of patriotic symbols, Finkelstein had suggested the date. Leading scientists, politicians, and university presidents spoke on defending the atmosphere of open inquiry that allowed scientists to maintain the integrity of their research. Finkelstein festooned the academic world with press releases and helped to arrange a hundred hours of radio coverage, much of it national. The coverage was aided by a compelling February 6, 1939, press release that used memorable words supplied for this purpose by President Roosevelt's secretary of the interior, Harold Ickes (1874–1952): "In an age as critical as ours, if a scientist or scholar remains in his ivory tower he stands a good chance of being blown up with his tower."[85]

Emboldened by the success of the manifesto and the Lincoln's Birthday event, Boas and Finkelstein decided to transform the ad hoc University Federation for Democracy and Intellectual Freedom into a larger, national organization to include university faculty in both science and the humanities; elementary and secondary school teachers; as well as those outside of academia. They named the group the American Committee for Democracy and Intellectual Freedom (ACDIF). "Founded on Lincoln's Birthday, 1939" appeared on the letterhead, along with Finkelstein's name as executive secretary. Finkelstein threw himself into the challenge of getting the group organized. Boas attempted to keep the expanded group's agenda away from the heated controversies between the Stalinists and the anti-Stalinists, fearing that internecine disputes would tear the organization apart. Plans included a *Manifesto of Educators* as a companion piece to the scientists' manifesto (this was completed within a month); opposition to the Devaney Bill in New York State, a bill to prevent Communist Party members from employment in public schools and colleges; removing the "misuse of the term *race*" from school textbooks; recruitment drives among school teachers at summer programs; and arrangement of a Columbus Day conference on "The Democratic Tradition in American Education."[86]

The assault on racism in school texts was carried out with impressive professionalism. A committee of scholars reviewed 166 textbooks. The committee prepared a pamphlet, "Can You Name Them," that remains a masterpiece of economy, effective writing, and sophisticated public presentation of social science findings. Finkelstein was justified in speaking about it with great pride.[87]

The scale on which the ACDIF carried out its mandate was likewise impressive. In June 1939, copies of the *Manifesto on Freedom of Science* and the *Manifesto of Educators* were mailed to 1,600 college presidents and

2,200 school superintendents. Finkelstein also coordinated a speakers' bureau, forum series, radio programs, and cooperation with public schools—activities that brought increasing awareness of the group's aims and summer recruitment project.[88]

Boas and Finkelstein also communicated about what they viewed as two provocations in the summer of 1939. In June, a report on immigration was released by the Chamber of Commerce of the State of New York. Eugenicist Harry H. Laughlin, whose dubious studies on criminality and intelligence among immigrants from southern and eastern Europe were used to justify restrictions on immigration in the 1920s, prepared the report. Boas was outraged when he read the following quotation from Laughlin's report in *The New York Times*:

> No wise nation . . . would admit as an immigrant anyone whose "blood"—that is, whose natural inheritance in energy, intellect and character, when reproduced by his future-born near kin—would not constitute a desirable addition to the reproductive stock of the receiving nation. The new blood should be definitely better than the average already established here, else it should not be admitted at all.[89]

"Blood?" What, an expert ethnographer like Boas must have asked himself, is the scientific content of such a term, and why is it being used now, after half a century of increasingly sophisticated scientific study? How is "natural inheritance in character" any less outrageous a conceit than Johannes Stark's "White Jews"?[90]

Finkelstein composed the ACDIF response to the Laughlin report under Boas's name. On July 11, Finkelstein reported that he consulted with coauthors, pulling the argument together and fashioning an effective final sentence. The next day he told Boas:

> I hope you do not mind the words which I am putting into your mouth in the press release, but that is the only way that this material can get proper publicity. You will no doubt recognize some of these sentences as being taken from your radio speech and letters.

The statement was released to the media the following week, gaining coverage in major newspapers.[91]

The second "provocation" concerned a major conference on "Education and Democracy" organized by William F. Russell, the conservative dean of Columbia's Teachers College who aspired to succeed the elderly Nicholas Murray Butler as the university's president. Russell's views on education and culture were far more traditional than those of Boas, and Russell wanted to give business leaders a prominent role in setting education policy and priorities. In addition, Russell regularly launched tirades in the press against Communism and unionization of teachers.

The goals of Russell's democracy conference were to promote capitalism and "character" within American education. Boas and Finkelstein treated Russell's conference as a serious form of resistance to the more liberal ideas they had been advocating, ideas that included a diminished emphasis on race and dominant culture, greater choice in textbooks, and union membership for teachers. Furthermore, the choice as a keynote speaker of former Conservative British Prime Minister Stanley Baldwin (now Earl Baldwin of Bewdley), a politician who had opposed labor unions at home and did not support the Loyalists in the Spanish Civil War—two causes extremely dear to New York intellectuals in the 1930s—guaranteed protests by radicals outside the conference venues. Boas had not been invited to participate. In an August 14, 1939, letter, Finkelstein suggested that Boas show up anyway and provoke a confrontation. Boas did not take up the suggestion, perhaps correctly gauging that there was no need. Other ACDIF members who were invited promoted Boas's more open and democratic prescription for American education.[92]

By late August 1939, the ACDIF was moving forward on several fronts. It had funding from the American Jewish Committee, the textbook project was well underway, and the organization had responded quickly and forcefully to a racist report from the Chamber of Commerce.[93] But the ACDIF now had competition.

In the spring of 1939, New York University philosophy professor Sidney Hook (1902–1989) and his mentor, retired Columbia University philosopher and education reformer John Dewey (1859–1952), announced the formation of the Committee for Cultural Freedom (CCF). In contrast to Boas's ACDIF, Hook and Dewey's CCF claimed from its inception to oppose all totalitarianism, whether fascist or Communist. The CCF's origin was intrinsic to the increasing acrimony between Stalinists and anti-Stalinists among the American Left. Exacerbating these tensions was the growing stature among New York intellectuals of Leon Trotsky, a hero of the Russian Revolution now in exile in Mexico. In 1937, when the exiled Trotsky was put on trial in absentia in Moscow, Hook organized an inquiry that included a trip to Mexico to visit the famed revolutionary. The inquiry was headed by Hook's mentor, John Dewey. On their return to the United States, the members of the Dewey Commission vigorously assailed Stalinism on the American Left.[94] Hook's association with Dewey gave him particular weight among academics and journalists.

From the Hook and Dewey perspective in founding the CCF, leftist ideas were acceptable. Hook and Meyer Schapiro, another key figure in the group, were still revolutionary socialists. What was not acceptable was the Communist Party USA, which Hook portrayed as so fully in the grip of the Soviet government that its members gave up the chance for independent action and thought. The CCF, with its fiercely anti-Stalinist leadership, threatened the effective but potentially unstable alliance of Stalinists, Socialists, centrists, and others that Boas had created in the ACDIF.[95] Furthermore, Boas believed that Hitler was far more of a threat than Stalin, and that the CCF's equation of the two blurred this important distinction.

The CCF's initial manifesto received coverage in *The New York Times* on May 15, 1939. The story highlighted the contrast with Boas's organization and included the implication—which in later stories would be made explicit—that the ACDIF was carrying out the program of the Communist Party. As reported in the *Times*, "One of the signers who helped to draft the statement said last night that it was not aimed at Professor Boas, whose sincerity in his devotion to democracy and freedom was not doubted, but against those members of his committees . . . who have insisted on a 'one-sided' policy." Within two days, the *Times* published a letter from Boas insisting that his group was intent primarily on promoting intellectual freedom, both here and abroad. Boas was clearly upset at the implication that his committee was subject to outside control. In a companion letter, Hook acknowledged that he was the "signer" who had criticized some "members of [Boas's] committees."[96]

Letters from Dewey to his old friend and colleague Boas—one on the day of the *Times* story, and one ten days later—sought to smooth all this out by blaming the *Times* reporter, who was, Dewey claimed, a Roman Catholic upset by Boas' position on the Spanish Civil War. Dewey's effort to explain away Hook's behavior is noteworthy. At the same time, a separate message from Dewey to Hook (on May 27) revealed that the education reformer truly believed that the ACDIF had been hijacked by the Communist Party: "The enclosed from Boas gave me a chance to say something about the Federation without . . . lugging it in too boldly. I don't know whether even now he will see the contra[di]ction between what he says . . . and the use actually made of his organization."[97]

Boas was quickly aware of potential problems. On the day the *Times* reported on the CCF's creation, he complained to an official at the American Jewish Committee that another AJC official, Frank Trager, was already involved with the rival organization. Boas was concerned that financing for the ACDIF might dry up, and that the success he had gained fighting Nazi propaganda on race might be lost. Germany, Boas insisted in the letter, remained the key potential enemy. "[W]e feel the pressure from there more directly" than from any other country, he explained.[98]

On May 25, 1939, Dewey and Hook met with Boas to propose merging the two committees. The pair wanted a program that not only favored "intellectual freedom" but directly opposed "totalitarianism" everywhere, including the Soviet Union.

How was Boas to respond? We have no record of what he said, but the meeting was unfruitful and quickly became contentious. All three men recognized the widening rift between pro- and anti-Moscow leftists. Boas had built a big tent that accommodated a range of members and undertook worthy tasks that all could accept, with a particular focus on combatting racism. Dewey and Hook, however, saw in Stalin an immediate danger to freedom, both within the Soviet Union and, through Moscow's control of the Communist Party USA, on these shores as well.[99]

Finkelstein seems not to have attended the Boas-Dewey meeting, but he was aware of it. The Hoover Institution has Hook's letter to his friend Frank Trager of the American Jewish Committee remarking that Boas "said he was instructing Finkelstein to send me a statement [of the ACDIF's principles] but I have heard nothing from F."[100] This is one of Hook's few direct mentions of Finkelstein. For the next fifteen years these two men, brilliant squires of famed antagonists, would execute a dance made all the more chilling by their failure to use each others' names. By the early 1950s, Hook was incessantly proclaiming that Communism and the Fifth Amendment had no place in the academy, while Finley remonstrated that he, the accused Communist who took the Fifth Amendment, deserved such a place.[101] There is almost a literary neatness to the final act, in which Rutgers trustees would proclaim in 1952 that Finley was "unfit to teach," and Finley, reportedly holding back tears, responded, "I am fit to teach."[102]

Pro-Moscow intellectuals felt an urgent need to respond to Dewey and Hook's Committee for Cultural Freedom. The response was to become notorious as one of the most disastrous public relations moves in American history. A "Committee of 400" was developed. Whether it really had four hundred members is unclear, and only half that number is known. The group put together a detailed Open Letter refuting Hook's condemnation of the Soviet Union as "totalitarian" and insisting that Stalin's Russia was a peace-loving country with humane and enlightened practices, and that it was a bulwark against Nazi aggression. A fairly wide variety of leftist intellectuals (including prominent ACDIF members such as the socialist Leslie Dunn) put their names on the letter, though Boas did not.[103]

What did Finkelstein do? His name is not among the published signatures. But he may have played a more profound role. George Watson has claimed in a recent essay that "Moses organized a statement signed by four hundred intellectuals denouncing the outrageous rumor that Stalin would soon sign a pact with Hitler. It was published a few days after a public announcement that Stalin had done just that."[104]

This is an amazing claim, putting Finkelstein at the center of a major, and disastrous, political movement. It is certainly possible that Watson is correct. The Open Letter was organized from Columbia University, and

Finkelstein had the skill to contribute significantly. Watson's essay, however, contains a number of errors, and Watson admitted, "By the time I knew him [Finley] as a colleague at Cambridge in the 1950s and later, his own ancient history was seldom mentioned."[105] Although Watson's claim seems to be based on first-hand testimony, the assertion requires careful handling.

The Open Letter was first published on August 14, 1939. Eight days later, news was announced that Hitler and Stalin had agreed to a non-aggression pact, which was signed in Moscow by their foreign secretaries the following day. Nine days after the signing, German troops invaded Poland from the west, and Soviet troops followed from the east two and a half weeks later. The news from Europe discredited the Communists in the eyes of many American leftists and made any further cooperation between Stalinists and anti-Stalinists nearly impossible. While the "majority of American Communist—leaders, cadres, and rank and file—remained in the party and, . . . would stick with it for the twenty-two month life span of the Nazi-Soviet pact," the damage was severe to the leftist coalition of intellectuals and artists known as the Popular Front.[106]

Stalin's deal with Hitler is not even mentioned in the correspondence between Boas and Finkelstein. The two continued to keep busy with preparations for an exhibit on racial prejudice that opened on September 18 at the New York World's Fair, while more than two hundred similar exhibits appeared around that time at libraries and bookstores across the country. The ACDIF also issued a rebuttal to a second report produced by the Chamber of Commerce of the State of New York, this time dealing with education. Along with teachers' unions and other groups, the ACDIF condemned "the conception of democracy revealed in the report, when it says the purpose for which our schools were founded 'was to preserve and strengthen the state by making better, abler citizens.' This concept is fascist, not democratic. It implies that citizens exist for the sake of the State, whereas in a democracy the State exists for the sake of its citizens." Finally, Boas's plans for "American Rediscovery Week" in October involved roughly two hundred clergymen nationwide preaching special sermons on diversity, meetings and lectures held in cities and towns across the country promoting freedom of speech and racial equality, and a panel discussion at the New York World's Fair dealing with scientific understandings of race.[107]

But while ACDIF did not "promptly dissolve" as Watson claimed, enthusiasm and support were diminishing.[108] The American Jewish Committee ended funding that autumn.[109] Allegations that the organization was little more than a Communist front became more common and were sometimes used to explain Boas' refusal to merge his organization with the CCF. In December 1939, labor reporter Benjamin Stolberg, an associate of Dewey and Hook, wrote a fierce attack in the *Washington Post* against Communist front organizations.

> Probably the most interesting "innocent front" was the American Committee for Democracy and Intellectual Freedom, which under the chairmanship of Professor Franz Boas, of Columbia University, enlisted over a thousand American scientists and educators, among them several Nobel Prize winners. Behind Dr. Boas, who disclaims being a Stalinist, the important work is done by Rabbi Bernhard Stern, a Columbia instructor, and M. I. Finkelstein, a notorious Stalinist in the history department of the College of the City of New York.[110]

This is a harsh indictment, but a very peculiar one. Hook's friend Stolberg, a veteran of the Dewey Commission's investigation of Trotsky in Mexico, would have known little of Finkelstein firsthand. Why, then, did Stolberg label Finkelstein "a notorious Stalinist"? Furthermore, Stolberg's essay is the only contemporary document I know of that links Finkelstein with Bernhard Stern, the Columbia sociologist, Marxist, founding editor of the journal *Science and Society*, and a longtime foe of Sidney Hook. What Stern and Finkelstein primarily had in common in 1939 was that both had recently crossed Hook.[111]

It should not be surprising if the combative Hook told Stolberg that Finkelstein was a Stalinist. Stolberg's essay seems to have been the starting point for notices pegging Finkelstein to the Communist Party. The claim also turned up in a personal memo from J. Edgar Hoover to Attorney General Francis Biddle on December 12, 1941:

> Boas is one of the leading 'stooges' for Communist groups in the U.S. He is used to put over propaganda. . . . Among other positions which he holds is that of Chairman, ACDIF, of which organization Mr. Moe Finkelstein is Executive Secretary.[112]

Using similar language, Roger Baldwin (1884–1981), the founder and director of the American Civil Liberties Union, wrote to the physician and social activist Walter B. Cannon (1871–1945) in April 1942:

> I know considerable about the American Committee for Democracy and Intellectual Freedom. . . . There is no doubt that the Committee . . . has a strong pro-Communist slant and that its paid secretary, Finkelstein, is either a member of the Communist Party or a close associate.[113]

It may seem surprising that the chief American defender of civil liberties should talk like this. Finkelstein at this time had been "named" only in the hearings of the Rapp-Coudert Committee, by a single witness, without full benefit of counsel or right to cross-examine. But the civil libertarians by this point had thrown in their lot with the investigators. We now know that Morris Ernst, ACLU General Counsel, conducted a decades-long secret correspondence with J. Edgar Hoover, forwarding copies of mail from friends and offering to help Hoover deal with troublesome sorts like I. F. Stone.[114] The ACLU had made its own non-aggression treaty with the House Un-American Activities Committee nearly three years before Baldwin wrote Cannon, after the committee chairman Martin Dies had sought indictments against it for "failing to register as an agent of a foreign power":

> In October 1939 [Dies] had a few drinks with . . . Ernst and Arthur Garfield Hays at the Hay-Adams Hotel in Washington. No one present revealed what they talked about, but Dies soon issued the ACLU a clean bill of health. The fact that a draft ACLU report with unexpected praise for HUAC started circulating . . . convinced many liberals that Ernst had cut an unholy deal with Dies.[115]

Both Hoover's memo and Baldwin's letter were written after Canning publicly identified Finkelstein as a party member before the Rapp-Coudert Committee in 1941. Finkelstein soon saw the end of his City College teaching appointment. Rapp-Coudert was simply an investigative committee without power to dismiss faculty, a task that was handled by the New York Board of Higher Education, often so quickly after the Rapp-Coudert hearing as to blur the distinction. We have accounts of the individual hearings for his fellow teachers Benjamin Paskoff and the Foner twins, but none concerning Finkelstein. (Finley mentioned his Rapp-Coudert hearings in a 1951 letter to his Rutgers dean.)[116] Paskoff, the Foners, and Theodore Geiger also saw their appointments come to an end. One of Finkelstein's teaching colleagues faced much worse. Morris Schappes, the only individual named by Canning who admitted having been a party member, was sent to prison for perjury. Schappes testified that he knew of no other current City College employees who were Communists. Schappes clearly lied, but the precedent was set for accepting the entirety of Canning's testimony as the truth. Canning's naming of Finkelstein was certainly less detailed than his accusations against the Foners, since Canning did not provide any secret party names belonging to Finkelstein.[117] World War II, however, made the United States and the Soviet Union allies, and anti-Communist furor seemed to subside. Finkelstein worked for Russian War Relief, and after the war's end he and others earlier suspected of Communist activities were once again able to find teaching positions in academia.

The onset of the Cold War and the ascendancy to power of Mao's Communists in China brought renewed attention to those who openly displayed Communist sympathies in the months before World War II. In this new environment of the early 1950s, the hunt for Reds ended or retarded the American academic careers of the renamed Moses Finley and several of his friends and associates from the late 1930s. Daniel Thorner, then an assistant professor at the University of Pennsylvania, went to India on a research fellowship in 1952 and ended up staying there for eight years. Thorner learned after his arrival in India that his refusal to name names before the McCarran Committee resulted in his being denied tenure and losing his faculty position. Thorner eventually gained a prestigious academic post in France.[118] Naphtali Lewis lost a Fulbright scholarship in 1953 after he and his wife, Helen, appeared before the infamous Senate Permanent Subcommittee on Investigations chaired by Joseph McCarthy (1908–1957). Helen Lewis refused to say whether she had been a member of the Communist Party. Naphtali Lewis and his colleague, Meyer Reinhold, were compelled to resign from Brooklyn College in 1955. Lewis was reinstated a few years later. It took a decade for Reinhold to gain another academic appointment, this time at the University of Southern Illinois at Carbondale. Reinhold later moved to the University of Missouri and finished his career at Boston University at the age of 85.[119]

The most recurrently asked question about Finley's activities in the late 1930s concerns, of course, membership in the Communist Party. "Was he or wasn't he?" Finley denied ever being a party member in 1952 to the Rutgers deans. Before the McCarran Committee, he stated that he was not currently a member of the Communist Party, but he refused to answer whether he had ever been a member. This refusal has been ascribed to a fear that his testimony would be used to convict him of perjury and to send him to prison, as had happened to Morris Schappes a decade earlier. Such a refusal was not an admission of anything, save the realization that in 1952, the testimony of Canning and Wittfogel was taken as more credible than his own.

And there was good reason to be concerned. Perjury was one of the favorite charges leveled at defendants during the Red Scare. In the seventeen years or so in which Communist Party membership could be criminalized, suspected Communists were often contradicted by witnesses and convicted of perjury. We now know that several of these professional witnesses were perjurers themselves, a circumstance that their compensation arrangements and book projects certainly encouraged, and contributed to the fact that an embarrassed Department of Justice "disbanded its stable of paid informer-witnesses" in 1955.[120] One paid informer and book author was Louis Budenz, who specifically accused Boas of being a secret Communist. Robert Lichtman described the "fail-safe" technique pioneered by Budenz: he could name someone listed on a Communist Front letterhead, without specific information that a defendant could attack.

Only a Communist Party official would be able to provide useful evidence against the charge, but declaring oneself as an official would, of course, bring criminal proceedings, since party membership was illegal.[121] Exposure of dishonest informants brought the need for the Fifth Amendment to the fore, but universities continued to use "taking the Fifth" as grounds for dismissal.

Finley's FBI file, obtained under the Freedom of Information Act, reveals that he had a lot to worry about. From December 22, 1952, the bureau was actively exploring an indictment for perjury based on the questions posed before the McCarran Committee, including whether the Finley's Sunday soirées were "Marxist study groups." In March, Wittfogel told the bureau that he saw no party cards at these sessions at what he called Marxist study sessions but heard people address each other as "comrade." In December, an anonymous informant reported that Mary Finley was a party member, and the Newark Office tried unsuccessfully to track down this claim. Also in December, the special agent reported that Wittfogel "does not know the subject to be a CP member." By February 15, 1954, the special agent reported that "there are no outstanding leads and no additional investigation to be conducted."[122]

In other words, throughout the period when he was seeking employment, the bureau was actively involved in seeking an indictment, seemingly on the matter of whether Sunday night meetings fifteen years previously could qualify as a "Marxist study group." With charges this nebulous floating around, the Fifth Amendment seems like a very worthwhile right for any citizen to have.

Besides Canning and Wittfogel, the only other witness to accuse Finley of having been a party member was Bella Dodd, herself a former party official who had helped organize the legal defense during the Rapp-Coudert hearings, then left the party and became a government witness. She testified in 1952 that she took it for granted in the late 1930s that Finley had been a party member, though she admitted she "never saw his Party card."[123] It has to be remembered that Communist Party membership after about 1938 was a fluid thing. It was clearly dangerous to be tagged as an official member, so not everyone who was active formally joined the party. During the Popular Front period, Finkelstein does not appear to have engaged in activities that expressed criticism of the party or its goals, and he carried out his ACDIF tasks with determination and efficiency. The suspicions of Bella Dodd, who had been a veteran party functionary, are not entirely improbable.

At the same time, we have to ask, what did this mean? Did Finkelstein's Communist sympathies affect his teaching at City College? Did he stifle dissenting points of view? This claim has repeatedly been leveled at Marxists and other leftist instructors from the 1930s to the present day. As

Canning told the Rapp-Coudert Committee, "All the historian needs to do
. . . is to implement the famous saying of Karl Marx . . . that the history of
all previously existing societies is the history of class struggle." Canning
said that many history department instructors made class struggle the primary topic of their teaching, and also used phrases such as "dialect [sic]
materialism," "Soviet Republic," "proletariat," and "other Communist
terms" in class, but said little about how these terms were used.[124]

It is hard to believe Finkelstein spouting vulgar Marxism in front of his
City College students. Sidney Hook, however, strongly asserted as early
as 1939 that Communist professors stealthily included propaganda into
their teaching, which justified not only the removal of any instructors
who were party members or "fellow travelers," but even denying Communists the full protection of the Bill of Rights. On October 24, 1939, at
the annual forum sponsored by *The New York Herald-Tribune* and held at
the Waldorf-Astoria Hotel, Hook gave a speech on "Academic Freedom
and 'The Trojan Horse.'"

> One has a right to represent or defend any cause, provided he hon-
> estly declares what that cause is, provided he does not masquerade
> under false labels, provided he does not have a secret program that
> he plans to substitute for the public program on which he solicits
> confidence. The difference between the man who invokes the Bill of
> Rights to profess his beliefs—whatever they are—and the man who
> invokes it to conceal them, is the difference between honest opposi-
> tion . . . and conspiracy. No democracy can survive which does not
> recognize the essential nature of this distinction.[125]

Hook went on to urge universities and professional groups to take
action against Communists and their sympathizers. Party members,
Hook would maintain for the next fifty years, were "conspirators" using
their positions of trust to indoctrinate and proselytize.[126] His 1939 speech
was printed in the *Bulletin of the American Association of University Professors*, an organization that failed to act forcefully on behalf of suspected
and fired teachers until McCarthy had left the scene in the late fifties.[127]
Certainly there were City College history instructors who brought leftist
ideology into the classroom. Benjamin Nelson was later praised for doing
just that by one of his students from the period, none other than the CIA-
funded Cold War anti-Communist Melvin Lasky (1920–2004), who in
1950 joined Hook in founding another organization, the Congress for
Cultural Freedom.[128]

Did Finkelstein indoctrinate his classes? One of his most famous students testifies to the contrary. Captivated by Finkelstein the social historian, the student changed his field at City College from anthropology to
ancient history and took two seminars with him. Here, if anywhere, was

a case of the seductive leftist professor misleading his charges. Except that he did not. The student was the young Daniel Bell, who went on to become a leader of anti-Communist liberalism, even dedicating *The Age of Ideology* to Hook and joining him in the Congress for Cultural Freedom. Did Hook realize, as he and Bell attended their endless meetings, that he was looking at a walking refutation of his own obsession with Communist professors, a man who was grateful to have been taught by Finkelstein?[129]

In the Talmud, the Greeks and Romans are regularly portrayed as the enemies of the Jews, and the ancient rabbis warned about the dangers of excessive interaction with these pagan civilizations.[130] A generation of radical Jewish intellectuals in the New York of the 1930s—a generation admittedly antagonistic towards Talmudic strictures—made massive contributions to the study of human societies, with some attention to classical antiquity. Few ancient historians, however, Jewish or Gentile, brought to their research the social science sophistication Finkelstein had acquired.[131] Working with Boas and, after World War II, with political economist Karl Polanyi (1886–1964) studying Marx and Weber, and maintaining relationships with social scientists like Daniel Thorner and (later) Orlando Patterson, Finkelstein/Finley provided an avenue of communication across disciplines, periods, and cultures that was particularly useful for scholars wrestling with topics like slavery, feudalism, and peasantry. He helped to bring a social-scientific approach to the study of the Greeks and Romans by asking new and different questions.

Finley's activity was dialectical in at least two senses. First of all, his work rests on dialogue with others, sometimes across decades. The association with Horkheimer and Boas took some time to become evident, and he was always ready to disagree, as he had done with Westermann and then with Polanyi. An adequate study of the mature Finley's intellectual world has yet to be made. Second, the "dialectic" involves constant adjustments in position under the pressure of reality or history. Throughout his career, though less often than his critics might wish, the historian's reality testing pulled him away from an overly systemic view of things: from Polanyi's "primitive models," from Engels's notions of post-antique society, and from easy formulations about "class struggle." One of Finley's fiercest debates involved not a shallow and "antiquarian" ancient historian, but a sociologist who had spent time at the Institute of Social Research, Alvin Gouldner. Finley found him wanting: "The data, in sum, have here been tailored to suit the explanation, as happens often. The historical anchorage is too sandy and shifting for the superstructure it is asked to carry."[132]

One way to view Finley's work, then, would be to recognize the dialectic required to understand another culture or era. Models are necessary, but in favoring a Weberian "ideal type" model Finley was rejecting "misleading polarities" for a "purely ideal limiting concept with which the real situation is compared and surveyed for explication of certain of its significant components."[133] A worthwhile consideration of Finley's resistance to rigid "polarities"—it is the source of the term "misleading polarities" in the preceding sentence—is Richard Saller's recent essay, "Framing the Debate over Growth in the Ancient Economy," which emphasizes the "common ground" between Finley and the historian to whom he is often contrasted, Rostovsteff, and mentions that as long ago as 1973, Finley was stressing the involvement of the "peasantry" in a "wider economic system."[134]

This essay marks the first step of a larger research project on Moses Finkelstein's intellectual and political development. There seems to be ample evidence that intellectual and political activity went hand in hand for Finkelstein in the period under consideration, but we have only begun to develop a satisfactory picture of these. Further work will require further immersion in the thinkers who influenced Finley and continued efforts to extract a biography from the unpromising desert of facts Finley left behind. Finley's family and friends have been extraordinarily generous in assisting this research during this first stage, and will likely provide more assistance in the near future. We have barely begun to discuss Mary Finley who was extraordinarily close to her husband and politically active on her own. Further study of Finley's Jewish connections may yield fruit, and further archival work at Darwin College and in the collections of friends may shed light on Finley's early years.

An epilogue may be permitted. Robert Morris, who served as chief counsel for both the Rapp-Coudert and McCarran committees, ended a long career of flushing out suspected Communists by accusing then Secretary of State Henry Kissinger in 1975 of acting in the interests of the Soviet Union.[135] This is one of the many wonders Sir Moses Finley might have commented on while secure in his reputation and livelihood at Cambridge University. The fact that he did not do this, did not engage in a dispute with Sidney Hook, and did not publicly take on Karl August Wittfogel, makes the biographer's task more challenging. Finley's reticence, however, contributed to a dignity that is found wanting in many of Finley's detractors.

Chapter 8

Thucydides and the Cold War

—Lawrence A. Tritle

> For ourselves, we shall not trouble you with specious pre-
> tences . . . [but] will aim at what is feasible, holding in view
> the real sentiments of us both; since you know as well as
> we do that right, as the world goes, is only in question
> between equals in power, while the strong do what they
> can and the weak suffer what they must.
> —*Thucydides 5.89 (adapted from the Crawley translation)*

From Machiavelli and Hobbes to George Marshall and Henry Kissinger, political theorists and practitioners have regarded Thucydides as a paradigm for studying the ways of the world and the interactions of states. His definition of power, cited in the above epigraph from the Melian Dialogue, is surely the first such analysis in the Western tradition. Its military essence is self-evident, and modern political theorists have redefined it only slightly. With his history of the Peloponnesian War (431–404 B.C.) recognized as the inspiration for the realist school of international relations that dominated American foreign policy in the decades after World War II, Thucydides was extensively studied for his concept of the balance of power and his distinctions between underlying and immediate causes

127

of war.[1] Writing in 1981, political scientist Robert Gilpin (born 1930) questioned whether modern students of international relations know anything that Thucydides and his contemporaries did not.[2]

In February 1947 at the beginning of the Cold War, Secretary of State George Marshall (1880–1959) gave an important address at Princeton University in which he called for continued American vigilance in world affairs. Much of the speech dealt with the lessons to be learned from history, and among his examples Marshall noted the intellectual impact and legacy of Thucydides. "I doubt seriously whether a man can think with full wisdom and with deep convictions regarding certain of the basic international issues today who has not at least reviewed in his mind the period of the Peloponnesian War and the Fall of Athens," Marshall said.[3]

Thucydides's influence continued to be reflected in the Cold War writings of political scientists such as Robert Gilpin, Henry Kissinger (born 1923), Hans Morgenthau (1904–1980) and Kenneth Waltz (born 1924). All of them regarded Thucydides as a guide illustrating the ambitions and actions of superpowers, as well as the problems that engulfed smaller states caught up in the wake of superpower conflict. In the second edition, published in 1954, of Morgenthau's influential work *Politics Among Nations*—the "Bible" for proponents of political realism—he approvingly cited the statement of the Corinthians before the second congress at Sparta in 432 B.C. (when Sparta and her allies together voted to go to war, 1.124.1),[4] that "an identity of interest is the surest of bonds whether between states or individuals." Thucydides was employed to justify the primacy of national interest over international idealism in forging alliances and setting foreign policy. Morgenthau kept the citation in the subsequent editions of the book published throughout the duration of the Cold War (third edition, 1960; fourth, 1967; fifth, 1972; sixth [posthumously], 1985).[5]

Journalists and historians during the Cold War era also looked to the Peloponnesian War for ideas and arguments in interpreting the events they saw and recorded. In 1953, William H. McNeill compared Stalin's refusal to aid the Warsaw uprising in 1944 to Thucydides's account of the failure of the Spartans to assist the Melians in their vain attempt to stave off destruction of their island home by the Athenians in 416 B.C.[6] Writing in 1969, historian Donald Kagan compared Spartan refusal to participate in an Athenian-proposed congress in 449 B.C. to the Soviet Union's refusal to participate in the Marshall Plan in 1947.[7] At a news conference while serving as secretary of state, Henry Kissinger suggested that the Cold War was a new Peloponnesian War between a United States "Athens" and a Soviet "Sparta." An astute journalist asked, "Does that mean we're bound to lose?"[8]

Cold War political scientists operated from two basic assumptions about Thucydides' history of the Peloponnesian War: that he described a group of states divided into two factions, with each faction under the domination of a single state—a concept called *bipolarity*—and that competition for power between Athens and Sparta, the two dominant states, made conflict inevitable. Such assumptions present a simplistic view of an author so dense and complex in both his style and aims. Nonetheless, this view of Thucydides was extremely common in the United States from the 1940s through the 1980s, to the point that these assumptions were often taken for granted.

These assumptions gave Thucydides's history an immediacy and relevance during the conflicts that arose between the Soviet Union and the United States. In 1952, State Department policy planner Louis J. Halle (1910–1998) recommended that those interested in current international relations read Thucydides. "The present, in which our country finds herself, like Athens after the Persian wars, called upon to assume the leadership of the free world, brings him virtually to our side. . . . [Y]ou will be surprised to discover how his meaning has been heightened by the events of our day, how the history that he wrote has become altogether more vivid and poignant," Halle wrote.[9] Classicist and historian W. Robert Connor, writing in 1984, remembered first studying Thucydides in the 1950s as "a simple but awesome allegory for our own times. Thucydides' work revealed a precedent for our own polarized world, and might, we hoped, provide a guide through the perils of contemporary international affairs."[10] In his 1966 book on *Thucydides and the Politics of Bipolarity*, Peter J. Fliess emphasized the "psychological reality" of having only two superpowers among the Greek city-states of the fifth century B.C. Fliess argued that both the other Greek city-states, and the superpowers of Athens and Sparta themselves, were constrained in their strategic policy-making because their actions were always interpreted—by themselves and others—primarily in terms of how those actions affected the balance of power between Athens and Sparta.[11]

This sense of immediacy and relevance ascribed to Thucydides came in spite of the fact that most Cold War political scientists never studied the Greek language in which Thucydides wrote. Louis J. Halle remarked that by the time he went to high school in the 1920s, classical antiquity was regarded as "obsolete" and that in school he was "burdened with something called 'social studies'—but not with Greek and Latin." Nevertheless, as an adult Halle was able to read Thucydides in English translation, and he recommended to his readers R. W. Livingstone's 1943 abridged version of Richard Crawley's 1874 translation.[12] The Greeklessness of American political scientists may, in fact, have aided in Thucydides's immediacy, since they experienced him first and exclusively in their native language, English. Comparisons to current events were made easier by the availability of English translations.

Finding parallels between the history of the Peloponnesian War, as told by Thucydides, and more recent conflicts was nothing new. Comparisons also were made throughout the twentieth century to the events of World War I. Classicist Louis E. Lord (1875–1957), writing in 1943, recalled the Melian Dialogue being publicly read at the University of Toronto in 1914, with the name of Germany substituted for Athens, Great Britain for Sparta, and Belgium for Melos.[13] Donald Kagan in 1969 compared the conflict between Corinth and Corcyra that sparked the Peloponnesian War with Austria-Hungary's declaration of war against Serbia after the Sarajevo assassination of Archiduke Franz Ferdinand.[14]

The assumed bipolarity of Thucydides' account led political realists during the Cold War to concentrate their attention upon perceived similarities with the contemporary global struggle between capitalist nations led by the United States and communist nations under the sway of the Soviet Union and the People's Republic of China. The question that arises, however, is how well did these political scientists understand Thucydides and his observations and arguments? Did they slide too easily from one era to another, neither taking the time to place Thucydides and his world in its context nor to examine carefully enough the nuances of his text? There are in fact real dangers in so doing.

Gilpin, for example, asserted in 1981 that Sparta "initiated" the Peloponnesian War in order to crush Athens, a "rising challenger" to its power. In fact, by the beginning of the second half of the fifth century B.C., Athens possessed far greater wealth and influence than Sparta, and the Athenians had for decades shown themselves eager to assert their power. While it may be true that Spartan armies marched on Athens first, Athenian naval forces had already engaged Sparta's Corinthian allies at Corcyra. Identifying the aggressor or initiator of conflict would seem to be a matter of perspective. Gilpin also claimed that the Greek states in the later fifth century B.C. "were part of a greater system dominated by imperial Persia, which was temporarily diverted from Greek affairs by troubles elsewhere in its system." No sources are offered in support of this view, which is weakened by the fact that Persia simply did not figure in the outbreak of the Peloponnesian War. It only later participated as a result of Athenian defeat in Sicily that sparked a series of complex diplomatic moves by Greeks and Persians alike.[15]

Moreover, the idea that there are "lessons" or "laws" in history is far from certain, Thucydides' claim (1.22.4) to be writing for all time notwithstanding. As historian Arthur Marwick stated, "[T]he human past enfolds so many periods and cultures that history can no more form one unified body of knowledge than can the social sciences. The search for universal meaning or universal explanations is, therefore, a futile one."[16] This point merits consideration in the case of Thucydides' influence on modern day policy planners.

Those who have read Thucydides in the original Greek know all too well that the language is terribly compressed and that he experiments with both forms and ideas throughout. The famous Melian Dialogue (5.85–113) is but one example of the former, while his analysis of such concepts as power and justice represent the latter. More critical, perhaps, is the belief among Thucydides's modern disciples that he saw the outbreak of the Peloponnesian War between Athens and Sparta as "inevitable," that war was simply bound to happen.[17] A close reading of his text—the sort of thing done by classicists and ancient historians but not necessarily by political scientists, journalists and State Department officials—suggests that when war came it was not inevitable, but an action seen as forced upon Athens and Sparta, and, as will be argued below, by Corinth.

The discussion of inevitability rests in part on a mistranslation of the Greek verb *anankasai* in Thucydides' famous remarks (1.23.6) on the "truest explanation" for the war. The standard English translations of Crawley and Warner render the verb as "made inevitable."[18] The verb is more accurately translated as "forced" or "compelled," a definition briefly discussed with great subtlety by the classicist and political philosopher Leo Strauss (1899–1973) in his 1964 book *The City and Man*. The careful definition was used for a different purpose (to analyze the distinction between justice and necessity) and may not have been retained by Strauss's Greekless readers.[19]

Even so, the interpretation that Thucydides believed the Peloponnesian War was inevitable found plenty of Cold War proponents even among classicists and ancient historians. Donald Kagan, writing in 1969, found only one twentieth-century scholar, the Cambridge don F. E. Adcock (1886–1968), who rejected inevitability. Even Kagan felt "compelled" to accept that Thucydides himself may have believed the war inevitable, even though Kagan argued that the facts revealed otherwise.[20] Thucydides understood the reasons behind the actions of individuals and states too well to be satisfied with arguments of inevitability in explaining what happened in Greece between 433 and 431 B.C.[21] An interpretation against inevitability in Thucydides's narrative finds support in his explanation of the war's short and long term causes, the "necessary" cause in the Theban attack on Plataea, and his own interpretation that the growth of Athenian power led Sparta to conclude that there was no recourse but war when diplomatic overtures failed.

Not without merit is the comparison, by Kagan and others, of the outbreak of the Peloponnesian War with the outbreak of World War I. In both instances we observe complex causes that combined to bring about war: the apparent enthusiasm of young men who were inexperienced in war and thereby drawn to it, the willingness of many to imagine that a war would follow a predictable course (an idea not unknown among modern politicians and statesmen), or the hard "no negotiations" line assumed by one of the parties in the conflict. That we can glean all this from Thucydides's sophisticated account suggests that the author had thought long and hard on what happened in 433–431, and that he saw war not as inevitable but rather the result of failed politics and decisions made by those caught up in the events. These factors require further examination.

In discussing the aftermath of the initial Theban attack on Plataea in the spring of 431, Thucydides observed (2.8) that there was widespread enthusiasm for war. Many Peloponnesian and Athenian young men had never been to war and were thrilled at the prospect. These young men feared that unless they became personally involved, the whole effort itself would be handicapped.[22] Thucydides further noted that support for the Spartans was widespread in Greece. Athenian suppression of Naxos and Samos, for example, had created widespread bitterness and fear that others might be next. Enthusiasm for war, then, was nourished by youthful exuberance for the unknown, and a wider belief that Athens was indeed the "tyrant city" as the Corinthians said, that those upholding the "freedom" of the Greeks were the Spartans, as they themselves increasingly proclaimed.[23]

Enthusiasm for war was matched by the popular belief that its course was predictable. Thucydides countered this popular belief in several passages early in his history where he emphasized the unpredictability of war. In a speech after the Theban attack on Plataea, Archidamus of Sparta reminded the allies that war is uncertain and that too often attacks are made in a sudden impulse (2.11.4). This reference to what we know today as the Clausewitzian "fog of war" seems to undercut the idea that Thucydides reckoned both the outbreak and the outcome of wars to be predictable and inevitable. How can that which is subject to uncertainty be reckoned as certain?[24]

A close reading of Thucydides's language argues against the view that the Peloponnesian War was inevitable and that its outbreak represents anything other than another example of how failed diplomacy, popular agitation, and misguided leadership can bring states to war. But the issue of inevitability points to another concept that Cold War political scientists discussed, namely the "security dilemma." As John Herz noted in 1950, whenever a state gains power, another loses, and the natural inclination is for a state to enhance its own security by acquiring more and more power. The net effect of this is easy to see—states compete for power and security which in turn sparks a struggle for survival.[25]

Modern political scientists have observed that states fear each other in the absence of a central authority that can protect them from the aggressions and ambitions of other states.[26] There can be little doubt that as early as Homer, the Greeks recognized the same problem. Only the gods could resolve the dispute between Agamemnon and Achilles over Briseis at the beginning of the *Iliad*.[27] But divine intervention was not always possible. The Aristophanic hero Trygaeus, upon arriving in heaven to find the goddess Peace, discovers that the gods have left Mt. Olympus in disgust, unable to resolve the disputes that led the Greeks to war.[28]

Thucydides stated that Athens offered arbitration to the Spartans (1.144.2), which they refused. The Spartan refusal, and their presumed responsibility for plunging Greece into war, is not an argument that should be accepted at face value. The Spartans, for their part, conducted an ancient version of "shuttle diplomacy" that was dismissed and ignored by most Cold War readers. If the Spartans indeed provoked war, they followed a most unusual diplomatic strategy. For on at least four occasions, Spartan ambassadors approached the Athenians attempting to find some way to stop the escalation to violence.[29] What did the Spartans hope to accomplish with these negotiations? Why did the Athenians refuse to deliberate?

In late fall of 432, the Athenians took up the issue of war with Sparta, which had been brewing for a year. A Spartan embassy now arrived and announced, "Sparta wants peace. Peace is still possible if you give the Hellenes their autonomy" (1.139.3). Pericles, architect of Athenian power, responded with a speech intended not only to incite rejection of the Spartan overture but also to serve as a vote for war with Sparta. It was in this speech that Pericles claimed the Spartans were plotting against Athens and had refused offers of arbitration. He referred specifically to a clause in the Thirty Years Peace of 445 stipulating the grant of arbitration upon the offer of one party in a dispute, and that until a decision, "each side should keep what it has" (1.140.2, 144.2). This statement would appear to indict the Spartans for causing a war that the Athenians scrupulously tried to avoid. Yet the Spartans, as Thucydides made clear (1.85.2) in a speech by Archidamus, knew of the obligation to accept arbitration.

Some scholars have maintained that the Spartan embassies and demands were only buying time to prepare for war and to gain the moral advantage in the dispute.[30] After all, Thucydides later asserted that some Spartans admitted to their city's responsibility in not preventing the Thebans from attacking Plataea or in taking up the Athenian offer to seek arbitration.[31] But this admission, placed in the context of the Sicilian expedition, comes some fifteen years after the war's outbreak. If the statement is genuine and not simply Thucydidean editorializing, it might just as easily reflect the limited knowledge and understanding of younger men to events of which they had no direct knowledge. How well did these *anonymous* Spartans know their own history—of the efforts made by Archidamus, Polyalces, and others, most if not all now dead—to stop the march to war?[32]

A greater problem in accepting the sincerity of the Athenian offer of arbitration involved the obvious difficulty in identifying an acceptable arbitrator. The only major non-aligned state in Greece proper was Argos, a community that had a long history of disputes with Sparta. The Spartans would never have consented to Argive mediation.[33] In western Greece, Corcyra had been the major non-aligned state, but Corcyra was now party to the dispute and could not possibly act as an arbitrator. There were several other non-aligned communities in western Greece, but these—Aetolia and Achaea—lacked the necessary political organization, sophistication, and authority to negotiate the complex issues involved. Syracuse, the dominant state in Greek Sicily, might have been considered as an alternative. Yet Syracuse had been founded by Corinth and the two states maintained close ties, which would have made Syracusan mediation unacceptable to Athens.

The difficulties of implementing arbitration played into the hands of the Athenians.[34] In those speeches that Thucydides creates for the Athenians, as well as in the words of the Corinthians and Spartans, the Athenians come across as argumentatively clever and intellectually quick.[35] The Athenians seem to have seized upon arbitration as a diplomatic technicality that allowed them to assume the role of the injured party in the negotiations. They could always claim that they were prepared to submit their quarrel to a third party, even though they knew full well it would be difficult if not impossible to settle on one. With such delaying tactics they could put off negotiations and at the same time continue their provocative policies, which were at the root of Spartan fears and anxieties. Even if the strategy backfired—which it did—Pericles and many other Athenians believed the resulting war could be beneficial to the longterm stability and prosperity of their city.

After the Persian Wars and the withdrawal of Persian forces from mainland Greece in 479, Athens and Sparta had taken divergent paths. Sparta remained an old-fashioned community whose goal remained that of preserving the status quo, which fundamentally meant maintaining control over the serf-like helots who provided the labor for an agriculture-based economy. Athens, however, was becoming increasingly a "modern" and commercial state where, as the Thucydidean Pericles emphasized, democracy had reshaped its citizens into lovers of the polis (2.43.1).[36] Democratic institutions established at the end of the sixth century B.C. continued to be expanded and refined throughout the fifth: magistrates with defined tenures of office, a functioning assembly that wielded real authority, law courts and juries that expressed the will of the people. The rise of democracy, commerce, and empire were inextricably linked. To maintain these political and economic developments, Athenians believed they needed to stay the course, to exercise power and authority wherever possible.[37]

Influenced by the new and "enlightened" thinking of the sophists, Thucydides recognized that this quest for power drove the "modern" state that Athens had become.[38] Power brought unprecedented security, prosperity, and social harmony to a city that less than half a century earlier had been sacked by the Persians. Thucydides saw that states flourish or decay based upon their military effectiveness, and that success in wielding power allows them to rule others as an empire. This situation was altogether preferable to being ruled and enabled states to achieve that greatest of political values, freedom.[39] The Greeks had long cherished the memory of military exploits. The purpose of Homer's *Iliad* and the Persian War history of Herodotus was understood as keeping the deeds of brave men from being forgotten. Thucydides also had this purpose in mind when he composed his own history of the Peloponnesian War, but he went further in showing how men's exploits in war enabled states to become strong and successful. The widely perceived connection between external military capability and internal prosperity and political stability was central to Thucydides' conception of the events leading up to the outbreak of the war.

In many ways the Athenians imagined that war would bring out the best in them, and it would protect their power and predominance as they prevailed over their adversaries as recent history had demonstrated. One Athenian who suffered no illusions about what was at stake was Pericles. He realized that war brought with it the opportunity to increase Athenian power and wealth and so took advantage of a legalistic interpretation of the arbitration clause of the Thirty Years Peace to disguise an Athenian bid for domination.[40]

Pericles himself argued that it would be interpreted as a sign of weakness for the Athenians to end their economic boycott of Sparta's ally Megara—an action that would clearly have prevented an immediate outbreak of hostilities with Sparta (1.140.4–141.1). Such an admission of weakness might well lead to further external conflicts that could deprive the Athenians of their empire. During the debate over Mytilene in 427, Thucydides attributed this very idea to the Athenian politician Cleon as justification for imposing a reign of terror over the subjects of the empire (3.37.2, 40.4). In his Melian Dialogue, Thucydides ascribed to the Athenians the same motivation: they must conquer and/or control Melos in order not to appear weak or indecisive to the subjects of their empire (5.91–96). This weakness was also understood as a retreat from the prospects of winning even greater power. So long as increasing the empire was perceived as the concomitant of increasing commerce and democracy, this linkage encouraged Athenians to believe that any setback in external domination would necessarily lead to internal decline. Driven by such perceptions, Athens was "compelled" to frustrate and deny Spartan overtures and go to war in 431.

But this argument may be taken a bit further. Political scientist John Mearsheimer has recently argued that democratic states are as driven by power politics as their authoritarian counterparts and will practice the same sort of policies that lead to aggression and expansion.[41] Such a notion seems to conflict with received wisdom. Athens, as a democracy, could not possibly have started, or "wanted," the Peloponnesian War, since those who would do the fighting and dying had a direct say in the decision. The desire for self-preservation should have made the average Athenian man hesitant to initiate war. Under this reasoning, militaristic and oligarchic Sparta must surely have been the culprit. Yet democracies, as shown as recently as the American-led war into Iraq in 2003, are as aggressive as other states. Although scholars seem to wish that what happened in 431 could not possibly have been Athens's fault, when the evidence is examined, that is exactly what appears to have occurred.

In stark contrast to slow and "conservative" Sparta, as the Corinthians emphasize in an illuminating comparison (1.70), Athens was constantly looking for opportunity wherever it could be found. The dispute that erupted between these two states was not only between a "land" power and a "sea" power, but between two communities that, as we have seen, for more than two generations had developed in diametrically opposed directions.

Yet the very emphasis placed on contrasting Athenians with Spartans—a rhetorical commonplace whose popularity was amply evidenced by Thucydides—masks the reality underlying fifth-century Greek politics. The Greek states confronted one another not in a bipolar world but in one that was, at least in the few years leading up to the outbreak of the Peloponnesian War, multipolar. The tendency to see the classical Greek world as consisting of two power blocs, the Athenian Empire and Sparta's Peloponnesian League, simplifies a much more complex political reality that must take into account Corinth and the sphere of influence it began carving out in northwest Greece in the 440s.[42] This gave Corinth the clout to assume an assertive stance not only against Athens, but also with Sparta, its titular hegemon. Certainly Corinth lacked the strength to confront either Athens or Sparta directly on its own, but it could assert its will and power in other ways, such as by threatening to abandon Sparta's leadership and lead others in an act of secession, as it did in the debates before war erupted (1.71.4). Corinth also maintained good relations with its colony Syracuse, a state that possessed extensive military power and wealth.

In explaining how states pressure and influence each other as they attempt to balance power, John Mearsheimer has identified one method which he calls "buck-passing," whereby a state that chooses not to act, pressures another to act in its place.[43] In this instance, Corinth—unwilling and unable to challenge Athens' greater power—maneuvered its leader and protector Sparta to do exactly what it could not. Buck-passing remains a familiar diplomatic technique today. Its practice among the ancient Greeks helps explain why political scientists look to Thucydides as a guide to power and politics, and why the Peloponnesian War feels so "modern."

This excursus on Thucydides and the Peloponnesian War suggests that while Thucydides could surely be described as a political realist, it should be clear that the views expressed in his history have sometimes been misrepresented or misunderstood. Furthermore, as an apologist for Athens and Athenian imperialism, Thucydides presented the Athenian side of the story without a fair or complete reckoning of other perspectives, particularly those of the Corinthians.[44] Nonetheless, despite the diminished attention given to the evidence for multipolarity in fifth-century Greece, such evidence can be gathered quite easily from Thucydides's text. Cold War interpretations on the outbreak of the Peloponnesian War that omitted Corinth's role and position are surely incomplete.

By the early 1990s, the fall of the Soviet Union made the bipolar model of international relations outdated. Political scientists in the United States began to look back on the Cold War and question exactly what bipolarity meant.[45] For some political scientists, the reexamination of their assumptions about the Cold War led to a reexamination of their assumptions about Thucydides.

It is instructive to compare the interpretation of the Peloponnesian War made by Robert Gilpin in his 1981 book, *War and Change in World Politics*, with what appeared a decade later in his essay "Peloponnesian War and Cold War."[46] In fact, both interpretations initially date from the Cold War, but from very different periods. Gilpin's earlier study originated in the Brezhnev era, while his later essay was first delivered at a conference in June 1988, when Mikhail Gorbachev was at the height of his power and before the spectacular collapse of the communist regimes in Eastern Europe the following year. The essay was subsequently revised during 1989, and Gilpin was able to declare in the published version that "the Cold War . . . has come to an end."[47]

In 1981 Gilpin presented the Peloponnesian War as a conflict originating in the bipolar struggle between Athens and Sparta for the dominant position over the Greek states.[48] By the end of the 1980s, he became convinced of the crucial role played by Corinth in fomenting the war. He contrasted the Peloponnesian War, in which the major parties were receptive to excuses that could be used to justify direct confrontation, with the Cold War, where both the United States and the Soviet Union sought to avoid direct confrontation. Both Cold War superpowers, Gilpin argued, believed that history was on its side. For the Soviet Union, Marx demonstrated that capitalism's collapse and replacement by communism was inevitable. For the United States, the belief in democracy and in the productivity of the market convinced politicians that communism would not survive in the long term. Direct confrontation, such as the Cuban missile crisis, was quickly defused, and the occasional "hot" wars in the period (Vietnam in the 1960s and 1970s and Afghanistan in the 1980s) involved one superpower confronting only surrogates of the other. The two modern superpowers tended to refrain from the more directly provocative actions that sparked the Peloponnesian War, such as the economic boycott of Megara (the Megarian Decree) imposed by Athens, or the various ultimatums made by Sparta.[49]

Furthermore, Cold War politics included a number of neutral states. In Europe, several nations both capitalist and communist (e.g., Sweden, Yugoslavia) refused to join either of the strategic alliances. Countries throughout Latin America, Africa, and Asia—many of which had only recently gained sovereignty after roughly three-quarters of a century of European colonial control—formed a bloc of states under the banner of the Non-Aligned Movement. Large sections of the world were not part of the bipolar structure that was the focus of Cold War international relations.

Yet these neutral and non-aligned states often became the locations where Cold War conflict was played out between the United States and the Soviet Union. In 1984 Gilpin's Princeton colleague, the classicist W. Robert Connor, noted the challenge of understanding the Cold War implications of Thucydides in a world in which communist China and communist Russia were antagonists, and in which countries in the "Third World" (a term that seems to have fallen out of fashion in the post-Cold War period), such as Vietnam, were often thrust into the forefront.[50] By the end of the decade, Connor was more explicit in his critique of those who ignored the independent actions of the various Greek states related in Thucydides' history.[51]

Reexamining the Cold War continues to encourage reexamination of Thucydides.[52] Political scientist Richard Ned Lebow has recently characterized United States foreign policy in the Cold War as overwhelmingly "expedient."[53] In other words, the realist mantra from Thucydides, about "identity of interest," became simplified to "the enemy of my enemy is my friend." "Interest" was understood primarily as military advantage and only for the short term. A shared vision of democracy seemed to be included in "identity of interest" only with regard to a few select countries in Western Europe. Actions taken by the United States in the immediate aftermath of World War II—the recruitment of German scientists and officials known to have been members of the Nazi party; assisting the French in their attempt to reoccupy Indochina; support for authoritarian regimes such as that of Franco in Spain, Syngman Rhee in South Korea, and Shah Reza Pahlavi in Iran—often contradicted the ideological foundations of American government and society. Did Thucydides describe similarly contradictory actions during the Peloponnesian War?

Athens frequently supported democratic factions in other Greek states against their oligarchic opponents.[54] Yet the Athenians were not always consistent in their treatment of fellow democrats. Perhaps the best example of this came in 427 when the island city of Mytilene attempted to throw off Athenian control and ally with Sparta. After suppressing the revolt, the Athenians initially condemned to death all adult citizens, including the common citizens who had been responsible for the city's surrender to Athenian forces (3.36.2, 3.37.2–3). In 416 the Athenians desired the acquiescence of the tiny island city-state of Melos and its enrollment in the Athenian empire. When the Athenian delegation met with the Melian councilors, the Athenians chided them for not allowing them to speak with the commons and so win their support (5.85.1). This comment implies that a democratic faction existed on Melos and that Athens could have attempted to gain its objectives through that faction. Finally, when the Athenians voted to dispatch the great, and ultimately disastrous, expedition to Sicily, the object of the Athenian attack was the island's largest city, democratic Syracuse.[55] Clearly in this instance, the similarity of political institutions was no obstacle to imperial aggrandizement.

No other "hot" spot in the history of the Cold War had more impact on the United States than the Vietnam War. It was also an event that has drawn comparison to Thucydides and the Peloponnesian War, particularly the Athenian expedition to Sicily that came to ruin in 413. By the mid 1960s, political realists were split over American involvement in Vietnam. Hans Morgenthau opposed support for the South Vietnamese government, arguing that U.S. military actions there were damaging American prestige and eroding American influence in the world. That influence, he argued, was as much based upon the ethical principles of equality and freedom that formed America's sense of identity, as it was the military and economic power the United States exercised throughout the world.[56] Henry Kissinger, on the other hand, argued that military involvement was necessary, primarily because of the concern over the reliability of the United States to maintain military commitments made in other parts of the world. For Kissinger, the goal of "ending the war honorably" involved preserving, as much as possible, the appearance of American military might.[57]

Clearly, support for both Morgenthau's and Kissinger's views could be found in Thucydides, but it depended very much on how Thucydides was read. Is the passage from the Melian Dialogue that began this essay to be understood as an honest and unsentimental depiction of the truth about the power of one state over another? Or did Thucydides, in the spareness of his language and the employment of the dialogue form, invite his readers to contemplate the consequences of a world without justice?

What would seem to unite the experiences of the Vietnam War and the Peloponnesian War is the corrosive effect of violence. In his history, Thucydides narrated the civil war that destroyed the city-state of Corcyra, one of the principal parties to the war's outbreak. As the internal power struggle continued and worsened, with horrific acts of brutality committed by all sides, Thucydides noted that violence is a harsh teacher, that it erases from human beings any sense of shared humanity (3.83–84). From my own personal experience in Vietnam, few Americans serving there knew much about Thucydides or the Peloponnesian War. But like him and the Greeks he wrote of, they too had experienced firsthand the ugly sorts of things of which human beings are capable. These experiences could not but change their notions of what constituted acceptable moral behavior.[58]

Because history does not necessarily always teach lessons, the use of Thucydides in an exemplary sense is surely misleading. To argue that his analysis of the balance of power in fifth-century Greece applies to the Cold War era amounts to little more than a truism that might be applied to any other era when powerful states challenge each other. That such comparisons were popular during the period does not make them valid. Evidence may be found in the reporter's astute question, "Does that mean we're bound to lose?" posed to Secretary of State Kissinger. Kissinger asserted that the Cold War was a struggle between an "Athenian" United States and a "Spartan" Soviet Union. The fact that the Soviet Union collapsed in 1991, ending the Cold War, surely reveals the fallacies of Kissinger's analogy.

Chapter 9

Senator Robert C. Byrd and the Wisdom of the Ancients

—Robert F. Maddox

George Stephanopoulos, in his book *All Too Human*, recalls an encounter with Senator Robert C. Byrd of West Virginia during the early days of President Bill Clinton's administration. The encounter took place in a meeting with members of the Senate Armed Services Committee in the White House cabinet room. The issue under discussion was gays in the military. Stephanopoulos described Byrd as a "compact man with pale blue eyes, a long, straight nose, white hair tapered to a widow's peak, and tightly tailored three-piece suits." To the young presidential aide, "Byrd looked like his name—an elegant, elderly popinjay."

In the cabinet room, Byrd rose to speak. He assumed an orator's pose and began his disquisition on gays in the military with an examination of homosexuality in ancient Rome.

> "Suetonius writes that [the emperor] Tiberius . . . had young male prostitutes in his service," Byrd began, before reeling off other tales of emperors, generals, and the men who served and serviced them. "We're talking about something that has been going around for centuries," he stated flatly, echoing one of the president's central arguments. *Wow,* [Stephanopoulos thought,] *are we going to get Byrd? Can't be. . . .*

> After a pause for emphasis, [Stephanopoulos reported, Byrd] deliv-
> ered the opening blow. "But Rome fell when discipline gave way to
> luxury and ease." Then he traveled through time from the decline of
> the Roman Empire to the Christian Coalition's slippery slope.
> "Remove not the ancient landmarks thy fathers have set. I am
> opposed to your policy because it implies acceptance. It will lead to
> same-sex marriages and homosexuals in the Boy Scouts.'"[1]

This was not the only time that Senator Byrd differed with his party's
president, nor was it unusual for Byrd to invoke the wisdom of the
ancients on his side. Although somewhat rare, references in the *Congressional Record* to classical antiquity were not entirely uncommon at the end
of the twentieth century. Regular communion with the ancients was, and
a predilection for offering advice from Cicero and other ancient worthies,
was characteristic of one of the most unlikely men ever to have become
a leading figure in the United States Senate.

Robert Carlyle Byrd was born on November 20, 1917, in North
Wilkesboro, North Carolina, as Cornelius Calvin Sale, Jr. His mother died
in the influenza pandemic the following year, and his father, with four
other children to rear, gave the baby to his childless sister Vlurma and her
husband, Titus Byrd. The couple adopted the boy and renamed him. The
future senator grew up in poverty in several small towns in southern
West Virginia, eventually ending up in Beckley, where he graduated from
high school in 1934. Unable to afford college, Byrd worked in a gas station, then as a produce clerk in a grocery store, and finally as a meat cut-
ter. He also served as an organizer for the Ku Klux Klan. During World
War II, he worked in Baltimore and Tampa as a welder in the shipyards.
By the war's end, Byrd returned to West Virginia where he opened his
own grocery store in Sophia and became well known as a teacher of an
adult Bible class that was broadcast on a local radio station.[2]

In 1946 Byrd filed for the Democratic nomination to one of three
Raleigh County seats in the West Virginia House of Delegates in the
August 6 primary election.[3] Ironically, a Republican lawyer took an interest in the young man's political career and advised Byrd, "Make your fiddle case your brief case. Your identity will become known. You make
yourself a little speech, and they won't forget you because of that violin."
Byrd took that advice, and the fiddling butcher won his first election by
a wide margin. Throughout his career, Byrd used his fiddle for political
self-promotion.[4]

Byrd's populist image served him well in his swift rise in West Virginia
politics, from the House of Delegates to the state Senate to the U.S. House
of Representatives and, finally, to the U.S. Senate, winning election in
1958 only a dozen years after he entered his first race. Byrd's background,
however, also made him a target for Republicans and progressive Demo-

crats alike during the 1940s and 1950s. A butcher who never graduated college, who did not fight in World War II, and who had once been a member of the Ku Klux Klan, Byrd was derided as an uncouth, fiddle-playing clown. Even organized labor was never fully comfortable with Byrd. On more than one occasion, the United Mine Workers of America, a powerful force in West Virginia politics, tried to block Byrd's ambitions.[5]

In the U.S. Senate, Byrd associated himself with other Southern Democrats, most notably with Richard B. Russell of Georgia, who was a master of the rules of the Senate and a voracious student of history.[6] Russell was often described as a "nineteenth-century man adrift in the twentienth century."[7] Byrd considered Russell a mentor and always showed him the utmost respect, and Russell's influence enabled Byrd to rise into leadership positions in the Senate. Most famously, the dying Russell signed a proxy letter in support of Byrd's successful bid to oust Edward M. Kennedy as Democratic whip, the deputy leadership position, in 1971. Byrd kept a framed copy of Russell's letter on his Senate office wall.[8]

Six years later, upon the retirement of Mike Mansfield, Byrd became the leader of the Democrats in the Senate. He maintained the position for twelve years, serving as majority leader when the Democrats were in control of the chamber (from 1977–1981, and again from 1987–1989), and as minority leader when the Republicans dominated (from 1981–1987). Byrd stepped down as majority leader in 1989, after the 100th Congress. He became the ranking Democrat on the powerful Appropriations Committee, serving as chair of the committee under Democratic majorities (1989–1995; and later, for most of the 107th Congress). As the longest serving Democratic senator, Byrd also fulfilled the role of President Pro Tempore when his party controlled the Senate.[9]

Social motives are easily found to explain Byrd's interest in history and his extensive use of historical references in Senate debate. Richard B. Russell provided a powerful model of a traditional orator who could combine immense knowledge with genteel charm. Although Russell's speeches employed historical references far more economically, emulation of Russell was one important factor in Byrd's development as a senator.[10] A desire to overcome the stereotype of a rural West Virginia background was another. Byrd's showy displays of classical allusions have been called "indicative of a country boy's need to show himself to be educated and erudite."[11]

Byrd's career demonstrated that knowledge of the ancient Greeks and Romans continued to be a way to gain the respect of voters and fellow politicians in the later twentieth century, but it should not be overlooked that these interests conformed to long-evident features of the senator's individual personality. A former classmate at Mark Twain High School in Beckley remembered Byrd as "a bookworm who thought more about studying than sandlot baseball games." In fact, "he wouldn't play basket-ball or football with us. He stuck to himself and stuck to his studies."[12]

Byrd maintained that he always wanted to pursue higher education but as a young man lacked the financial means to do so. He began taking college courses when he served in the West Virginia Senate, and at various times was enrolled at Marshall University in Huntington, Morris Harvey College in Charleston, and Concord College in Athens. Despite not finishing an undergraduate degree, once Byrd became a congressman in 1953, he gained permission to attend law school in Washington, first at George Washington University and then at American University. It took him ten years, but Byrd earned his law degree *cum laude* in 1963. The commencement speaker was his former senate colleague, President John F. Kennedy, who handed Byrd his diploma.[13] Byrd finally received a B.A. in political science, *summa cum laude*, from Marshall University in 1994.[14]

The career of one of Byrd's Senate contemporaries, Bob Dole of Kansas, provides a contrast to ascribing much political usefulness to knowledge of classical antiquity. Dole, only six years younger than Byrd, grew up in a modest home in small-town Kansas. Dole's college education was interrupted by service in World War II. He eventually returned to Kansas, where he began his political career in 1950. Two years later, Dole finally became a college graduate, earning concurrent B.A. and law degrees from Washburn University. Dole was elected to the United States House in 1960 and the Senate in 1968. Dole eventually served as the Senate Republican leader for over eleven years, alternating as majority leader (1985–1987, 1995–1996) and minority leader (1987–1995).[15]

As party leaders during the 1980s, Byrd and Dole shared other characteristics. Both were seen as "solo operators" who tended on their own to manage their party's agenda in the chamber. Both placed a high regard on collegiality and were reluctant to trample wantonly over the concerns of opposing senators in the fashioning of legislation.[16] Only Byrd, however, showed any interest in employing the wisdom of the ancients. Dole never aspired to eloquence, did not make classical allusions in his speeches, nor was he concerned with his intellectual image. The Kansan's senatorial career owed nothing to Cicero.

In the 1980s and 1990s, Byrd and Dole found themselves on opposing sides in the debate over the line-item veto. As far back as Ulysses S. Grant in the 1870s, presidents have wanted the authority to block individual appropriations in bills passed by Congress without having to veto the entire bill. The governors of most states have for many years enjoyed such an authority. From time to time, presidents have refused to spend money allocated by Congress for specific projects, but these impoundments of funds were of limited scope and short duration. Franklin D. Roosevelt, who as Governor of New York had such a line-item veto over the state budget, regularly requested a similar authority from Congress. In 1938, the House passed an appropriations bill that gave Roosevelt this power. The Senate, however, refused to go along, and the line-item veto provision was removed in the conference committee.[17]

Richard Nixon's aggressive use of impoundment to avoid funding programs he disliked led Congress to pass the Congressional Budget and Impoundment Control Act of 1974. This law allowed a single house of Congress the right to overturn a temporary impoundment, while a permanent impoundment (a rescission) required approval of both houses. Federal court rulings in the 1980s invalidated the temporary impoundment provisions, adding impetus to the calls for a line-item veto by Ronald Reagan, another former governor to serve in the White House. The issue gained widespread Republican support during the ballooning budget deficits of the late 1980s and early 1990s.[18]

In the 1992 presidential election, both the incumbent George H. W. Bush and his Democratic challenger, Bill Clinton (yet another governor), supported the line-item veto.[19] Late in the campaign, the Democratic-controlled House passed a bill giving the president slightly enhanced rescission authority (only up to twenty-five percent of the budgeted amount and subject to congressional approval).[20] Passage of the bill was seen merely as political cover for House Democrats, most of whom generally opposed the line-item veto. Members of the House were well aware that the Democratic majority in the Senate, which had rejected the idea in a separate vote earlier in the year, was unlikely to take up the matter again before the end of the 102nd Congress.

Clinton's election significantly raised the likelihood that the 103rd Congress would pass some form of the line-item veto, even though both houses remained under Democratic control. Speaker of the House Thomas S. Foley had agreed to support the new president's request. Within one hundred days of Clinton's inauguration, the House approved and sent to the Senate a bill even stronger than what had been passed the previous year, giving the president full rescission authority subject to overturning by simple majorities in both houses.[21] Although the Senate had voted 54–44 the previous year to reject the line-item veto,[22] a handful of incoming senators publicly supported the veto in some form. Others in the Democratic majority were sympathetic to the new president and willing to consider an idea that was an important part of Clinton's agenda.

In this atmosphere, Senator Byrd sprang into action to convince his colleagues to maintain complete congressional control over government spending. As chair of the Senate Appropriations Committee, Byrd stood to lose much of his influence in the chamber, as well as his ability to fund projects in West Virginia should the line-item veto become law. Byrd's traditional views on the mechanics of American governance were the real driving force behind his fierce opposition to the line-item veto. The seventy-five-year-old senator, who cherished his reputation as the "most ardent protector of the powers of the legislative branch," planned a series of fourteen hour-long speeches in opposition to the line-item veto that he delivered on the Senate floor from May through October of 1993.[23] The primary subject of these speeches was the development of the Roman senate, from its origins until the end of the republic. Byrd wanted to use the history of the Roman senate as a model and a warning to his U.S. Senate colleagues.

"What does Roman history have to do with the line-item veto? Where is the relevancy?" Byrd himself asked in his seventh Roman history address, given on June 22.[24] In this speech and elsewhere, Byrd presented three reasons for the relevancy of analyzing the senate of ancient Rome. The study of history provides access to the experiences of previous generations, allowing human beings to gain additional wisdom and foresight in the decision-making process. One of Byrd's favorite quotations from Cicero dealt with this idea: "To be ignorant of what occurred before you were born is to remain always a child."[25]

Another reason for studying Roman history was the influence the subject had on the framers of the United States Constitution, both directly through their own classical education, as well as in the political theory of the French philosopher Montesquieu (1689–1755), whose ideas on the separation of powers were inspired by his interpretation of Roman history.[26] The ultimate reason was Byrd's insistence on the parallels and similarities between the senate of ancient Rome and its American namesake two millennia later. On May 11, for example, Byrd interpreted the support of the Roman senate for the accession of the king Servius Tullius as analogous to modern confirmations by the U.S. Senate. "Here, then," Byrd remarked, "was a primordial form of separation of powers and checks and balances—the people chose but the Senate could approve or disapprove."[27] On July 13, Byrd compared the Lex Caecilia Didia, a Roman law of 98 B.C. that prohibited the inclusion of extraneous matter in legislation and forbade omnibus bills, with one of his own contributions to Senate lawmaking, the Byrd Rule, which requires a three-fifths affirmative vote in the Senate to allow extraneous matter in a budget reconciliation bill.[28]

Byrd repeatedly asked his colleagues to compare themselves to the senators of ancient Rome. On June 9, Byrd recounted the story of the Roman consul Regulus during the First Punic War (264–241 B.C.). Regulus and his army met defeat in Africa at the hands of the Carthaginians, who allowed him to carry a proposal of peace to Rome if the consul took an oath to return. Living up to his oath, Regulus returned to Carthage knowing that he would receive a horrible death. Byrd took that example and wondered before the Senate how many senators took their Senate oath seriously. He pointed out that the "Constitution provides that the power of the purse shall be vested in the Congress of the United States. We swear before God—our Maker, Creator of life and life eternal—and before man that we will support and defend that Constitution. Yet, there are those in this body who would support the shifting of that power over the purse, at least in part, to the chief executive." He admonished senators to be "serious" about the oath, and that the "Constitution vests the power of the purse in the legislative branch." After all, "Regulus was true to his oath, and we should be true to ours."[29]

The underlying theme woven throughout Byrd's speeches was that the rise of the Roman Republic was due to an independent senate that safeguarded its authority and maintained control over Rome's finances. Once that senate began to cede its authority to individual officeholders, the Roman state traveled on the path toward tyranny and totalitarianism. The lesson for a United States Senate considering the line-item veto was obvious. As Byrd stated on June 22, "by delivering the line-item veto into the hands of a president—any president, Republican or Democrat or Independent—the U.S. Senate will have set its foot on the same road to decline, subservience, impotence, and feebleness that the Roman Senate followed in its own descent into ignominy, cowardice, and oblivion."[30]

This theme crystallized in the eighth address in the series, delivered one week later on June 29. The speech examined Roman history during the second century B.C., as well as the tensions leading up to the reforms of the brothers Tiberius and Gaius Gracchus. The speech's delivery less than a week before Independence Day infused the topic with an even greater concern for the future path of American democracy.

Byrd discussed the concept of *auctoritas* (authority). "In practice," he said, "the term meant the prestige and esteem that the Senate possessed, based on custom and precedent and the outstanding qualities of its members." One source of this authority was the traditional power exercised by the Roman senate in its roles of ratifying the decisions of the popular assembly, approving the election of magistrates, issuing advice to those magistrates, and controlling public finances. The other source was the traditional Roman virtues of honesty, frugality, flexibility, and respect for law. These two sources flowed together to maintain responsible government. Virtuous Romans accepted the political balance that existed in their state and deferred to the authority of the senate to uphold that balance.

The authority of the senate was the cornerstone. Byrd alluded to a phrase in Cicero's *Republic* that the ideal state allotted executive power to the magistrates, authority to the senate, and liberty to the people. Modern comparisons were also made. The senator connected the relationship between the Roman senate and the popular assemblies with that of the

U.S. Senate and the House of Representatives. Byrd also described Roman virtues as "so much like the religious and family values and other virtues in American life that we have known since the beginning and prior thereto, of our own republic."[31]

Byrd recognized the urgent social problems created in the second century B.C. by the displacement of the Italian peasantry after wealthy Romans used slave labor to set up large plantations on conquered lands. Yet he could not excuse Tiberius and Gaius Gracchus for subverting the traditional Roman constitution in their attempts at land reform and at diminishing the power of their opponents in the senate. The reforms of Gaius Gracchus in particular earned Byrd's wrath. Byrd saw subsidized grain distribution as opening the door to the welfare state. He compared the establishment of equestrian juries to affirmative action. The contracting out of provincial tax collection to private companies enabled business interests to pollute the Roman political process. Byrd wondered, "As we endure the assaults of modern Gracchans on the legislative branch and the Constitution's checks and balances, are we to conclude that history must always and inexorably repeat itself?"[32]

In the following four speeches, Byrd reviewed the turbulent events of the first century B.C.; the rise of domineering leaders like Marius, Sulla, Pompey, Caesar and Augustus; and the demise of the Roman Republic. The senator's thirteenth address, delivered on September 20, summarized the role of the Roman senate in the republic's fall. Although Byrd recognized that senators had been intimidated by Caesar's armies and that their numbers had been packed with Caesar's supporters, he insisted that these senators had themselves to blame for acquiescing to Caesar's desire for solitary and permanent control over all aspects of Roman government.

"Gaius Julius Caesar did not seize power in Rome," Byrd flatly declared. "The Roman Senate thrust power upon Caesar deliberately with forethought, with surrender, with intent to escape from responsibility. The Senate gave away power; the members . . . abandoned their duty as senators, and, in doing so, created in Caesar the most powerful man in the ancient world and one of the most powerful men in all history."[33]

This interpretation of the demise of the Roman Republic fit with Byrd's understanding of the nature of political power. The senator saw political power as an attitude of assent and acquiescence in the minds of the people. This attitude creates the authority that exists in those who become the people's leaders. When that assent is channeled through long-established constitutional norms, in a system where power is balanced between those who make the laws and those who enforce them, government is more likely to satisfy the people and promote an environment of freedom. If, however, constitutionally sanctioned leaders acquiesce in disrupting that balance to concentrate political authority in a single executive, the resulting tyranny will eventually compel the people to fashion a new form for their governance.

This is why Byrd passionately urged his U.S. Senate colleagues to contemplate "the surrender of the Roman Senate's power to Caesar, and . . . consider the implications of our own surrender—God forbid—to any president, of power that is unchecked by a Senate and House of Representatives.[34] The rest of the speech warned of the dangers of the already expansive power of the executive branch. Just as Julius Caesar had been the most powerful man in the ancient world, so, too, the president of the United States was the most powerful person in the modern world, directing a vast bureaucracy that regulates activities both at home and abroad. Limitations to the president's power were eroding. Modern presidents lacked a sense of accountability, and the senator mentioned a version of the famous, "Son, they're all my helicopters" quip of Lyndon Johnson.[35]

Byrd's fears fit into an American tradition of warnings against Caesarism. Presidents who asserted an expansive view of their authority— such as Abraham Lincoln, Theodore Roosevelt and Franklin D. Roosevelt—regularly faced the criticism that they tried to use their popularity to extend executive power beyond constitutional limits.[36] Critics complained that each of these presidents aspired to become a new Julius Caesar. Openly connecting himself to this tradition of anti-Caesarism, Byrd in this speech brought up Henry Clay's comment in 1832 that President Andrew Jackson's use of the veto was already transforming the presidency into an "elective monarchy."[37]

In Byrd's final address on the relevance of Roman history, the senator on October 18 recapitulated the ideas and rationale underlying his series of addresses. Byrd's central emphasis was on the separation of powers and system of checks and balances that drove the mechanics of both the American and Roman republics. For Byrd, the "basic lesson" from ancient Rome relevant to the line-item veto was "that when the Roman Senate gave away its control of the purse strings, it gave away its power to check the executive. From that point on, the Senate declined and, as we have seen, it was only a matter of time. Once the mainstay was weakened, the structure crumbled and the Roman Republic fell."[38]

Byrd concluded his series of speeches by quoting the remarks of Daniel Webster in 1832 on the centennial anniversary of George Washington's birth. Webster had employed architectural metaphors to describe the American constitution. What, Webster mused, would happen if the "columns of constitutional liberty" should collapse? Byrd related Webster's prediction: "Bitterer tears . . . will flow over them than were ever shed over the monuments of Roman or Grecian art. For they will be remnants of a more glorious edifice than Greece or Rome ever saw." With a thank you to his colleagues, Byrd ended his fourteenth and final exposition on the senate of the Roman Republic.[39]

The effectiveness of Byrd's addresses, in and of themselves, was minor. Although the speeches were nationally televised over the C-SPAN 2 cable network and generated appreciative comments from members of the general public as well as from Byrd's senatorial colleagues, newspaper editorial writers derided both Byrd's motives and his message.[40] The speeches did little to stem political agitation for the line-item veto. While the message may have been ridiculed and ignored, the messenger could not be. Byrd's control of the Appropriations Committee ensured that his colleagues took note of his strong opposition to the line-item veto, or to any improvements to the president's rescission authority under the 1974 Budget Act. None of the bills in the 103rd Congress dealing with rescission, either those passed by the House or those proposed in the Senate, made it beyond hearings in the Senate Budget Committee. No votes were ever taken.[41]

The Republican Revolution of 1994 changed the situation dramatically. The G.O.P. gained control of both the House and the Senate, and the 104th Congress passed the Line-Item Veto Act, giving the president rescission authority that could be overturned only by a two-thirds majority in both the House and the Senate. President Clinton signed the act into law on April 15, 1996.[42]

In January 1997, Byrd and several of his colleagues challenged the constitutionality of the Line-Item Veto Act in court, and a United States District Court ruled in April that the act was unconstitutional. However, the U.S. Supreme Court ruled in June that Byrd and others did not have the legal standing to bring the suit.[43] After Clinton began using the line-item veto, some of those local governments and organizations whose funding was cut did bring suit. A federal court again ruled the act unconstitutional, a ruling affirmed by the Supreme Court in June 1998. The majority opinion, written by Justice John Paul Stevens, followed the same arguments used a decade and a half earlier to strike down the temporary impoundment provisions of the 1974 Budget Act, namely that the text of a law was subject to alteration after the legislative process was complete. The only acceptable means of establishing a line-item veto was through the laborious method of amending the Constitution.[44] When informed of the Supreme Court decision, Byrd saluted and proclaimed, "God save this honorable court."[45]

Ultimately, the wisdom of the ancients counted for little in the fight over the line-item veto, whose adoption and subsequent striking down were almost entirely driven by contemporary political and constitutional arguments. Byrd's speeches on Roman history should not, however, be dismissed as an ego-driven exercise in intellectual self-promotion. Byrd was sincere in his adherence to tradition and to the value of studying ancient history and political thought. That love of tradition may not have had much resonance among other politicians and journalists at the end of the twentieth century, but it had enough among the general public to gain some recognition and awareness for paying attention to the Greeks and Romans.

Byrd's promotion of the wisdom of the ancients was testament to the fact that comparisons between the United States and classical antiquity maintained a residual fascination among some political observers. Such comparisons are always tinged by the knowledge that both Athenian democracy and the Roman Republic eventually disappeared, and by what the implications may foretell for the United States. Byrd's speeches on the Roman Republic played upon the fears of the possibility of America's own decline, fears that resonated far more widely in late twentieth-century America than did references to the ancient world. Bestselling books presented historical cycles, economic data, and changes in morality as evidence for the imminent decay of American civilization.[46]

Byrd's addresses blended the traditions of American classicism and American fatalism in an attempt to curb political enthusiasm for the line-item veto. The Supreme Court eventually did what Byrd could not, stopping the line-item veto and removing the idea from the center of political debate. Yet the speeches on Roman history that resulted from that debate provide an insight into one senator's unique perspective on what the ancients can teach modern Americans about government.

Chapter 10

Platonism in High Places
Leo Strauss, George W. Bush and the Response to 9/11

—Neil G. Robertson

Various articles in a number of reputable newspapers, magazines and journals—including the *The New York Times, Le Monde, The New Yorker*, and *Harpers*—have made the surprising claim that the response of the Bush White House to the events of 9/11 is deeply connected to the thought of Leo Strauss.[1] On the face of it, Leo Strauss would seem to be an unlikely figure to be linked with the policies and practices of the Bush White House. Born in 1899 into a fairly observant Jewish family in Germany, Strauss studied philosophy at the University of Marburg and earned a Ph.D. from the University of Hamburg. He became a researcher at the Academy for Jewish Research in Berlin, and at the time the Nazis came to power, he was in France on a research fellowship. The following year, he moved to England. In 1937, he came to the United States, eventually securing a tenured position at the New School for Social Research in New York City. In 1949, Strauss began two decades of teaching in the Department of Political Science at the University of Chicago. He retired as an emeritus professor in 1968 but continued teaching and giving guest lectures at several universities until his death in 1973.[2]

Strauss spent his career writing very difficult, nuanced interpretations of works from the history of political thought, and he is noted for demanding a return to the ancients and, especially, to the thought of Plato. That George W. Bush would consult the writings of Strauss or Plato—neither of whom said a great deal about international affairs or anything about Islamic terrorism—in order to sort out how to respond to the events of September 11, 2001, seems to require a suspension of disbelief usually called upon only by the annals of pulp fiction. Yet many important and established organs of the media have drawn a very strong connection between Leo Strauss and the Bush White House.

The explanation for this unlikely claim lies in the mediating role of what has been called *neo-conservatism*. The neo-conservatives are a loosely connected movement—or, as the "godfather" of neo-conservatism, Irving Kristol (born 1920), prefers, "persuasion"—that has been seen as very influential in formulating the White House's response to 9/11. In turn, the argument suggests, the neo-conservatives have been influenced by the thought of Leo Strauss; indeed, a number are former students of Strauss, or students of students of Strauss, and so are often described as Straussians. Both terms, *neo-conservative* and *Straussian*, are contentious and used very loosely, often as terms of abuse. However, while there are dangers in using these labels, often resisted by those to whom they are applied, they can be useful as ways of characterizing the "persuasion," and identifying a fairly limited, and certainly not homogeneous, group of intellectuals and government officials who have various overlapping intellectual and personal ties to one another.

Among the most prominent and influential of those identified as "neo-conservative" during George W. Bush's first term and who became involved in the response to 9/11, were Paul Wolfowitz (deputy secretary of defense at the time); Lewis Libby (vice president's chief of staff); Abram Shulsky (pentagon's office of special plans); Richard Perle (pentagon policy board); Douglas Feith (undersecretary of defense for policy); Stephen Cambone (undersecretary of defense for intelligence); John Bolton (state department); David Wurmser (state department); Eliot Cohen (defense policy board); and Elliot Abrams (national security council). The claim of those who see a Straussian conspiracy or a neo-con "cabal" at work in the formulation of the response to 9/11 in general and in the decision to go to war in Iraq, in particular, is that these individuals, operating in the context of support from friendly think tanks and institutes on the one hand, and the right wing media, especially that owned by Rupert Murdoch, on the other, were able to "hijack" the Bush White House foreign policy to fulfill their own ideological (Strauss-inspired) objectives.[3] Stefan Halper and Jonathan Clarke make this claim:

> The situation of unending war in which we find ourselves results in large part from the fact that the policies adopted after 9/11, the ini-

tial strike against the Taliban aside, were hardly specific to the event. . . . [T]he post-9/11 policy was in fact grounded in an ideology that existed well before the terror attacks and that in a stroke of opportunistic daring by its progenitors, has emerged as the new orthodoxy. The paper trail is unambiguous.[4]

Further, in his book, *The President of Good and Evil*, Peter Singer writes:

If we are persuaded that there is a Straussian conspiracy, we will view Bush as the "gentleman" of suitably patrician background, being used by Straussians for their own political purposes. . . . I'm not particularly keen on conspiracy theories myself, but I have to admit that, as an explanation of why the Bush administration was so determined to go to war with Iraq, this one has some plausibility.[5]

So we are faced with the claim that Leo Strauss has, posthumously, through his teaching and his students and their role in the Bush White House, brought about a transformation of American foreign policy. This transformation is seen as an ideological shift from the post-1945 orthodoxy of multilateral containment, diplomacy, and support for international law and institutions, to a foreign policy that is resolutely nationalistic, imperialistic, unilateral, pre-emptive, and militaristic in orientation, and whose first clear result is the war in Iraq.

This shift in foreign policy is the most obvious way in which Straussian neo-conservatism has been seen to influence the White House. But beyond this, the claim is made that Strauss's influence through his neo-conservative acolytes has altered not only the character of American foreign policy, but also the very way the American government understands its relationship to the American people. Strauss's position, and his turn to Plato and the ancients, has been understood as a radical break with the ideals and principles of modern liberal democracy. In his writings, Strauss pointed to the role of what Plato, *Republic* 414b–415e, described as "the noble lie" in political life. Further, Strauss famously developed from Plato, *Republic* 494a, *Timaeus* 28c, *Seventh Epistle* 332d and 341c–e (as well as from other texts and authors), the distinction between esoteric and exoteric teachings. So, for Strauss, in the writings of philosophers there is one obvious level that is for public consumption, and another level reserved for the philosopher, or would-be philosopher, who can read "between the lines" and discern a secret teaching the "many" could not recognize or stomach. Strauss argued that there are different ranks of people and that this entails different standards of justice and of the virtues more generally. Further, Strauss criticized modernity in general, seeing it as a leveling and ultimately nihilistic "project" whose failings bring to light the need to return to ancient principles and teachings. All of this has led commentators to see Strauss not only as an enemy of liberal democratic principles, such as equality, freedom, and the responsibility of government to the people, but also as negating all objective principles.

One of the most prominent scholars of Strauss and his influence on American politics, Shadia Drury, has argued that what Strauss discovered in his reading of the ancients is indistinguishable from Nietzsche—a philosophy of the weak and the strong, of the citizens and the philosophers.[6] In Drury's view, the Straussian neo-conservative influence is seen not simply in the fact that the Bush White House has taken up a new foreign policy, but in the way they are perceived to have done so—through the most manipulative use of dishonesty, misrepresentation, and a whole array of practices and policies aimed to undermine the principles, procedures, and safeguards of liberal democracy.[7] From this point of view, the Bush White House, insofar as it engaged in untruth and incomplete disclosure of information, was not just carrying on with the follies and foibles of government as usual, but actually doing so out of ideological principle, self-consciously and with a good conscience.

Now, if this were true—that the White House had been taken over by a group that had views fundamentally opposed to the principles of the American Constitution, and so were not only leading America into a new and potentially dangerous foreign policy, but were doing so out of fundamental opposition to liberal democratic principles—the integrity of the American regime would be in dire straits. Does the presence of Straussian Platonism in the White House really mean the undoing of the American order?

In an attempt to throw a little light into this murky and rather overwrought debate, this paper makes three fundamental claims.

1) In spite of clear lines of influence, neo-conservatism is not identical to the position articulated by Strauss, and, in particular, Strauss's rather limited account of foreign affairs is opposed to the policy and goals of the neo-conservatives. Whether Strauss would or would not have supported the war in Iraq, I cannot say, but he would not have supported the rationale provided by the neo-conservatives.

2) Strauss is misunderstood as a Nietzschean or moral nihilist: Strauss's position is far more subtle than either a simple advocate for fixed moral principles or an annihilator of all moral order. Strauss's turn to Plato was an effort to escape these alternatives. So while there may be good reason to complain about the honesty, lack of openness, and the manipulation of the public by the Bush White House, it is problematic to lay this at the door of Leo Strauss—or at least to do so in the way that critics, such as

Shadia Drury, have done. Strauss would have understood his own thought, including his turn to Plato, as supportive of, not undermining, liberal democracy.

3) While I deny any direct connection of Strauss to the policies and practices of the Bush White House, I do want to argue for an indirect or more general connection. Strauss himself described Marx as the "father of communism" and Nietzsche as "the step-grandfather of fascism."[8] I am not quite sure how to state the exact familial relationship of Strauss to the neo-conservatives in the Bush White House, but the recognition of some connection is useful in order to get at the background assumptions that inform the political views of the neo-conservatives and at least some aspects of the Bush White House.[9]

Before I turn to fleshing out these claims, I must be clear about what this paper is not trying to do. I am not trying to discover the extent of the actual influence of the neo-conservatives in the White House nor whether they "hijacked" American foreign policy. I am not trying to get at the motivations of the president or his staff in deciding to invade Iraq. While the war may have been underdetermined from the perspective of international law, it seems to have been overdetermined from the perspective of alternative motivations (such as the war on terrorism, spreading democracy, geopolitics, oil, the defense industry, and so forth). And finally, I am not trying to discern the level, if any, of what Machiavelli calls "the fox and the lion," force and fraud, in the way the Bush White House represented and sought to convince America and the world of the need to invade Iraq. Rather, this paper seeks to articulate the stated views of the neo-conservative "persuasion," to compare them to those of Leo Strauss, and so to discern the extent to which a Strauss-inspired Platonic understanding can illuminate and be seen to inform the policies of the Bush White House.[10]

While neo-conservatism has come to prominence with the presidency of George W. Bush and has come to be identified almost exclusively with an interventionist, imperialist or hegemonic foreign policy, its roots go back much further and its breadth is much wider. As has been described in a number of commentaries, the neo-conservatives were originally a small group of New York intellectuals, generally Democrats, who broke with the increasingly powerful "liberal" wing of the Democratic Party in the 1960s. Most of the first neo-conservatives were originally, in the 1930s, Trotskyists—a fact noted by a number of commentators as an explanation of the group's sense of alienation from the liberalizing, leveling aspects of North American life and of an incipient tendency to radicalism. The label *neo-conservative* actually began life as a term of abuse by former colleagues on the left trying to caricature this new-found conservatism. Irving Kristol famously described a neo-conservative as "a liberal mugged by reality."[11]

It might be useful to bring out what Kristol means by "liberal." *Liberal* here is not being used in the same sense the term is used in the phrase *liberal democracy*—something not always recognized by critics of the neo-conservatives. *Liberal* in *liberal democracy* traditionally means upholding or protecting individual rights, being in favor of individual liberty. How individual rights can best be upheld and protected, and the character of those rights, is a matter of interpretation; the *liberal tradition* in the widest sense would encompass both "neo-conservatism" and the "liberalism" they oppose. Certainly, the neo-conservatives would understand their own position as liberal-democratic, and indeed they argue that they are seeking to strengthen liberal democracy against the self-destructive tendencies of the "liberal" interpretation of liberal democracy. The neo-conservatives (and here they draw, in part, from the analysis of Leo Strauss) see "liberalism" as a break with the older individualist, natural rights account of liberal democracy—realized most fully in the American Revolution—and as a turn to the more deeply socialized account of liberty that underlay the French Revolution and the general turn to social democracy that has largely characterized European political development since the Second World War.[12] Kristol saw the distinctive mark of neo-conservatism within the history of conservatism as due to its criticizing not the intrusive welfare state, but rather the moral ends being pursued by the welfare state in accord with a prevailing liberalism. Kristol saw this refocusing of the debate as due in large measure to the thought of Leo Strauss. Kristol, in 1996, wrote:

> Strauss' analysis of the destructive elements within modern liberalism, an analysis that was popularized by his students and his students' students, has altered the very tone of public discourse in the United States.[13]

The overriding characteristic of neo-conservatism is its demand that moral distinctions be used to guide the formulation of policy, whether in domestic or foreign affairs. At the heart of the neo-conservative critique at the level of domestic affairs is its claim that liberalism undermines the moral integrity of the individual through producing dependence on the state, the reduction of the individual to subjective desire, and the occlusion of all standards—thus moral relativism. What is interesting in the analysis of the neo-conservatives here is that this analysis need not mean eliminating the welfare state; rather it would rework it to be supportive of, and not undermining of, moral and practical engagement. The fundamental move for the neo-conservatives is to shift from an "equality of results" that produces dependency to an "equality of opportunity" that would strengthen and encourage moral activity. However, along with the removal of the actively destructive elements of liberalism, the neo-conservatives also see the need for moral resources that transcend modern social and political life: the need for religion and an older, indeed premodern, sense of virtue. Here also the neo-conservatives are drawing on Strauss's analysis.[14] For neo-conservatives, a purely secular liberal standpoint—the standpoint that came to prevail more and more in the United States over the course of the twentieth century through various Supreme Court decisions and a culturally neutral bureaucracy—is incapable of sustaining the kind of activities and ends necessary for a vibrant and morally effective polity. People have to see themselves as more than pure choosing selves acting in the context of a neutral, secular, procedural state.[15] Kristol, who spoke of his own Jewish roots as influential here, argues that inner belief or religious conviction is not as important as religious practice. The importance of religion is not its truth so much as its moral worth, its capacity to give moral structure to human personality. At the heart of religion in America, according to Kristol, is not dogma and doctrine, but a sense of moral activity and purpose. For Kristol, the strength and dynamic character of American liberal democracy resides in its implicit relation to older moral religious sources—a relationship that underlies the constitutional order. Further, Kristol also made the claim that this turn to older sources does not undermine America's dynamic engagement with the world, but rather, paradoxically is the necessary support for it.

The most obvious aspect of this critique of liberalism is the neo-conservative view of foreign policy. Just as the neo-conservatives see domestic liberalism as self-destructive to the goals of American social and political life, they see liberalism in international affairs to be equally self-destructive. Liberalism at the international level involves the assumption that the ideal world order is either a universal homogeneous state or a league of nations that recognize and affirm one another's sovereignty. This assumption leads to an analogous dissolution of moral categories in the international sphere to that which liberalism affects at the domestic level. To act as if the ideal is realistic in international relations is to suppose that all countries are to be treated identically and given the same recognition: liberal democracies and totalitarian tyrannies are somehow to be given equal status. In particular, the neo-conservatives in the 1970s were strongly opposed to détente and the political realism of Henry Kissinger, and demanded a much more direct confrontation with the Soviet Union. As a result, Ronald Reagan was lauded and even mythologized by the neo-conservatives.[16]

Underlying the neo-conservative foreign policy of the 1970s and 1980s, in contrast to that of Kissinger, was an optimism about the capacity and the strength of the United States to develop at all levels, to shake off its economic malaise, and to dispell the sense of confusion that had arisen from the Vietnam War and other failures in international affairs. It is unclear what the ground for this optimism was, but it was certainly connected to a sense of the exceptional character of the United States and the religious foundation of that sense.[17] Kristol wrote:

> Neo-conservatism is not merely patriotic—that goes without saying—but also nationalist. Patriotism springs from love of the nation's past; nationalism arises out of hope for the nation's future, distinctive greatness.[18]

But, in spite of this sense of dynamism and optimism, the foreign policy advocated by the first generation of neo-conservatives in the 1970s and 1980s was essentially reactive, characterized by renewed efforts at "containment" of communism in both hemispheres, and with a primary focus on the Soviet Union.

As Halper and Clarke note in their book *America Alone*, the collapse of the Soviet Union posed a fundamental problem for the first generation of neo-conservatives, and responding to this challenge marked a generational shift in the neo-conservatives. The dissolution of the USSR was a huge victory for neo-conservatism insofar as it could claim a connection to the Reagan presidency, but now that America was unrivalled and essentially unthreatened, the purpose of American military might—the strengthening of which had been the central platform of neo-conservative foreign policy—seemed empty. So Irving Kristol, Jean Kirkpatrick, and Norman Podhoretz, all members of the first generation of neo-conservatives, saw this as a time in which the United States could become like other nations, "normal." They abjured the lure of Wilsonian idealism to try to use American power to make the world a better place.[19]

It was the next generation of neo-conservatives who moved from this earlier reactive posture to a proactive foreign policy. In the 1990s, William Kristol (Irving Kristol's son), Paul Wolfowitz, Richard Perle, Robert Kagan (son of historian Donald Kagan), Charles Krauthammer, and others began outlining the foreign policy most identified with neo-conservatism today. They claimed that the United States should seize this moment of unparalleled power to shape a world that fulfills American principles and serves American interests, to realize an era of a *Pax Americana*. The implication of this shift for the neo-conservatives was to turn outward to promote democracy and eradicate the sources of "evil" that threatened democracy and American interests.[20] One of the first important documents supporting this shift was the controversial *Defense Planning Guidance* of 1992.[21] This document from Paul Wolfowitz's office in the White House of George H. W. Bush defined a notion of American pre-eminence that was later taken up in *National Security Strategy* of 2002.[22] The launching of the *Project for the New American Century* in 1997 was the clearest articulation of this new policy. As is now widely known, a central part of this policy, well before 9/11, was the plan to bring about "regime change" in Iraq.[23]

The claim of those who see a Straussian influence in the White House of George W. Bush concerns more than the taking up of a moralizing and hegemonic foreign policy. They also assert a Straussian connection in the apparently "opportunistic" way this foreign policy, embodied in the decision to invade Iraq, was attached to the events of 9/11. They argue that Straussian influence brought about the misleading way in which the case to invade Iraq was presented to the American people, not only by the government, but also with the assistance of think tanks, institutes, foundations, and media organizations allied with the neo-conservatives. Politicians, however, do not have to read Plato to learn how to lie. And, oddly enough, there is little written by neo-conservatives actively arguing for the use of Machiavellian politics or demonstrating contempt for liberal democracy and its institutional forms.[24]

Those who want to claim that the perceived lies and deceptions of the Bush White House in trying to justify the war in Iraq were intentional, and were part and parcel with neo-conservatism, tend to do so by making direct reference to Leo Strauss and his presentation of the Platonic principles of the "noble lie," the exoteric/esoteric distinction, and the use of myths in establishing the polity. The connection seems reasonably plausible: the Bush White House appears to have misled the American people about what it knew about ties between Iraq and Al Qaeda and about Iraq's possession of weapons of mass destruction. Many of the neo-conservatives, inside and outside of the Bush White House, were students of Strauss or of Straussians, or at least influenced by Strauss. And Strauss had called for a revival of Platonic political philosophy with its justification of deception and its critique of democracy. So Strauss seems to provide exactly the interpretive background by which to understand the actions of the Bush White House. This all has a certain plausibility, until one starts to look at what Strauss actually wrote.

Leo Strauss was rightly known for seeking to reawaken the quarrel between the ancients and the moderns. Strauss's position began from a critique of modernity and specifically of modern moral and political thought. The fullest development of modernity, according to Strauss, results in moral relativism and, indeed, moral nihilism. To counter this result, Strauss sought a return to ancient political philosophy, and especially to that of Plato, where, in contrast to relativism or nihilism, there was expressed "an eternal and immutable order within which history takes place."[25] On the face of it, then, Strauss's teaching seems to be a corrective for moral disorder offering a return to stable, external standards.

Strauss was, however, also well known for advocating the exoteric/esoteric distinction: the idea that philosophers present a public or exoteric teaching for ordinary citizens, while at the same time a concealed or esoteric teaching for philosophers or would-be philosophers is also being conveyed. So we cannot stop with our own first impressions. Perhaps there is an esoteric teaching in Strauss. Indeed a number of commentators, especially those who see a pernicious influence of Strauss on the neo-conservatives, argue that Strauss's secret teaching is in fact Nietzschean.[26] Strauss presents a distinction between the philosopher and the citizen that can be seen as a parallel to Nietzsche's distinction between the strong and the weak. The philosopher (which critics of neo-conservatism elide with the Straussian) is seen to rule secretly and without moral compunction, much as Nietzsche envisaged the *Übermensch* would rule creatively over the weak; both Strauss's philosopher and Nietzsche's *Übermensch* are "beyond good and evil," and certainly beyond the principles of equality, freedom, and openness that are central to the liberal democratic order. In this view, all of Strauss's language about reviving moral principles and standards is a cynical contrivance; for morality, religion, and tradition are but the means by which the philosopher shapes the citizens to be pliable to his ends. This same cynical use of morality, patriotism, and religion is seen by critics of the neo-conservatives to underlie the neo-conservative pursuit of the war in Iraq and their wider foreign policy aspirations.

The reading of Strauss as a Nietzschean does have some supporting evidence. In a letter of June 23, 1935 to Karl Löwith, Strauss wrote that between his twenty-second and thirtieth years he "literally believed everything that [he] understood of [Nietzsche]."[27] Yet this only establishes that Strauss's mature position developed out of an intellectual confrontation with Nietzsche. Strauss himself asserted that the possibility of a return to the ancients arises out of the most extreme development of modernity as articulated by Nietzsche. It is out of the crisis of the West that there emerges the possibility of a release from modernity and an apprehension of a principle that is beyond, but forgotten by, modernity. Strauss's account of this path of return in fact parallels the arguments of both Nietzsche and Heidegger. However, in striking contrast to both men, Strauss turned not to the pre-Socratics, but to Plato and Aristotle— the very thinkers Nietzsche and Heidegger charged with creating the metaphysics that produced modern nihilism.[28] Strauss's very different assessment of the ancients had its roots in a different conception of the character of modernity's crisis. For Strauss, the problem of modernity was not captured so much by phrases like "the death of God" or "the forgetting of Being," as by "relativism" or "the rejection of natural right." In other words, Strauss characterized the crisis of modernity as primarily moral and political rather than existential, more about the Good than about Being.

So while Strauss in crucial ways built upon the thought of Nietzsche and Heidegger (and Strauss knew that his own position was a development upon their radicalization of modernity), it is a misreading of Strauss and a failure to grasp his position to align it simply with this radicalization. Indeed, Strauss's position and the motivations for that position become deeply incoherent unless it is distinguished from Nietzsche's or Heidegger's: if Nietzsche opened wide the door of moral nihilism, why stay in the closet and maintain the pretense of a stable morality? It is altogether more plausible to take Strauss at his word when he argued that Nietzsche and Heidegger represented the third and most radical wave of modernity. Far from providing a genuine release from the crisis of the West, in Strauss's eyes, the pair embodied that crisis *in extremis*. Nietzsche and Heidegger failed to escape modernity, according to Strauss, because they failed to grasp its true character and so deepened the crisis. The root of their failure is that their effort to escape modernity continued to assume the basis of modernity. And for Strauss, the basis of modernity is the break with the older understanding of nature and, in particular, the break with what Strauss termed *natural right*. Faced by relativism and the loss of moral standards, Strauss called upon the West to return to the ancients, and above all to Plato, to reawaken our understanding of natural right.

On the face of it, Strauss's return to Plato and to natural right contradicts the claim that Strauss is a Nietzschean. Nietzsche spoke of being beyond good and evil; Strauss placed humanity precisely within the context of a natural order of right or justice. Nietzsche saw Plato as the originator of the moral-metaphysical order from which he demanded we free ourselves; Strauss turned to Plato in order to repudiate the radical historicism propounded by Nietzsche. But this obvious refutation misses the crucial point for those who read Strauss as a closet Nietzschean: what Strauss found in Plato and what he meant by natural right do not contradict, but in fact conform to the teaching of Nietzsche.[29] So if we are to sort out this issue, we need to understand what Strauss meant by *natural right*.

According to Strauss, in the context of antiquity, the great alternative to natural right was *conventionalism*, namely, the notion that the laws that bind us, and the moral principles we use to justify them, have no natural foundation but are rather grounded in human convention. This, according to Strauss, was the standpoint of the pre-Socratic philosophers, the rhetoricians, and above all the sophists. Another way of stating the claim that Strauss is a teacher of deception is to say that he upholds the standpoint of conventionalism, that justice is not ultimately binding (the standpoint given voice by Thrasymachus in Plato's *Republic*).[30] Just as the assertion that Strauss is a Nietzschean is not without some foundation, this too is not entirely a misreading of Strauss's understanding of the ancient account.

For Strauss, natural right is *justice in accord with nature*. This definition follows the discussion of Aristotle, *Nicomachaean Ethics* 1134b–1135a, though the concept derives from Plato (e.g., *Apology* 19a–d).[31] Nature for Strauss involved two connected aspects: 1) nature appears as the standards and types available to natural or pre-philosophical understanding; and 2) nature is the eternal, articulated order of the universe, which can be properly recognized only through philosophy. For Strauss, these two aspects of nature are connected above all in the shift from pre-philosophic opinion to philosophic knowledge. This movement from nature-as-found-in-opinion to nature-as-found-in-knowledge involves the relationship of and distinction between the city (representing an organized human society) and the philosopher.

It can sometimes appear that Strauss placed, on one side, the city given to the fulfillment of its particular needs; and on the other side, the philosopher, free and independent of the city in his self-sufficient knowledge. However, it is precisely in contrast to such a "pre-Socratic" understanding that Strauss presented what he called *classic* natural right.[32] The relation of philosophy to the city transforms both. Strauss saw that philosophy arises within the city through the questioning of tradition. The recognition that there is a plurality of ways of life challenges the traditional, closed, pre-philosophic opinions that govern the life of the city, the unthinking mentality of "We do things this way because we've always done things this way." The philosopher benefits the city: 1) through assuring the city when its traditions have a foundation in nature; and 2) by making it aware of the standards of nature so that it may improve itself.

Just as philosophy benefits the city, so too does the city benefit philosophy, for the city is the condition for the philosophic life. Both philosophy and the city assist in each other's needs, and the philosopher fulfills a role as a citizen as well as his role as a philosopher. Indeed, Strauss argued that in this duality the philosopher comes to appreciate the distinctions among individual human beings and their affairs. This appreciation leads to an awareness of the full heterogeneity within nature, and, above all, of the difference between the human and the divine.[33] Further, the existence of the city allows philosophy to move beyond merely recognizing the fundamental problems, to a knowledge of the actual standards at work in natural right.

So there appears to be a natural symbiosis of philosophy and civic life. According to Strauss, however, while philosophy may wish to give this impression to the city, it is in fact a noble lie (and not all that dissimilar to the famous noble lie about the common origin of the citizenry described in the third book of Plato's *Republic*, 414b–415e). In truth, the way of the philosopher is utterly in contrast to, and destructive of, the way of the citizen. The philosopher leads a life open to the whole of existence; by contrast, the citizen's virtue and nobility depend upon his attachment to the closed world of his city. The citizen requires that the virtues by which he lives are confirmed as natural by the philosopher. The philosopher knows those virtues to be groundless in the sense intended by the citizen.[34] That is to say, what applies to the closed horizons of the city cannot be grounded in the open, universal, natural horizon of the philosopher. The citizen must believe certain things about the world which, while false, are necessary to the very being of the citizen. Strauss sees that deception is thus necessary, but not as simple manipulation by the philosopher for any nefarious or extra-civic purpose; rather, the philosopher "lies" in order to preserve and enhance the life of the citizen, while at the same time safeguarding the place of philosophy.

It is necessary to emphasize that in Strauss's account of the noble lie, the source and purpose of the deception is to preserve both philosophy *and* the city. A lie is not noble if used by rulers for personal or ideological ends. That the structures or virtues necessary to a properly human life within the city are not grounded in metaphysical "ideas" that stand outside the city is not to say that these structures are "not susceptible of rational legitimization."[35] Rather, the very necessity of these virtues for civic life—a necessity exposed in the interaction between the philosopher and the city—provides their rational legitimization. In other words, civic virtues have validity precisely because of their efficacy in preserving social order within the city, and thus preserving philosophy as well. Because these virtues are grounded in the nature of man as a political animal, they apply to the philosopher only insofar as he is a political animal.

In Strauss's account of classical political philosophy, the virtues of the city are necessarily conditional or dependent virtues. Precisely because the city is the necessary premise for civic morality, it is established in a situation lacking civic morality.[36] In other words, in order for human beings to learn how to behave properly when they live together in a society, they first have to form and maintain a society, which they do outside of the internal rules of behavior that make the society work. Thus the founding of the city and its preservation cannot themselves be subject to civic morality.[37] For Strauss, this freedom from civic morality was particularly apparent in the need to defend the city against destruction from both external enemies and internal strife.[38] He does not presuppose a beneficent nature that ensures that good will prevail between cities and across human societies.[39] The limitations of civic morality do not undermine its inherent worth for the citizenry within the city, but they point to a necessary tension between the conditions of civic life, where morality is sometimes lacking, and the purpose of civic life, where morality is a goal.[40]

Alongside these inherent tensions are the contradictions between philosophy and civic morality. The philosopher affirms civic morality as necessary to the city insofar as the continued existence of the city is a necessary condition for the continued existence of philosophy. But at the same time, he would limit civic morality not only because it is problematic for the city in its worldly existence (as it struggles to survive against its enemies), but also because it destroys the freedom of thought necessary to philosophy. In this sense Strauss's philosopher, like Nietzsche's *Übermensch*, is beyond good and evil; his "morality" is strictly provisional to the requirements of philosophy, which is seen as a non- or post-civic activity.[41] The philosopher lives beyond the moral and political imagination, engaged as he is in intellectual enquiry into the permanent problems of the universe that both structure and render questionable that imagination.[42] Yet for Strauss, this rise beyond civic morality on the part of the philosopher was not the appearance of nihilism. Philosophic activity is not simply self-willed. Rather, it is an activity given to the philosopher out of the relation of humanity to nature.[43] The classical philosopher remains within the phenomenology of what is good even as he questions it.

For Strauss, the recognition of philosophy as the only fully complete and fully "natural" activity renders the city and its virtues conditional and problematic.[44] Strauss made this point a number of times by contrasting the "vulgar" or "political" virtue of the city with the "genuine" virtue of the philosopher. It is inherent to the city that its virtues can and must not be simply "natural." The city is closed, built on opinion, and therefore on lies and conventions. It needs the support of myth, poetry, and religion to sustain its claims to authority and legitimacy. It exists in a world that is not without evil and violence and contending claims. It therefore rests on violence and depends, at least in its leaders, on a sense of its continuing vulnerability.

All of this seems to undermine Strauss's claim to found the city on natural right, on a sense of higher ends and excellencies grounded in the very nature of things. But it is important to see that this inescapable element of "unnaturalness" that belongs to every city did not, for Strauss, dissolve the city into sheer conventionalism or Nietzschean constructivism. Strauss argued that Plato exposed two "roots" to virtue: the vulgar, utilitarian root and the genuine, philosophic root (*Phaedo* 68b–69c, 82a–c; *Republic* 500d–e).[45] In truth, civic morality is not reducible to the vulgar root; it shares as well, though incompletely, in the genuine root.

From this genuine root springs a sense of nobility, excellence, striving, and openness to the universe, which fleetingly belongs to the city even as it must return to its necessary focus on its own, particular needs. According to Strauss, it was above all the work of Aristotle (*Nicomachaean Ethics* 1095b, 1177b; *Politics* 1278b) that articulated the inherent truth of the moral virtues, the virtues of the gentleman.[46] While from the viewpoint of the ever-questioning activity of the Platonic philosopher, these Aristotelian moral virtues are inherently problematic, for Strauss, they are, even in their problematic and limited character, grounded in and reflective of nature, and so an aspect of natural right.

Does this mean that Strauss and the neo-conservatives (insofar as they are following him) are not simply being hypocritical and deceptive in invoking moral virtues, a sense of nobility, or a sense of piety? These virtues and sensibilities, according to Strauss, answer to natural wants and needs of the soul, and indeed apply to the philosopher insofar as he is a citizen and moved not only by a love of what is good, but also by a love of his own city and its well-being. Strauss was, however, equally clear that these virtues are limited to the horizon of the city during periods of normalcy. The philosopher must detach himself from his love of his city, and from the "spiritedness" necessary to moral virtue, in order to pursue his fearless quest for the truth. The philosopher must break through the horizon of the city in order to pursue the natural horizon of the permanent problems. Equally, in extreme situations, the city must be able to abandon its virtues for its own sake. Strauss wrote, "In extreme situations the normally valid rules of natural right are justly changed, or changed in accordance with natural right; the exceptions are as just as the rules."[47] This sense of the limited character of the moral virtues can appear to be a justification for all manner of Machiavellian actions. But Strauss addressed this concern directly: "Machiavelli denies natural right, because he takes his bearings by extreme situations . . . and not by the normal situations in which the demands of justice in the strict sense are the highest law."[48]

So Strauss's explanation of natural right as he discovered it in the texts of Plato and Aristotle does not provide a justification for lying or manipulation to avoid electoral defeat. In a democracy, the defeat of one party is hardly an extreme situation. The concepts of natural right and the noble lie do not justify undermining the political order or violating the constitution—except to save that order or constitution. They do not justify the government enriching its friends. They do not justify consciously governing for the sake of one's own interests or those of a part and not for the common good. All these, Strauss would say, the ancients characterized as actions of a corrupt government and ultimately as belonging to tyranny. But more directly relevant to those who see Straussianism in the perceived lying and manipulation in the Bush White House's efforts to draw America into war with Iraq, the doctrine of natural right, as Strauss presented it, does not justify ignoring ordinary moral and political virtues to create the impression of an extreme situation when, in fact, none exists. This seems to be the heart of the issue. If the Bush White House did have to respond to an extreme situation for the United States, then Strauss's account of the ancients would provide principles of justification for necessary measures that are not in accord with normal civic or moral virtue. But in the absence of this condition, such actions are open to condemnation on those very same principles.

There is a further aspect to the claim that Strauss's teaching and influence has, through the neo-conservatives, corroded the constitutional norms of American government. Critics maintain that Strauss was opposed to and even despised modern liberal democracy.[49] Here there is a case to be made. The nub of the case rests in Strauss's account of modernity.

Strauss divided modernity into three stages or "waves." The first wave began with Machiavelli and was crucially modified by Hobbes and Locke to produce the modern doctrine of natural right. Its contemporary correlate is capitalist liberalism, the acquisitive consumer society dedicated to fulfilling human needs.[50] The second wave, initiated by Rousseau, absorbed nature as a standard by taking it into human history, which now served as the source of moral and political guidance.[51] Freed from notions of a natural necessity, this wave produced a more radically utopian—and hence more deeply alienated—form of humanism. Its contemporary correlate is communism.[52] The third wave, which Strauss saw as our contemporary crisis, began with Nietzsche's questioning of the rationality or "humanity" of both history and nature—humanity finds itself in the midst of a terrifying existence, where it is free to create the values by which to live. The contemporary correlate of this wave is fascism.[53]

The three waves by which Strauss defined the historical stages of modernity are, at the same time, all contemporary political standpoints. But while Strauss saw these positions as distinct, they also belong together as a common development. The waves of modernity exposed with increasing explicitness the nihilism at its heart.[54] The assumption that the human will has a positive content is shown to be simply the residue left from antiquity that was inadequately liberated by the preceding waves. The second wave dissolves the assumption of a human nature adumbrated by a fundamental guiding passion, which could form the basis of modern natural right. And for Strauss, the third wave dissolves the assumption of a human right or rational right that came to replace natural right. The third wave brings to light that the sole basis of the will's guidance is its own free activity, beyond both nature and reason.[55]

Strauss was able to support liberal democracy as the best available form of government in the modern world. While still modern, liberal democracy belongs to the first, least radical wave of modernity, and gives space to both virtue and philosophy—the excellence of both the citizen and the philosopher. Strauss argued that modern liberal democracy at a certain level depends on a continuing presence of the residue from antiquity, the premodern moral and religious life within its citizens. And yet because liberal democracy belongs to modernity, it retains a tendency towards reduction and levelling that is destructive of virtue and religion. The inner truth of liberal democracy as revealed in the thought of Hobbes and Locke leads to the dissolution of premodern virtue and piety through the release of the capitalist passions of acquisition and self-preservation.

In particular, Strauss's account of the American foundation and its status as a liberal democracy is obscure, and is contested by Straussians themselves. Some—the so-called "East Coast" Straussians whose most prominent scholars have been Harvey Mansfield (born 1932) of Harvard and Walter Berns (born 1919) of Georgetown—argue that the United States is best understood as fully a part of the first wave of modernity and inherently Lockean, and that what residual aspects of pre-modern virtue remain will tragically be dissolved over time. Others, such as the "West Coast" Straussians under the leadership of Harry Jaffa (born 1918) of the Claremont Institute in Southern California, argue that the United States has always been inherently both ancient and modern and in a form that properly reinforces the two sides. But by either account, "liberalism" defined as the socializing, equalizing tendency of modern American life, is a corruption to be contested through awakening in Americans (especially through the work of a liberal arts education) a connection to the ancients and religion, and thereby to a sense of human excellence and elevated moral purpose. So for Strauss (and by and large for the neo-conservatives), America has consisted of two opposing tendencies: a modernist tendency that would level social differences and lead naturally to a more and more radicalized modernity, and a premodern tendency that in most Americans is represented as a residual attachment to religion.

This mixed view of the nature of the United States reveals the ambivalence of the Straussians and neo-conservatives toward American life. They are compelled to be simultaneously postmodern, fully cognizant of the nihilistic character of advanced modernity; and premodern, seeking to affirm an earlier relation to nature that is ignorant of liberalism's thrall and pre-dates modern nihilism. Irving Kristol's recounting of the neo-conservative relation to religion displays a similar tension. According to Kristol, many neo-conservatives (Kristol included) were not believers or practitioners of their religion, but recognized in the face of the emptiness of modern liberalism the need for the very religion they knew themselves liberated from. The solution is that neo-conservatives educate their children to believe in a religion they do not necessarily believe in themselves.[56]

For Strauss, there was something deeply ambiguous and vulnerable about American liberal democracy. Its institutions simultaneously make room for and depend upon an older sense of the liberal or aristocratic soul, and yet those self-same institutions have within them tendencies that would undermine the inequalities necessary to standards of excellence and of virtues.[57] By contrast, the neo-conservatives, especially in the last two decades, have a much less fragile sense, indeed a confidence, that American liberal democracy will not only retain, but indeed cultivate and develop a sense of the pre-modern moral personality. The neo-conservatives of the 1960s and 1970s wrote about the cultural contradictions of capitalism in a spirit similar to Strauss, but more recently, as Tod Lindberg has noted, this sense of vulnerability about the moral dimension of the American economic system has been dropped.[58] Among the neo-conservatives one finds a confidence and optimism about the United States that is lacking in Strauss. They assert that Americans can and must be both ancient and modern, as well as able to affirm simultaneously aspects that for Strauss were fundamentally opposed: religion and secularity, virtue and freedom. This confidence underlies the most notable area of distinction between Leo Strauss's teaching and the viewpoint of second generation neo-conservatives: foreign policy.

Certainly there are general aspects of Strauss's position, especially the notion of "regime" (Strauss's preferred translation of the Greek word *politeia*) and the use of moral categories to characterize and understand the action of "regimes," that neo-conservatives have explicitly adopted from Strauss.[59] I do not know whether Strauss can be credited as the source for the use of the term *regime* of the now famous phrase *regime change*, but clearly this aspect of Strauss's thought has been important to the neo-conservative way of understanding the political world. But, although they share some assumptions, Strauss and the neo-conservatives come to opposite conclusions. Strauss's own statements about foreign affairs are singularly critical of idealistic or imperialist foreign policy.

Strauss viewed the primary aim and purpose of any regime to be excellence: all regimes "look up" to something, as he put it. The regime informs the whole life of a city, and so determines the city's fundamental character and essence. Strauss viewed the tendency of political theorists to downplay the formative role of the regime in setting a city or state's character as a failing of modernity. Hobbes, for instance, was fundamentally indifferent to the type of regime in place in any given state. The ancient concentration on the internal excellence of the city meant that for

Strauss, foreign policy was only an external and derivative concern. So in a discussion of the fourth book of Plato's *Republic*, Strauss states:

> [T]he good city is [not] guided in its relations to other cities, Greek or barbarian, by considerations of justice: the size of the territory of the good city is determined by that city's own moderate needs and by nothing else; the relation of the city to the other cities belongs to the province of wisdom rather than of justice; the good city is not a part of a community of cities or is not dedicated to the common good of that community or does not serve other cities.[60]

There are two aspects of this quotation that need to be noted: 1) Strauss rejected a central role to foreign affairs in defining the city, and, in particular, rejected the subordination of the city to an international league of nations; 2) equally, he rejected imperialism. Let us discuss these points in turn.

Strauss's skepticism about, and indeed opposition to, the notion of a community of nations may well have influenced, or at least supported, similar tendencies in the neo-conservatives and the Bush White House. Strauss's essential argument here was developed in his introduction to *The City and Man*. In that work Strauss was writing in the context of the Cold War, though no doubt the experience of the failure of the League of Nations also provided an important background. But most fundamentally, he responded to what he saw as an international liberalism at work in the notion of a community of nations or an international law binding on all parties irrespective of their type of regime or intentions. At the heart of the Kantian vision of a community of nations moving to a "perpetual peace," Strauss saw two kinds of untruth: a denial of the ineradicable character of evil, and a denial of the regime as the space and context of civic loyalty and authority.

Strauss wrote in *The City and Man*: "[N]o bloody or unbloody change of society can eradicate the evil in man."[61] This claim has implications not only for the internal requirements of any regime, but also for international relations. The ineradicable presence of evil in international affairs means not only the ineradicable need to be wary of other regimes, but also that there will inevitably be worse and better regimes. For Strauss, the concept of a legal equality and legitimacy of all nations that belong to the "international community" is a "pious fraud."[62] The idea that a body like the United Nations could have overriding moral authority, or that international law has binding legitimacy, can for Strauss be necessary, and even useful, pieties, but they should not actually be believed or assumed. Behind the claim of an international law or a "community" of nations, Strauss detected a progressive, secular humanism fully implicated in modernity and its break with nature.

The most compelling exponent of this viewpoint for Strauss was his friend Alexandre Kojève, who argued on the basis of an interpretation of Hegel that the end point of history is the Universal and Homogeneous State (UHS). Strauss, however, argued that the truth of the UHS is not freedom and the fulfillment of humanity, but necessarily a tyranny that must eradicate all the intimations of a nature related to human excellence. He believed the international system, insofar as it is grounded in the ideal of the UHS, is not in accord with natural right, but rather presupposes the replacement of natural right by ideology. Following his interpretation of the classics and especially Plato (*Republic* 423a–c, 470c–471c), Strauss reckoned foreign affairs to be essentially amoral.[63] What provides limit and order is not an overriding principle of international law or a presumed community of nations but the internal character of nations, their regime.

He wrote in the face of the intransigent divide of the Cold War:

> All this amounts to saying that for the foreseeable future, political society remains what it always has been: a partial society whose most urgent and primary task is its self-preservation and whose highest task is its self-improvement.[64]

His problem with the concept of international law and a community of nations (in contrast to alliances) was that this subordinates the regime and its self-improvement to a spurious ideal that implicitly points to the dissolution of all regimes into the UHS. So George W. Bush, if he had needed it, could certainly have found support for his "unilateralism" in Strauss. Strauss would have concurred that international agreements tend to bind only the good and lawful nations and leave the evil all the freer to act. International laws and institutions may have some usefulness, but natural right would disallow any subordination to the international system that inhibited a regime's pursuit of its self-improvement or self-preservation. None of this, of course, prevents alliances or international agreements, but it does require the recognition that these must all be, in the end, provisional upon the well-being of the regime.

According to Strauss, the implication of this seeming amoralism and realism was not a defense of expansionism and imperialism (except where strictly necessary). Rather, he drew upon both Plato and Thucydides in his recognition that imperialist, expansionist foreign policy tends to undermine the moral and political order at home. The Straussian byword in politics, both domestic and international, is moderation. Thomas West, a former student of Strauss, remarks:

> We may sum up the Socratic approach by saying that although foreign policy is in principle amoral, because it is dictated by the self-

ish needs of the political community, it is also moderate, because the needs of the city are limited, given the primacy of its concern for civic virtue and therefore domestic policy.[65]

The good city is not a danger to its neighbors, as its end is not wealth and power, but virtue. The instability and danger in foreign policy has its root in corrupt regimes. So the source of international peace is achieved less through international institutions and laws (though these may have their uses) than through the presence of good regimes.

This is where Strauss parts company with the neo-conservatives. For Strauss, the great example of democratic folly in international affairs was the Sicilian expedition that Athens undertook in the disastrous Peloponnesian War and that was promoted by Socrates' most extravagant and politically effective student, Alcibiades.[66] It is not clear that there is an Alcibiades among the neo-conservatives that have joined the Bush White House, but the extravagant and idealist language of "hegemony" and "empire" seems to provide a strange parallel between some of Strauss's students and this particular student of Socrates. Behind the neo-conservatives' language of "benevolent hegemony" and bringing democracy to the world is not only the example of figures such as Woodrow Wilson and Theodore Roosevelt, but also Kojève's ideal of a Universal Homogeneous State.[67] Strauss's critique in *The City and Man* of the liberal idealism of his day seems, with some small modification, equally applicable to the neo-conservative agenda:

> The movement toward the universal society or the universal state was thought to be guaranteed not only by the rationality, the universal validity, of the goal but also because the movement of the large majority of men on behalf of the large majority of men: only small groups of men who, however, hold in thrall many millions of their fellow human beings and who defend their own antiquated interests, resist that movement.[68]

The only modification needed to what Strauss says about liberalism in order to make it apply to the neo-conservatives is that the "movement" of history, which for liberals was inevitable, requires, according to the neo-conservatives, a bit of a shove by American power. The neo-conservatives point to the need for the UHS to be actively willed.

So while Strauss may well be a crucial source for the neo-conservatives in their move to a post-liberal analysis of foreign policy involving a release from the moral demands of international law, nonetheless a liberal idealism re-emerges relative to the ends their post-liberal means are intended to pursue.[69] There are, of course, those who have questioned the benevolence in the "benevolent hegemony" recommended by

William Kristol and Robert Kagan, or have doubted the claim that the goal was ever to bring "democracy" rather than just American control to the Middle East. But, of course, even if the ends are more real than ideal, it is the imperialism itself that Strauss would criticize as destructive of the American regime. But this point about the material interests in the Middle East to the United States as a capitalist-consumerist society also reconnects us to a point of distinction made earlier. Strauss remained deeply apprehensive of the acquisitive passion of the United States as a modern regime. The neo-conservative confidence that capitalist-consumerism need not be destructive, and indeed may be positively supportive of virtue and the well-being of the American regime, parallels their similar confidence in the positive effects of a new idealistic imperial American foreign policy.

One can say that Strauss's critique of modernity, and revival of what he took to be the standpoint of Plato and antiquity generally, provided a crucial background for neo-conservatism. Students brought up in the age of ascendant liberalism, who came to Strauss or to one of his many students, would have found in their teaching a release from liberal moralism and idealism. This is the Nietzschean moment of revolt against secular humanism. But together with this release—embodied in the philosopher's break from the city—they would equally have discovered a retraction of this release in the name of nature and of natural right. It is this retraction of Nietzschean will in the face of an always already existing natural teleology that returns these students back to political life—but from a standpoint of already having transcended it. For Strauss these two moments must be carefully kept apart: the philosopher may be given to divine madness in his philosophizing, but remains moderate and promotes moderation in political life. The spirit of an Alcibiades is of one who has sought to tear down the sacred veil that separates philosophic immoderation and practical moderation.

It is impossible to say whether Strauss would have recommended the war in Iraq, what he would have made of a unipolar world, or what he would have seen as the appropriate response to 9/11. But what one can say is that in the neo-conservative rationale for the war in Iraq that emanated from within the administration of George W. Bush, Strauss may well have detected more the spirit of Alcibiades than of Socrates.

Afterword

—Michael Meckler

In 1997, Garry Wills wrote an essay for the *The New York Times Sunday Magazine* suggesting that classical antiquity was undergoing a revival of interest and relevance in the United States as the twentieth century drew to a close. Contemporary social and political issues—such as the nature of imperialism, the tension between dominant and minority cultures, the role of warfare in a democracy, and the growing prominence of homosexuality—are posing precisely the sort of questions that the ancients are well equipped to answer. Wills argued against a transcendent classicism that enables moderns to join themselves to a timeless antiquity. Instead, he claimed that revivals are more about turning the ancients into moderns than the other way around. "The classics are not some sort of magic wand that touches and transmutes us," Wills wrote. "We revive them only when we rethink them as a way of rethinking ourselves."[1]

Wills placed great emphasis on the role of translation in classics revivals. He claimed that the incipient revival he recognized taking place would be independent of any changes in the teaching of ancient languages. Nonetheless, he suggested that greater interest in learning ancient Greek and Latin was emerging among Americans.

Although accurate data are hard to come by, it appears that the study of Latin in American secondary schools has continued a steady, though not spectacular rise since falling to its nadir in the late 1970s. Enrollments have grown by more than twenty-five percent in the last quarter century to exceed 200,000 students, despite a demographic decline in the total number of Americans of high school age. The number of students taking national, standardized tests in Latin and classical mythology has skyrocketed, as has membership in the National Junior Classical League, suggesting that the connections being fashioned between American teenagers and classical antiquity are becoming stronger.[2]

Certainly popular culture over the past decade has reflected greater awareness of the ancient Greeks and Romans. A sidebar to Wills's essay mentioned classically themed books, museum exhibits, and film and television programs of the mid 1990s (such as the syndicated television series *Xena: Warrior Princess*, and the animated Disney movie *Hercules*), but popular interest in antiquity has blossomed even further since, and in a wide variety of media.[3] In 1998, Dark Horse Comics released a five-issue series by Frank Miller and Lynn Varley titled *300*. The comic books related the story of the Battle of Thermopylae involving the Spartans and the Persians in 480 B.C., and the popularity of the comic books led to the series being reissued the following year as a graphic novel in a hardcover binding. The military exploits of the ancient Greeks have served as the inspiration for the best-selling novels of Stephen Pressfield. The motion picture *Gladiator* (nominally about the reign of the Roman emperor Commodus) was released in 2000 to both commercial and critical acclaim, garnering five Academy Awards including Best Picture and Best Actor for star Russell Crowe. Two of the most popular movies of 2004 were set in antiquity: *Troy* (a rather free retelling of Homer's *Iliad*) and *The Passion of the Christ* (a retelling of the gospels). For 2005, both the broadcast television network ABC (with the program *Empire*) and the cable subscription channel HBO (with *Rome*) prepared limited-run series set in the final, tumultuous years of the Roman Republic. Even the children's cartoon *The Grim Adventures of Billy and Mandy* (broadcast on cable television's Cartoon Network) contains the recurring character of Eris, the Greek goddess who was the personification of conflict and strife. In the cartoon, Eris is regularly depicted wearing a chiton (modified into a sort of white tank-top and skirt) and holding an apple—an allusion to the apple that, in classical mythology, she provided as the prize for the Judgment of Paris.

In the political sphere, classical antiquity has gained greater attention and interest through the well-publicized efforts of the neo-conservatives, whose devotion to the ancients verges on the fetishistic. Creators of conservative Weblogs and their visitors regularly employ classical-sounding nicknames to reveal their ideology while masking their true identities.[4]

Furthermore, the national prominence among conservatives of the ancient historians Donald Kagan and Victor Davis Hanson has served to cement a popular conception that the ancients are more often invoked by the Right than by the Left.

Yet those on the Left are often equally eager to claim the ancients as their own. *The New York Times Sunday Magazine* essay by Garry Wills was just such an attempt, in which he praised the Greeks and Romans for being "multicultural." Classics professor Page DuBois of the University of California, San Diego, has made even more extensive use of the ancients in her opposition to American conservatives and in support of liberal and progressive politics.[5] At the 2005 annual meeting of the American Philological Association in Boston, a panel discussion on "Can Public Intellectuals Think? Classics and the Public Sphere" drew a large crowd and spirited discussion that involved not only academic classicists but also public intellectuals such as Daniel Mendelsohn (on the panel) and Cornell West (in the audience).[6]

This renewed enthusiasm for classical antiquity in the early years of the twenty-first century is hardly monolithic. Then again, throughout American history, promoters of the political usefulness of the ancient Greeks and Romans have had various reasons for their devotion. Some have seen timeless truths in ancient texts. Others claim that the particularities of Greek and Roman society provide the necessary distance for allowing the ideas of the ancients to be viewed as alternatives to our own culturally bound policymaking. Some have interpreted classical political theory as canonically depicting three types of government (by a single ruler, by the few, and by the many), the ebb and flow of these types pointing to some degree of mixture as providing the best stability. Others have pointed out the wide differences in ancient forms of government, and that the Greeks and Romans themselves were aware of the shortcomings of their own political theory. Some have viewed the modern world as the heir and successor of classical antiquity. Others have argued for an inseparable gulf between the present and the distant past, between modernity and antiquity.

What has united the viewpoints of all those political observers in the United States who, for more than two and a quarter centuries, have promoted increased attention to classical antiquity, is the unmatched eloquence of the ancients in describing the trials and tribulations when human beings live together in organized groups. From Homer's depiction of the city at peace and the city at war on the Shield of Achilles in book 18 of the *Iliad*, to Augustine's contrast of the heavenly city and the earthly city in the *City of God*, the Greeks and Romans spoke about how communities should operate and be organized, and the conflicts that inevitably emerge between the individual and society. Regardless of whether we view the ancients as our kinsmen, or as utterly alien to our contemporary understanding of the world, we cannot but wonder at the studiousness with which they grappled with the problems that plagued the organization and operation of their own societies. Even when we are philosophically opposed to the solutions they devised (such as slavery, aristocracy, or civic cult), we learn something from examining how they justified these aspects of their polities, even if merely by negative example.

The "conflict between ancients and moderns" may well be overblown and a distortion of contemporary political discourse, yet it is certainly no cliché to connect the study of classical antiquity with the promotion of values in civic life.[7] Classical education is first and foremost values education. Page DuBois and Victor Davis Hanson will come to quite different conclusions over what those values may be, but both will aver that values are at the core of any meaningful study of antiquity. In this regard, the demand that the primary purpose of American education be the imparting of technical knowledge—whether the subject matter involves agriculture and machinery, or mathematics and engineering, or computer science and biochemistry—seems a dated, twentieth-century conceit. Knowing how to operate a cash register does not prevent an individual from stealing from the till. Without a focus upon the moral dimension of research and policymaking, education that is strictly technical leads to a society that employs its technological know-how for violent, destructive, and immoral ends.

Study of the ancients provides a bulwark against the mindless drifting of political activities and institutions into unrecognizable and uncontrollable forms. When in 1993 Senator Robert C. Byrd of West Virginia, worried about the growth in executive power inherent in the line-item veto, elocuted his lectures on the history of the Roman senate, some pundits found his obsession with the fall of the Roman Republic to represent a quaint, antiquarian notion of the sort of lessons to be drawn from classical antiquity. After all, the fall of the Roman Republic was a topic that had generally lost much of its popular and scholarly appeal during the second half of the twentieth century.[8] Yet Byrd was not merely tapping into an earlier obsession that the Founders had with the fall of the Republic.

The Founders were acutely aware of the fragility of constitutions and their susceptibility to decay. The tinkering with Roman constitutional norms in the course of the late second and throughout the first century B.C. found parallels in English constitutional history during the tumultuous seventeenth and eighteenth centuries. In establishing the new nation of the United States of America, the Founders feared that changes in the balance of constitutionally established authority, whether between the federal government and the states, or within the separate branches of the federal government, could likewise send the nation spinning headlong into the sort of crisis that finished the Roman Republic. Although the line-item veto seemed a fairly benign corrective to the uncontrolled spending of a profligate Congress, Byrd saw the tinkering with constitutional norms as having the potential to cripple permanently a Congress already having to deal with an increasingly powerful executive.

Now more than a decade later, the dynamics of American government after 9/11 present even greater tendencies towards the concentration of power in the federal government, especially in the executive branch. Although the final decades of the Roman Republic were disfigured by civil war and violence, the question of whether the tendencies toward concentration of power were already forming in the second century B.C. has again become particularly relevant. As the twenty-first century moves forward, the obsessions of the Founders with trying to understand the circumstances of the fall of the Roman Republic may once again become our own.

Notes

Introduction

1. Lester J. Cappon, ed., *The Adams-Jefferson Letters*, 2 vols. (Chapel Hill: University of North Carolina Press, 1959), 2:549.

2. Cappon, *Adams-Jefferson Letters*, 2:551.

3. Juvenal 6.293.

4. Cf. Paul A. Rahe, *Republics Ancient and Modern*, 3 vols. (Chapel Hill: University of North Carolina Press, 1994), 3:201–3.

5. E.g., Bernard Bailyn, *The Ideological Origins of the American Revolution* (Cambridge, Mass.: Harvard University Press/Belknap Press, 1967), 22–26.

6. These essays were collected to form Reinhold's book *Classica Americana* (Detroit: Wayne State University Press, 1984).

7. See, among others, Carl J. Richard, *The Founders and the Classics* (Cambridge, Mass.: Harvard University Press, 1994); Caroline Winterer, *The Culture of Classicism: Ancient Greece and Rome in American Intellectual Life, 1780–1910* (Baltimore: Johns Hopkins University Press, 2002); Rahe, *Republics.*

8. Elaine K. Swift, *The Making of an American Senate* (Ann Arbor: University of Michigan Press, 1996).

9. Charles A. Kromkowski, *Recreating the American Republic* (Cambridge: Cambridge University Press, 2002).

10.   The tension between biblical and classical influences on American thought in this period is discussed by John C. Shields, *The American Aeneas* (Knoxville: University of Tennessee Press, 2001).

11.   Cappon, *Adams-Jefferson Letters*, 2:335; cf. Richard, *Founders*, 83.

12.   Lee T. Pearcy, *The Grammar of Our Civility: Classical Education in America* (Waco, Tex.: Baylor University Press, 2005).

13.   I. F. Stone, *The Trial of Socrates* (Boston: Little, Brown, 1988). The book, which spent nine weeks on *The New York Times* bestseller list for non-fiction, was not reviewed in either *Classical Philology* or the *American Journal of Philology*, the two most important professional classics journals in the United States. For a review by an academic classicist that dealt as much with Stone's career as a journalist as it did with his view of Socrates, see Donald Kagan's comments in *Commentary* 85.3 (1988): 72–77.

14.   Cf. Sara Rappe's review of Mark L. McPheran, *The Religion of Socrates* (University Park: Pennsylvania State University Press, 1996), in *Classical Philology* 94 (1999): 99–103, esp. 101.

15.   *Congressional Record*, 107th Cong., 1st Sess., 2001, vol. 147, S. 7557–58.

16.   See the essay in this volume by Robert F. Maddox.

17.   John Finnis, " 'Shameless Acts' in Colorado: Abuse of Scholarship in Constitutional Cases," *Academic Questions* 7.4 (1994): 10–41; Martha Nussbaum, "Platonic Love and Colorado Law: The Relevance of Ancient Greek Norms to Modern Sexual Controversies," *Virginia Law Review* 80 (1994): 1515–1651; cf. Daniel A. Farber, "Adjudication of Things Past: Reflections on History as Evidence," *Hastings Law Journal* 49 (1998): 1009–38, esp.1013–15. In 1996, the United States Supreme Court, in *Romer v. Evans*, upheld lower court rulings finding the Colorado amendment unconstitutional.

18.   Lawrence W. Reed, "Are We Going the Way of Rome?" (pamphlet published by the Mackinac Center, Midland, Michigan, 1994, based on a lecture originally given in 1979); Bruce Bartlett, "How Excessive Government Killed Ancient Rome," *Cato Journal* 14.2 (1994): 287–306; Richard J. Maybury, *Ancient Rome: How It Affects You Today* (Placerville, Calif.: Bluestocking Press, 1995).

19.   Martin Bernal, *Black Athena: the Afroasiatic Roots of Classical Civilization*, vol. 1 (New Brunswick, N.J.: Rutgers University Press, 1987); Shelley Haley, "Black Feminist Thought and Classics: Re-membering, Re-claiming, Re-empowering," in *Feminist Theory and the Classics*, edited by Nancy Sorkin Rabinowitz and Amy Richlin (New York: Routledge, 1993), 23–43.

20.   Victor Davis Hanson, *The Wars of the Ancient Greeks and Their Invention of Western Military Culture* (London: Cassell, 1999); idem, *The Soul of Battle* (New York: Free Press, 1999).

21.   See George A. Kennedy, "Afterword: An Essay on Classics in America since the Yale Report," in Reinhold, *Classica Americana*, 325–51; Pearcy, *Grammar of Civility*, 43–83.

22.   On Everett and Felton, see the essay in this volume by Caroline Winterer. On Hoar, see my essay in this volume.

23.   On Westermann, see the essay in this volume by John Milton Cooper, Jr. On Reinhold and Lewis, see the essay by Daniel P. Tompkins. Features of Donald Kagan's Cold War interpretation of Thucydides are discussed in Lawrence Tritle's essay, while Neil G. Robertson's essay examines Leo Strauss. See also Donald Alexander Downs, *Cornell '69: Liberalism and the Crisis of the American University* (Ithaca: Cornell University Press, 1999); Bruce Fellman, "Lion in Winter," *Yale Alumni Magazine* (April 2002): 44–47.

24.   Virgil, *Aeneid* 8.337–69.

Chapter 1

1.   Andrew A. Lipscomb, ed., *The Writings of Thomas Jefferson,* 20 vols. (Washington: Thomas Jefferson Memorial Association, 1903–1905), 18:255.

2.   See Douglas L. Wilson, "Jefferson and the Republic of Letters," in *Jeffersonian Legacies*, edited by Peter Onuf (Charlottesville: University of Virginia Press, 1993), 50–76, esp. 53–56, for a brief summary on the composition and printing of Jefferson's *Notes on the State of Virginia.*

3.   Merrill D. Peterson, ed., *The Portable Thomas Jefferson* (New York: Viking Press, 1979), 197.

4.   Peterson, *Portable Jefferson*, 198; Lipscomb, *Writings of Thomas Jefferson*, 2:206–7.

5.   Richard, *Founders*, 12–38.

6.   See James Michael Farrell, Jr., "John Adams and the Ciceronian Paradigm" (diss., University of Wisconsin, 1988).

7.   Letter of John Adams to John Quincy Adams, March 17, 1780: "As to Geography, Geometry and Fractions I hope your Master will not insist upon your spending much Time upon them at present; because altho they are Useful sciences, and altho all Branches of the Mathematicks, will I hope, sometime or other engage your Attention, as the most profitable and the most satisfactory of all human Knowledge; Yet my Wish at present is that your principal Attention should be directed to the Latin and Greek Tongues, leaving the other studies to be hereafter attained, in your Country"; letter of John Adams to Pechigny (the schoolmaster), May 16, 1780: "I will take this upon myself, and further I would not have them put any longer to the Master of Fencing and Dancing—let them attend the Drawing and Writing Masters, and bend all the rest of their Time and attention, to Latin, Greek, and French, which will be more useful and necessary for them in their own Country, where they are to spend their Lives." See *Adams Family Correspondence*, vol. 3 (1973), *April 1778–September 1780*, edited by L. H Butterfield and Marc Friedlaender (Cambridge, Mass.: Harvard University Press/Belknap Press, 1963–), 308, 348. For the life, education, and career of John Quincy Adams, see Paul C. Nagel, *John Quincy Adams: A Public Life, A Private Life* (New York: Knopf, 1997).

8.   See Jefferson's comments in a January 27, 1800, letter to the scientist Joseph Priestly, in Lipscomb, *Writings of Jefferson*, 10:146–47; see also Adrienne Koch and William Peden, eds., *The Life and Selected Writings*

of Thomas Jefferson (New York: The Modern Library, 1944), 554. On the classics as "useful knowledge," see Reinhold, *Classica Americana*, 50–93.

9.   Kemp P. Battle, *History of the University of North Carolina*, vol. 1 (Raleigh: Edwards & Broughton, 1907); F. N. Boney, *A Pictoral History of the University of Georgia*, 2nd ed. (Athens: University of Georgia Press, 2000); Roy J. Honeywell, *The Educational Work of Thomas Jefferson* (Cambridge, Mass.: Harvard University Press, 1931).

10.   L. H. Butterfield, *Letters of Benjamin Rush*, vol. 1, Memoirs of the American Philosophical Society 30.1 (Philadelphia: American Philosophical Society, 1951), 517–18; Reinhold, *Classica Americana*, 116–41. For a sampling of the religious, cultural, and social attacks on the classical heritage from the period immediately following the Revolutionary War through the Jacksonian era, see Edwin Miles, "The Young American Nation and the Classical World," *Journal of the History of Ideas* 35 (1974): 259–74.

11.   Reinhold, *Classica Americana*, 124, 131.

12.   See Koch and Peden, *Life and Selected Writings of Jefferson*, 4; brackets are mine. For Jefferson's views on education, books, and the classical world, see Merrill D. Peterson, ed., *Thomas Jefferson: A Reference Biography* (New York: Scribner, 1986), 135–79, 233–51.

13.   Samuel Eliot Morison, *The Founding of Harvard College* (Cambridge, Mass.: Harvard University Press, 1935; repr. 1968), 333, 433.

14.   Pauline Holmes, *A Tercentenary History of the Boston Public Latin School 1635–1935* (Cambridge, Mass.: Harvard University Press, 1935), 260–62; cp. Samuel Eliot Morison, *Three Centuries of Harvard, 1636–1936* (Cambridge, Mass.: Harvard University Press, 1937), 103.

15.   Edwin Oviatt, *The Beginnings of Yale, 1701–1726* (New Haven: Yale University Press, 1916), 199. It was not until 1745 that the trustees of Yale changed any of the original entrance requirements. Then they stated that applicants, in addition to their knowledge of Greek and Latin, should also understand the rules of "Common Arithmetick." See Richard Warch, *School of the Prophets: Yale College, 1701–1740* (New Haven: Yale University Press, 1973), 186–88.

16.   Thomas Jefferson Wertenbaker, *Princeton, 1746–1896* (Princeton: Princeton University Press, 1946), 91–92.

17.   For a description of the 1705, 1859, and 1862 fires that, to varying degrees, ravaged the records and the main building of the College of William and Mary, see Marcus Whiffen, *The Public Buildings of Williamsburg* (Williamsburg: Colonial Williamsburg Foundation, 1958), 23–24, 188–98. Also, for some indication of the social and educational environment which Thomas Jefferson experienced while a student at William and Mary, see A. J. Mapp, Jr., "Young Thomas Jefferson at William and Mary," *William & Mary Alumni Magazine* 55 (1988): 10–15; J. A. C. Chandler, "Jefferson and William and Mary," *William and Mary Quarterly*, 2nd ser. 14 (1934): 304–7.

18.   In time, the Greek requirement was leniently interpreted, as the entry for the May 11, 1803, faculty meeting at the College of New Jersey attests: "Mr. George Harston was likewise admitted to study with the sophomore class, without being considered as a candidate for a

diploma, unless he acquires a competent knowledge of the Greek language, with which he is totally unacquainted," Princeton University Archives, Faculty Minutes 1787–1810. In the late eighteenth century, especially under the presidency of John Witherspoon (1768–1794), exceptions to thorough preparation for admission to the College of New Jersey were very rare, as Alexander Hamilton discovered when his request for admission with advanced standing was denied; see Ron Chernow, *Alexander Hamilton* (New York: Penguin Press, 2004), 42–49.

19.   Louis Franklin Snow, *The College Curriculum in the United States* (New York: Teachers College, Columbia University, 1907), 93.

20.   For a reproduction and discussion of Williams' text, see Holmes, *Tercentenary*, 258–61. See also K. B. Murdock, "The Teaching of Latin and Greek at the Boston Latin School in 1712," *Publications of the Colonial Society of Massachusetts* 27 (1932): 21–29; John Rexine, "The Boston Latin School Curriculum in the Seventeenth and Eighteenth Centuries: A Bicentennial Review," *Classical Journal* 72 (1976): 261–66; and Robert Francis Seybolt, *The Public Schools of Colonial Boston, 1635–1775* (Cambridge, Mass.: Harvard University Press, 1935; repr. New York: Arno Press, 1969), 69–71.

21.   In the early eighteenth century there were available several "accidences" (grammar books), of which the two most popular were William Lily's *Latin Grammar*, first published in England in 1509, and its American counterpart, *Cheever's Accidence*, first formally published in Boston in 1709. Many "nomenclators" (dictionaries) were also available at this time. J. A. Comenius's *Orbis Sensualium Pictus*, first published in Nuremberg in 1658 (and appearing with an English translation by Charles Hoole in a first London edition the following year), was, perhaps, the most popular because of its many illustrations. Leonhard Culmann's *Sententiae Pueriles* (an elementary Latin text containing collections of moral maxims) was first published in Nuremberg in 1540; an English edition was prepared by John Brinsley and first published in London in 1612. "Cato" refers to the *Catonis Disticha de Moribus* (a collection from late antiquity of moral sayings, primarily in simple poems) based upon the sixteenth-century edition by J. J. Scaliger; in circulation were many editions of Aesop and of the introductory Latin textbook of Mathurin Cordier (1479–1564; whose name was rendered in Latin as "Corderius") including the very popular one (with English translation) by John Clarke, *Corderii Colloquiorum Centuria Selecta*, first published in London in 1718. All brackets explaining the abbreviations in Williams's text are mine. The parentheses are part of the original text.

22.   None of the examples "on backside A" mentioned by Williams have survived. The most commonly studied essays of Erasmus were his *Colloquia Familiaria, De Copia Verborum*, and his *Adagia*, for each of which there were many editions in circulation. *Propr: As in pres.*: refers to William Lily's *Propria quae maribus, Quae genus, As in praesenti, Syntaxis, Qui mihi construed*, a series of short essays which were frequently attached to Lily's *Latin Grammar*. J. Garretson, *English exercises for school-boys to translate into Latin, comprizing all the rules of grammar, and other necessary observations; ascending gradually from the meanest to higher capacities*, was first published in London in 1683.

23.   Florus in the early second century A.D. wrote *Epitome Bellorum Omnium Annorum DCC*; it is a history of Rome in abbreviated form.

24.   Justin's *Historia* was written in the third century A.D. Thomas Godwin's *Romanae historiae Anthologiae*. An English exposition of the *Romane antiquities wherein many Romane and Englishe offices are parallelled and divers obscure phrases explained*, was first published in London in 1658. William Walker, *Treatise of English Particles, showing much of the variety of their significations and uses in English, and how to render them into Latine according to the propriety and elegancy of that language. With a praxis on the same* was first published in London in 1655.

25.   See, for example, Worthington C. Ford, *The Boston Book Market, 1679–1700* (Boston: The Club of Odd Volumes, 1917).

26.   For the complete English text of Mather's *Corderius Americanus*, see Wilson Smith, ed., *Theories of Education in Early America, 1655–1819* (Indianapolis: Bobbs-Merrill, 1973), 32–38. Mather's original eulogy concluded with nearly forty additional lines of Latin verse.

27.   Smith, *Theories of Education*, 36.

28.   Marcus Boas, *Die Epistola Catonis,* Verhandelingen der Koninklijke Akademie van Wetenschappen n.s., 33.1 (Amsterdam: Noord-Hollandsche Uitgevers-Maatschappij, 1934), 41.

29.   Edwin L. Wolf, "Classical Languages in Philadelphia," in *Classical Traditions in Early America*, edited by John W. Eadie (Ann Arbor: University of Michigan Press, 1976), 68–69; Snow, *College Curriculum*, 129–34.

30.   Holmes, *Tercentenary*, 275–76.

31.   It should be noted that *English* educational influence dominated in New England and the South, while *Scottish* influence was greatest in the middle colonies of New Jersey and Pennsylvania. The sixteenth-century English background of the classical curriculum of early American education is splendidly described in T. W. Baldwin's two-volume work, *William Shakspere's Small Latine & Lesse Greeke* (Urbana: University of Illinois Press, 1944). See also, Courtland Canby, "A Note on the Influence of Oxford University upon William and Mary College in the Eighteenth Century," *William and Mary Quarterly*, 2nd ser. 21 (1941): 243–47. The reduplication of the English educational scheme was so rigid that Lyon C. Tyler, *The College of William and Mary in Virginia: Its History and Work, 1693–1907* (Richmond: Whittet & Shepperson, 1907), 26, stated the grammar school students in early eighteenth-century Virginia "studied the same books as were by law and custom used in England, but the master was permitted, with the president's consent to make criticisms on the grammar employed."

32.   An example of a mid-eighteenth-century Latin regulation for students at Yale College can be found in Walter C. Bronson, *The History of Brown University, 1764–1914* (Providence: The University, 1914), 112–13; the regulation forbade a student to drink tea with others outside of his own chamber room, at the penalty of one shilling: *Et si quis, in aliquo Coetu extra Cubiculum suum, Theam potaverit, mulctetur uno Solido.* Harvard College's laws were also written in Latin, and revised from time to time; see Samuel Eliot Morison, *Harvard College in the Seventeenth Century,* 2 vols. (Cambridge, Mass.: Harvard University Press, 1936), 2:477.

33.   Cf. Richard, *Founders*, 24–26.

34.   David Potter, *Debating in the Colonial Chartered Colleges* (New York: Teachers College, Columbia University, 1944).

35.   For a most interesting description of the pomp and circumstances, and even rowdy disturbances, which accompanied the commencement exercises of an early American college, see Ashbel Green's early nineteenth-century narrative of his visitation to Harvard College during commencement week, Joseph H. Jones, *The Life of Ashbel Green* (New York: R. Carter, 1849), 234–37.

36.   For a thorough discussion of the English university system as a backdrop to the development of the American university system, see Morison, *The Founding of Harvard College*, 1–116.

37.   Snow, *College Curriculum*, 58–59. See also, David C. Humphrey, *From King's College to Columbia, 1746–1800* (New York: Columbia University Press, 1976).

38.   Undoubtedly Sallust's *Catiline*, though his *Jugurthine War* might also have been included under this term.

39.   Probably only the *Gallic War*.

40.   Hugo Grotius's (1583–1645) *De Veritate Religionis Christianae* (translated into Latin in 1627 from a Dutch original written in 1620) was a popular work of Christian apologetics.

41.   The London schoolmaster Thomas Farnaby (1575?–1647) prepared a collection of Greek epigrams as an elementary text, *Florilegium Epigrammatum Graecorum* (first published in London in 1627).

42.   Oxford mathematician John Wallis (1616–1703) wrote *Institutio Logicae* (first published in Oxford in 1687) as an introduction to logic.

43.   English clergyman Robert Sanderson's (1587–1663) *Logicae Artis Compendium* (first published in Oxford in 1618) was another popular text on logic.

44.   Samuel Johnson (1696–1772), born in Guilford, Connecticut, and educated at Yale, was an Anglican clergyman and philosopher who served as the first president of King's College. He retired in 1763. While the assignment of the *Noetica*, the first part of his *Elementa Philosophica* (published by Benjamin Franklin in Philadelphia in 1752) may be seen as an early example of a professor teaching from his own book, the volume was widely acclaimed as the first important textbook on philosophy to have been written by an American.

45.   Antoine de Waele (1573–1639), professor of theology at Leiden, composed a synthesis of Aristotelian and Christian ethics, the *Compendium Ethicae Aristotelicae ad Normam Veritatis Christianae Revocatum* (first published in Leiden in 1620).

46.   Grotius's *De Jure Belli ac Pacis* (first published in Amsterdam in 1625), which established a system of natural law and rights, was modified by the German philosopher Samuel von Pufendorf (1632–1694) in his *De Jure Naturae et Gentium* (first published in Lund in 1672); their views were further developed by the Scottish philosopher Francis Hutcheson (1694–1746) in his posthumously published work, *A System of Moral Philosophy* (first published in London in 1755).

47.   Wertenbaker, *Princeton*, 214.

48.   Sarah N. Randolph, *The Domestic Life of Thomas Jefferson* (New York: Ungar, 1958), 340–41.

Chapter 2

1.   On competing conceptions of the Senate during the Constitutional Convention, see Jack N. Rakove, "The Great Compromise: Ideas, Interests, and the Politics of Constitution Making," *William and Mary Quarterly*, 3rd ser. 44 (1987): 424–57.

2.   Lance Banning, *The Jeffersonian Persuasion: Evolution of a Party Ideology* (Ithaca: Cornell University Press, 1988), 13–18, 92–93, 273–74; Drew R. McCoy, *The Elusive Republic: Political Economy in Jeffersonian America* (Chapel Hill: University of North Carolina Press, 1980), 189–95, 253.

3.   For a more detailed discussion of the understanding of classical mixed-government theory and classical pastoralism in revolutionary America, see Richard, *Founders*, 123–68; idem, "The Classical Roots of the U.S. Congress: Mixed Government Theory," in *Inventing Congress*, edited by Kenneth R. Bowling and Donald R. Kennon (Athens: Ohio University Press, 1999), 3–28.

4.   Algernon Sidney, *Discourses concerning Government* (London: A. Millar, 1751; repr. Farnborough, Eng.: Gregg International, 1968), 130, 139–40, 434; Alan Craig Houston, *Algernon Sidney and the Republican Heritage in England and America* (Princeton: Princeton University Press, 1991), 179–219; Paul K. Conkin, *Self-Evident Truths* (Bloomington: Indiana University Press, 1974), 146–47.

5.   J. G. A. Pocock, ed., *The Political Works of James Harrington* (Cambridge: Cambridge University Press, 1977), 172–74.

6.   Gordon S. Wood, *The Creation of the American Republic, 1776–1787* (Chapel Hill: University of North Carolina Press, 1969), 201–2, 211; Houston, *Algernon Sidney*, 236–55.

7.   Wood, *Creation*, 201, 203, 208, 213–15, 232–33, 436; John Adams, *A Defence of the Constitutions of Government of the United States of America*, 2 vols. (London: C. Dilly, 1787–1788; repr., New York: Da Capo Press, 1971), 1:xxi, 169–82, 209, 325; Richard M. Gummere, "The Classical Politics of John Adams," *Boston Public Library Quarterly* 9 (1957): 172; Houston, *Algernon Sidney*, 261–64.

8.   Max Farrand, ed., *The Records of the Federal Convention of 1787*, 3d. ed., 2 vols. (New Haven: Yale University Press, 1966), 1:422–23, 2:299; William T. Hutchinson and William M. E. Rachal, eds., *The Papers of James Madison*, vol. 6 (Chicago: University of Chicago Press, 1969), 76–77, "Report on Books," January 23, 1783.

9.   Alexander Hamilton, John Jay, and James Madison, *The Federalist: A Commentary on the Constitution of the United States* (New York: The Modern Library, 1941), 410–11, 415; Wood, *Creation*, 410, 473, 559.

10.   Farrand, *Records*, 1:299–300, 308, 424, 432; Wood, *Creation*, 55–58.

11.   Herbert J. Storing, ed., *The Complete Antifederalist*, 7 vols. (Chicago: University of Chicago Press, 1981) 2:138–39, 273, 380; 5:89–90; Farrand, *Records*, 1:402; Jonathan Elliot, *The Debates in the Several State Conventions on the Adoption of the Federal Constitution*, 2nd ed., 5 vols. (Washington: Printed by and for the editor, 1836–1845), 3:218, 421;

4:326–29. For greater detail on the views of the Federalists and Antifederalists on mixed-government theory, see Richard, *Founders*, 132–54; idem, "Classical Roots," 17–25.

12.   Hamilton, Jay, and Madison, *Federalist*, No. 10, 58–59; cf. Rackove, "Compromise," 434. Madison made the same argument in *Federalist*, No. 51.

13.   John F. Hoadley, *Origins of American Political Parties, 1789–1803* (Lexington: University of Kentucky Press, 1986), 77–85, 121–25, 150–51, 165–67; Swift, *Making of an American Senate*, 67–73.

14.   A. Whitney Griswold, "Jefferson's Agrarian Democracy," in *Thomas Jefferson and American Democracy*, edited by Henry C. Dethloff (Lexington, Mass.: D. C. Heath, 1971), 40; Dorothea Wender, ed. and trans., *Roman Poetry from the Republic to the Silver Age* (Carbondale: Southern Illinois University Press, 1980), 59–60.

15.   Rahe, *Republics*, 1:323.

16.   Griswold, "Jefferson's Agrarian Democracy," 40–42. For Harrington's statement see Rahe, *Republics*, 1:414.

17.   Shields, *American Aeneas*, 129–63.

18.   Douglas L. Wilson, "The American Agricola: Jefferson's Agrarianism and the Classical Tradition," *South Atlantic Quarterly* 80 (1981): 347–54; Karl Lehmann, *Thomas Jefferson: American Humanist* (Chicago: University of Chicago Press, 1965), 181; Gilbert Chinard, ed., *The Literary Bible of Thomas Jefferson: His Commonplace Book of Philosophers and Poets* (Baltimore: Johns Hopkins University Press, 1928; repr., New York: Greenwood Press, 1969), 32; Cappon, *Adams-Jefferson Letters*, 2:483, Jefferson to John Adams, July 9, 1819.

19.   Richard K. Matthews, *The Radical Politics of Thomas Jefferson: A Revisionist View* (Lawrence: University of Kansas Press, 1984), 43; Griswold, "Jefferson's Agrarian Democracy," 46–47.

20.   For a fuller discussion of classical pastoralism, see Richard, *Founders*, 159–64.

21.   Douglass Adair and John A. Schutz, eds., *The Spur of Fame: Dialogues of John Adams and Benjamin Rush, 1805–1813* (San Marino, Calif.: Huntington Library, 1966), 66–67, Adams to Rush, September 9, 1806; Gummere, "The Classical Politics of John Adams," 179.

Chapter 3

1.   This essay expands on ideas in my chapter, "The Rise of Greece," in Winterer, *Culture of Classicism*, 44–76; see also Charles Sellers, *The Market Revolution: Jacksonian America, 1815–1846* (New York: Oxford University Press, 1991); Gordon S. Wood, *The Radicalism of the American Revolution* (New York: Knopf, 1992).

2.   Richard Hofstadter, *Anti-Intellectualism in American Life* (New York: Vintage Books, 1963), 159.

3.   Sidney H. Aronson, *Status and Kinship in the Higher Civil Service: Standards of Selection in the Administrations of John Adams, Thomas Jefferson and Andrew Jackson* (Cambridge, Mass.: Harvard University Press, 1964), 166.

4.   Robert V. Remini, *John Quincy Adams* (New York: Times Books, 2002).

5.   Daniel Walker Howe, *The Political Culture of the American Whigs* (Chicago: University of Chicago Press, 1979), 44; Hoftstadter, *Anti-Intellectualism*, 157.

6.   Reinhold, *Classica Americana*, 239.

7.   Winterer, *Culture of Classicism*, 42–43, 47–48.

8.   *Journal of the Proceedings of a Convention of Literary and Scientific Gentlemen, Held in the Common Council Chamber of the City of New York, October 1830* (New York: J. Leavitt and G. & C. & H. Carvill, 1831), 180; Henry H. MacCracken and Ernest G. Sihler, *Seventy Years, A History of New York University, New York University: Its History, Influence, Equipment and Characteristics*, vol. 1 (Boston: R. Herndon, 1901), 53–62.

9.   Thomas Smith Grimké, *Reflections on the Character and Objects of All Science and Literature* (New Haven: Hezekiah Howe, 1831).

10.   Charles Caldwell, *Thoughts on Physical Education, and the True Mode of Improving the Condition of Man; and on the Study of the Greek and Latin Languages* (Edinburgh: Adam & Charles Black, 1836), 128.

11.   Reinhold, *Classica Americana*, 174–203.

12.   Wendell Garrett, *Neo-Classicism in America: Inspiration and Innovation, 1810–1840* (New York: Hirschl & Adler Galleries, 1991); Wendy A. Cooper, *Classical Taste in America, 1800–1840* (New York: Abbeville Press, 1993); Stuart P. Feld, *Boston in the Age of Neo-Classicism, 1810–1840* (New York: Hirschl & Adler Galleries, 1999); *Classical America, 1815–1845* (Newark: Newark Museum Association, 1963); Robert Sutton, *Americans Interpret the Parthenon: The Progression of Greek Revival Architecture from the East Coast to Oregon, 1800–1860* (Niwot: University Press of Colorado, 1992); Mills Lane, *Architecture of the Old South: Greek Revival and Romantic* (Savannah: Beehive Foundation, 1996); William Vance, *America's Rome*, vol. 1 (New Haven: Yale University Press, 1992); Joy Kasson, *Marble Queens and Captives: Women in Nineteenth-Century American Sculpture* (New Haven: Yale University Press, 1990).

13.   Cf. the writings of the Federalist essayist Fisher Ames (1758–1808), on which see Paul A. Gilje, *The Road to Mobocracy* (Chapel Hill: University of North Carolina Press, 1987), 5–6, 100–112.

14.   Michael F. Holt, *The Rise and Fall of the American Whig Party* (Oxford: Oxford University Press, 1999), 12–32, esp. 13.

15.   This shift has been documented in a number of recent studies, including Kenneth Cmiel, *Democratic Eloquence: The Fight over Popular Speech in Nineteenth-Century America* (Berkeley: University of California Press, 1990); Christopher Grasso, *A Speaking Aristocracy: Transforming Public Discourse in Eighteenth-Century Connecticut* (Chapel Hill: University of North Carolina Press, 1999); and Jay Fliegelman, *Declaring Independence: Jefferson, Natural Language, and the Culture of Performance* (Stanford: Stanford University Press, 1993).

16.   Walsh quoted in Edwin Miles, "The Young American Nation and the Classical World," *Journal of the History of Ideas* 35 (1974): 266.

17.   Cornelius Conway Felton, *An Address Pronounced August 15, 1828, at the Close of the Second Term of the Livingston County High School, Temple Hill, Geneseo, New York* (Cambridge, Mass.: Hilliard, Metcalf, 1828), 20.

18.   Felton, *Address*, 13, 16.

19.   J. C. Gray, "Demosthenes," *North American Review* 22 (1826): 48.

20.   David Potter, *Debating in the Colonial Chartered Colleges* (New York: Teachers College, Columbia University, 1944), esp. 33–63.

21.   Robert Bridges Patton, *A Lecture, on Classical & National Education; Delivered December 28, 1825, in the Chapel of Nassau Hall, before the Literary & Philosophical Society of New Jersey* (Princeton: D. A. Borrenstein, 1826), 5–6.

22.   Daniel Walker Howe, *The Political Culture of the American Whigs* (Chicago: University of Chicago Press, 1979), 218–19; cf. Thomas Brown, *Politics and Statesmanship: Essays on the Whig Party* (New York: Columbia University Press, 1985), 184–86.

23.   George E. Baker, ed., *The Works of William H. Seward*, 2nd ed., 5 vols. (Boston: Houghton Mifflin, 1887), 3:133.

24.   On Everett's career as a classicist, see Reinhold, *Classica Americana*, 204–13.

25.   Paul Revere Frothingham, *Edward Everett, Orator and Statesman* (Boston: Houghton Mifflin, 1925), 135–39.

26.   Edward Everett, "The Importance of Education in a Republic," *Orations and Speeches on Various Occasions*, 2nd ed., 2 vols. (Boston: Little, Brown, 1850), 2:317.

27.   Jonathan Messerli, *Horace Mann* (New York: Knopf, 1972), 392–96; on the contrasting views of Democrats and Whigs towards educational reform in Massachusetts in the 1830s and 1840s, see Carl F. Kaestle and Maris A. Vinovskis, *Education and Social Change in Nineteenth-Century Massachusetts* (Cambridge: Cambridge University Press, 1980), 208–32.

28.   Carl Diehl, *Americans and German Scholarship, 1770–1870* (New Haven: Yale University Press, 1978); see also the individual entries in Ward W. Briggs, Jr., ed., *Biographical Dictionary of North American Classicists* (Westport, Conn.: Greenwood Press, 1994); on Round Hill School, see Russel B. Nye, *George Bancroft, Brahmin Rebel* (New York: Knopf, 1944; repr. Octagon Books, 1972), 60–84.

29.   Diehl, *Americans*, 71–117, was dismissive of the notion that German classicism had much real influence over American higher education during the first half of the nineteenth century.

30.   Suzanne L. Marchand, *Down from Olympus: Archaeology and Philhellenism in Germany, 1750–1970* (Princeton: Princeton University Press, 1996), 24–35.

31.   [George Bancroft], "The Value of Classical Learning," *North American Review* n.s. 10, no. 44 (1824): 125–37, esp.129–30; cf. Nye, *George Bancroft*, 80.

32.   St. Leger Landon Carter, "Pinkney's Eloquence," *Southern Literary Messenger* 1 (1834): 94–96; F. S. Cassady, "Eloquence," *Ladies' Repository* 20 (1860): 360–61; C. C. Felton, *An Address Delivered at the Dedication of the New Building of Bristol Academy in Taunton, August 25, 1852* (Cambridge, Mass.: John Bartlett, 1852), 16.

33.   Gray, "Demosthenes," 36.

34.   D.S.G.C., "Modern Oratory," *Southern Literary Messenger* 18.6 (1852): 371.

35. G. B. Cheever, "Study of Greek Literature," *American Quarterly Register* 4 (1832): 277.

36. Cf. Bancroft, "Classical Learning," 126–28.

37. C. C. Felton, *A Lecture on Classical Learning, Delivered before the Convention of Teachers, and Other Friends of Education, assembled to Form the American Institute of Instruction, August 20, 1830* (Boston: Hilliard, Gray, Little & Wilkins, 1831), 28.

38. Daniel Walker Howe, *Making the American Self: Jonathan Edward to Abraham Lincoln* (Cambridge, Mass.: Harvard University Press, 1997).

39. Bancroft, "Classical Learning," 130.

40. Ronald F. Reid, *Edward Everett, Unionist Orator* (Westport, Conn.: Greenwood Press, 1990), 79–106.

41. See the prudent comments of Reid, *Everett*, 94–103; cf. Gary Wills, *Lincoln at Gettysburg* (New York: Simon & Schuster, 1992), esp. 54–55; the text of Everett's speech may be found on 213–47.

42. Wills, *Lincoln*, 213–15.

43. Wills, *Lincoln*, 215, 239.

Chapter 4

1. Alexander Crummell, "The Attitude of the American Mind toward the Negro Intellect," *American Negro Academy Occasional Papers* no. 3 (Washington: American Negro Academy, 1898), reprinted in *Civilization and Progress: Selected Writings of Alexander Crummell on the South*, edited by J. R. Oldfield (Charlottesville: University of Virginia Press, 1995), 204–14.

2. Edgar W. Knight and Clifton L. Hall, *Readings in American Educational History* (New York: Appleton-Century-Crofts, 1951; repr. Greenwood Press, 1970), 659–700; Carter G. Woodson, *The Education of the Negro Prior to 1861*, 2nd ed. (Washington: Association for the Study of Negro Life and History, 1919; repr. New York: Arno Press, 1968), esp. 151–78.

3. Knight and Hall, *Readings*, 669–70; Woodson, *Education*, 205–28.

4. Robert C. Morris, *Reading, 'Riting and Reconstruction: The Education of Freedmen in the South, 1861–1870* (Chicago: University of Chicago Press, 1981), 86–89.

5. Morris, *Reading*, 1–53.

6. Joe M. Richardson, *Christian Reconstruction: The American Missionary Association and Southern Blacks, 1861–1890* (Athens: University of Georgia Press, 1986), esp. 123.

7. Richardson, *Christian Reconstruction*, 123–40, esp. 135.

8. For a detailed account of Scarborough's life, see my edition of *The Autobiography of William Sanders Scarborough: An American Journey from Slavery to Scholarship* (Detroit: Wayne State University Press, 2005), esp. 23–29 for Scarborough's early years.

9. Scarborough, *Autobiography*, 37–59. For a detailed history of Lewis High School, see Titus Brown, *Faithful, Firm and True: African American Education in the South* (Macon, Ga.: Mercer University Press, 2002).

10. Eric Foner, *Reconstruction: America's Unfinished Revolution, 1863–1877* (New York: Harper & Row, 1988), 575–87.

11.   There is a small painting dated December 15, 1876, of the burned facility in the Sidney Lanier Cottage in Macon, Georgia. The painting was donated by Sarah A. Grant, Mrs. Scarborough's great-granddaughter.

12.   Scarborough, *Autobiography*, 60–67.

13.   See my introduction to Scarborough's *Autobiography*, 7–9.

14.   Readers should be aware, however, that the "W. S. Scarborough" briefly mentioned only by name in Foraker's autobiography, *Notes of a Busy Life*, 2 vols. (Cincinnati: Stewart & Kidd, 1916), 1:85, was not the classics scholar but rather a white Cincinnati attorney with the same initials and last name. This attorney's published remarks on the history of the *Cincinnati Law Library Association* (Cincinnati: The Association, 1875) have mistakenly been attributed to the classicist in several library catalogs.

15.   Philip D. Jordan, *Ohio Comes of Age, 1873–1900*, vol. 5, *The History of the State of Ohio* (Columbus: Ohio State Archaeological and Historical Society, 1943), 179–82; David A. Gerber, *Black Ohio and the Color Line, 1860–1915* (Urbana: University of Illinois Press, 1976), 230–44; Scarborough, *Autobiography*, 64, 69.

16.   Gerber, *Black Ohio*, 331–32, 351; Jordan, *Ohio*, 395; Scarborough, *Autobiography*, 90–91.

17.   Roy E. Finkenbine, "'Our Little Circle': Benevolent Reformers, The Slater Fund, and the Argument for Black Industrial Education, 1882–1908," *Hayes Historical Journal* 6 (1986): 6–22, reprinted in *African Americans and Education in the South, 1865–1900*, edited by Donald G. Nieman (New York: Garland, 1994), 70–86.

18.   Gerber, *Black Ohio*, 38–40; Scarborough, *Autobiography*, 97.

19.   *Sketch of Joseph Benson Foraker, with an Appendix* (n.p., 1885), 125–32, esp. 129.

20.   Scarborough, *Autobiography*, 194; Foraker, *Busy Life*, 2:128–29.

21.   Scarborough, *Autobiography*, 320.

22.   Joel Chandler Harris, *Life of Henry W. Grady, Including His Writings and Speeches* (New York: Cassell, 1890), 126; cf. Scarborough, "The Future of the Negro," *The Forum* (March 1889): 80–89.

23.   Walter Guild, "A Plea from the South," *The Arena* 4, no. 5 (1900): 483–88, esp. 487–88; Guild, who came from a prominent Democratic family and served in the Confederate army, is listed in Thomas Waverly Palmer, *A Register of the Officers and Students of the University of Alabama, 1831–1901* (Tuscaloosa: The University, 1901), 146–47.

24.   Frederick A. McGinnis, *A History and an Interpretation of Wilberforce University* (Wilberforce, Ohio [printed at Blanchester, Ohio: Brown Publishing Co.]: 1941), 103–9.

25.   Alfred A. Moss, Jr., *The American Negro Academy* (Baton Rouge: Louisiana State University Press, 1981), esp. 22–32.

26.   See Richard Wormser, *The Rise and Fall of Jim Crow* (New York: St. Martin's Press, 2003).

27.   Louis R. Harlan and Raymond W. Smock, eds., *The Booker T. Washington Papers*, 14 vols. (Urbana: University of Illinois Press, 1972–1989), 3:583–87.

28.   For Washington's thoughts about classical languages, see my article, "A Look at Booker T. Washington's Attitude toward the Study of Classical

Languages by People of African Ancestry," *Negro Educational Review* 53 (2002): 59–72.

29.   Crummell, "Attitude," 208–10.

30.   Published as W. S. Scarborough, "The Educated Negro and His Mission," *American Negro Academy Occasional Papers* 8 (Washington: American Negro Academy, 1903, repr. New York: Arno Press, 1969), 3–11.

31.   W. S. Scarborough, "The Negro and Higher Learning," *The Forum* 33 (1902): 349–55, esp. 349–50.

32.   Scarborough, "Higher Learning," 352–53.

33.   Scarborough, *Autobiography*, 193.

34.   John D. Weaver, *The Senator and the Sharecropper's Son: Exoneration of the Brownsville Soldiers* (College Station: Texas A&M University Press, 1997).

35.   "Burton for Senator; Taft, Foraker Out," *The New York Times*, January 1, 1909, 8; Foraker, *Busy Life*, 2:205–397, esp. 347–50.

36.   Harlan and Smock, *Booker T. Washington Papers*, 10:xxi–xxiii; cf. Scarborough, *Autobiography*, 208–10.

37.   Scarborough, *Autobiography*, 112–14; David Levering Lewis, *W. E. B. DuBois: Biography of a Race, 1868–1919* (New York: H. Holt, 1993), 152–53; cf. DuBois's 1940 commencement address at Wilberforce, reprinted in *DuBois on Education*, edited by Eugene F. Provenzo, Jr. (Walnut Creek, Calif.: AltaMira Press, 2002), 253–75.

38.   McGinnis, *Wilberforce*, 66–68.

39.   McGinnis, *Wilberforce*, 109–14.

40.   Scarborough, *Autobiography*, 270–77.

41.   Scarborough, *Autobiography*, 84.

42.   Judith de Luce, "Classics in Historically Black Colleges and Universities," *American Classical League Newsletter* 21 (1999): 10–12.

Chapter 5

1.   On this broad definition of populism, see the introduction to George McKenna, *American Populism* (New York: Putnam, 1974), xi–xxv.

2.   On the changes in American college education during the nineteenth century, see Frederick Rudolph, *Curriculum: A History of the American Undergraduate Course of Study Since 1636* (San Francisco: Jossey-Bass, 1977), 99–244.

3.   *New York Tribune*, April 13, 1890, 18.

4.   The creation of learned societies in the sciences is documented by Ralph S. Bates, *Scientific Societies in the United States*, 3rd ed. (Cambridge, Mass.: M.I.T. Press, 1965), 85–136.

5.   Diehl, *Americans*; Peter Drewek, "Limits of educational internationalism: foreign students at German universities between 1890 and 1930," *Bulletin of the German Historical Institute* 27 (2000): 39–63.

6.   Section 4 of the Act, as reprinted in *History of the Agricultural College Land Grant of July 2, 1862* (Ithaca: Journal Book and Commercial Printing House, 1890), 104.

7.   Winton U. Solberg, *The University of Illinois, 1867–1894: An Intellectual and Cultural History* (Urbana: University of Illinois Press, 1968), 111.

8. Alexis Cope, *History of the Ohio State University, 1870–1910*, vol. 1, *History of the Ohio State University* (Columbus: Ohio State University Press, 1920), 43, 103.

9. Michael Bezilla, *Penn State: An Illustrated History* (University Park: Pennsylvania State University Press, 1985), 32–33.

10. Orrin Leslie Elliott, *Stanford University, the First Twenty-five Years* (Stanford: Stanford University Press, 1937), 39–49, 65–74.

11. Hugh Hawkins, *Between Harvard and America: The Educational Leadership of Charles W. Eliot* (New York: Oxford University Press, 1972), 95–96, 173–74.

12. "A Criticism from Yale of the Last Harvard Educational Move—Greek and the Bachelor's Degree," *The New Englander* 44 (1885): 424–35.

13. James McCosh, *The New Departure in College Education, Being a Reply to President Eliot's Defense of It in New York* (New York: C. Scribner's Sons, 1885), as reprinted in *American Higher Education: A Documentary History*, edited by Richard Hofstadter and Wilson Smith, 2 vols. (Chicago: University of Chicago Press, 1961) 2:715–30, esp. 720; see also W. B. Carnochan, *The Battleground of the Curriculum* (Stanford: Stanford University Press, 1993), 9–21.

14. The culmination of these efforts was a conference organized at Princeton in 1917—after the battle to preserve classical education in American secondary schools and universities had really been lost—and the conference's corresponding publication in *Value of the Classics*, edited by Andrew F. West (Princeton: Princeton University Press, 1917).

15. See Edward Everett Hale's memorial of Hoar in *Proceedings of the American Antiquarian Society*, October 1905, 150–66.

16. Although the book is not free from bias, useful background on direct election may be found in C. H. Hoebeke, *The Road to Mass Democracy* (New Brunswick, N.J.: Transaction Publishers, 1995).

17. *Congressional Record*, Fifty-third Congress, First Session, pp. 101–10.

18. The allusion is to Cicero, *Pro Flacco* 7.15–16.

19. Cicero, *Philippics* 2.108.

20. Montana, Washington, and Wyoming each had one Senate seat unfilled during the Fifty-third Congress.

21. The quotation printed in the *Congressional Record*, Fifty-third Congress, First Session, p. 109, reads *Contempsi Catilinea gladios, non pertinescum tuos.*

22. Hoebeke, *Mass Democracy*, 14–60.

23. *Congressional Record*, Sixty-first Congress, Second Session, p. 7110.

24. *New York Tribune,* May 4, 1890, 19; Willard Hayes Yeager, *Chauncey Mitchell Depew, the Orator* (Washington: George Washington University Press, 1934), 34.

25. Merle Curti and Vernon Carstensen, *The University of Wisconsin, A History, 1841–1925*, vol. 1 (Madison: University of Wisconsin Press, 1949); Horace Samuel Merrill, *William Freeman Vilas, Doctrinaire Democrat* (Madison: State Historical Society of Wisconsin, 1954), 8–11, 15; David Paul Thelen, *The Early Life of Robert M. La Follette, 1855–1884* (Chicago: Loyola University Press, 1966), 21–50, esp. 25, 46.

26. Hoebeke, *Mass Democracy*, 91–97.

27. Information from the online *Biographical Directory of the United States Congress*; http://bioguide.congress.gov [accessed May 19, 2004].

28. *Congressional Record*, Sixty-first Congress, Third Session, p. 1977.

29. *Congressional Record*, Sixty-first Congress, Third Session, p. 2260; Philip C. Jessup, *Elihu Root*, 2 vols. (New York: Dodd, Mead, 1938), 2:238–42.

Chapter 6

1. On Westermann's appointment, see Robert Lansing to William L. Westermann, November 30, 1918, in William L. Westermann Diary, Columbia University Library.

2. Lawrence E. Gelfand, *The Inquiry: American Preparations for Peace, 1917–1919* (New Haven: Yale University Press, 1963).

3. The Jewish ambassadors in this period were Oscar S. Straus (1887–1889, 1898–1899, 1909–1910), Solomon Hirsch (1889–1892), Henry Morgenthau (1913–1916), and Abram I. Elkus (1916–1917).

4. Westermann to Sellery, May 12, 1919, University of Wisconsin-Madison Archives, Westermann File.

5. William Linn Westermann, "Greek Culture and Thought," in *Encyclopedia of the Social Sciences*, edited by Edwin R. A. Seligman, vol. 1 (New York: Macmillan, 1930), 8–41, esp. 27–28.

6. Entries, December 4, 6, 10, 1918, Westermann Diary. For other accounts of this meeting, which agree with Westermann's and reproduce the same words from Wilson, see memoranda by William C. Bullitt and Isaiah Bowman, December 10, 1918, in *The Papers of Woodrow Wilson*, edited by Arthur S. Link, 69 vols. (Princeton: Princeton University Press, 1966–1994), 53:350–56; and by Charles Seymour to family, December 10, 1918, 53:356–57.

7. Westermann Diary, January 2, March 25, May 7, 1919; Westermann to Avrina D. Westermann, January 26, 1919.

8. Westermann Diary, January 12, April 12, 1919; more than two decades later, Westermann expressed criticism of those swept up in the romanticism of Lawrence's exploits and his depictions of the Arabs; William Linn Westermann, *Peoples of the Near East Without a National Future* (New York: Council on Foreign Relations, 1944).

9. Westermann Diary, January 20, 1919.

10. Westermann Diary, March 23, June 9, 1919.

11. Westermann Diary, February 9, March 23, 1919.

12. Westermann Diary, February 4, 1919.

13. Westermann to Avrina D. Westermann, April 27, 1919; Westermann Diary, May 13, 1919.

14. Westermann Diary, December 29, 1918.

15. Westermann Diary, December 30, 1918, February 3, 1919.

16. Westermann Diary, February 8, 1919.

17. Westermann Diary, April 13, 1919.

18. Westermann Diary, May 22, 1919. This account is also in Link, *Papers of Wilson*, 59:374–76.

19. Westermann and Magie to Wilson, May 21, 1919, in Link, *Papers of Wilson*, 59:349.

20. Westermann to Sellery, May 13, 1919, Wisconsin Archives, Westermann File.

21. Westermann to Sellery, June 10, 1919, Wisconsin Archives.

22. Westermann to Sellery, June 20, 1919, Wisconsin Archives.

23. Westermann Diary, June 28, 1919.

24. Westermann Diary, July 2, 1919.

25. Herbert Hoover, *The Memoirs of Herbert Hoover*, 3 vols. (New York: Macmillan, 1951–1952), 1:13.

26. Ironically, Westermann's experience at the Paris Peace Conference (and the continuing paucity of American scholars of the Middle East) would render him an expert on the post-World War II arrangements for the Kurds; see Westermann, *Peoples*. Westermann's July 1946 article, "Kurdish Independence and Russian Expansion," *Foreign Affairs* 24 (1946): 675–86, was even excerpted and reprinted 45 years later in the immediate aftermath of the Gulf War in *Foreign Affairs* 70 (1991): 50–54.

27. Gelfand, *Inquiry*, 240–58.

Chapter 7

1. This essay could not have been written without substantial assistance. I have benefited from conversations and correspondence with John Albert Baumgarten, Daniel Bell, Victor Bers, Roger Bowen, W. G. Bowersock, Ward Briggs, Bruce Cumings, Robert DuPlessis, Edward Harris, Eric Foner, Henry Foner, David Goldfrank, Walter Goldfrank, Fred Greenstein, Judith Hallett, W. V. Harris, Patricia Hills, Richard Immerman, Martin Jay, David Konstan, Stephen Leberstein, Martin Ostwald, Peter Kuznick, Richard Saller, James Schmidt, Brent D. Shaw, Carol Smith, David Tandy, Thomas Wheatland, and G. Kevin Whitfield. I have also had the privilege to conduct extended interviews with Gertrude Finkelstein, M.D., and Sylvia Goldfrank, and to correspond with Sharon Finley. I am indebted to all of these individuals for their generous assistance. A debt must also be acknowledged to the wonderful archivists who have assisted my efforts. These include the entire staff at the American Philosophical Society as well as Bette M. Epstein, New Jersey State Archives; Thomas Frusciano, Special Collections and University Archives, Rutgers University; Susan Golding, Government Papers, Temple University; Gail Malmgreen, Donna Davie, and Peter Filardo, Tamiment Collection, New York University; Barbara Morley, Kheel Center for Labor-Management Documentation and Archives, School of Industrial and Labor Relations, Cornell University; and Dale Reed, Hoover Institution Archives, Stanford University.

2. Ellen Schrecker, *No Ivory Tower* (New York: Oxford University Press, 1986), 161–79. The official date of his Rutgers dismissal was December 31, 1952; his teaching in England apparently began in October 1954. See "Historical Background to the Academic Freedom Cases at Rutgers University" in Arda Aguilian, "Inventory to the Records of the Rutgers University Office of the President (Lewis Webster Jones). Series II: Academic Freedom Cases, 1942–58." Special Collections and University Archives, Rutgers University Libraries; http://www2.scc.rutgers.edu /ead/uarchives/Jones2b.html [accessed June 28, 2005]. For the

date of his position at Oxford, see correspondence from A. Andrewes, M. M. Postan, and A. H. M. Jones, March–May 1954, also in the Rutgers Special Collections and University Archives, Box 4.

3.   C. R. Whittaker, "Moses Finley, 1912–1986," *Proceedings of the British Academy* 94 (1996): 459–72, esp. 461.

4.   F. W. Walbank, "Finley, Sir Moses I," *Oxford Dictionary of National Biography* (Oxford: Oxford University Press, 2004), 620–21.

5.   George Watson, "The Man from Syracuse: Moses Finley, 1912–1986," *Sewanee Review* 112 (2004): 131–37, esp. 132.

6.   Whittaker, "Finley," 462.

7.   Walbank, "Finley," 620.

8.   M. I. Finley, *Ancient Slavery and Modern Ideology* (New York: Viking Press, 1980), 40.

9.   Moses I. Finkelstein finally followed his two brothers in changing the family last name to Finley, a change that was finalized on November 26, 1946; see Finley's FBI file and Finley's statement to Rutgers deans, 1951. A copy of the FBI file and other material related to Finley's dismissal are kept in the Records of the Office of the President housed in the Rutgers University Archives. On Finley's bibliography before the change in surname, see the early entries in M. I. Finley, *Economy and Society in Ancient Greece* (New York: Viking Press, 1982), 312, 315.

10.   Comments on the rabbinate and upbringing: Gertrude Finkelstein, M.D., personal communication, May 13–14, 2005, and Interviews with Murray Finley: May 12 and 21, 1990, Gail Malmgreen, Interviewer. Kheel Center, Cornell University. The bar mitzvah or "confirmation" speech, on the history of the bar mitzvah ceremony, was delivered on the festival of Shavuot, May 29, 1925, at Temple Adath Yeshurun in Syracuse, New York. Two years later, Finkelstein was asked to stand in for the temple's vacationing rabbi by giving another address to the congregation on Shavuot. Invitation to bar mitzvah (called a "confirmation" in English) and letter of Isaac Markson to Moses Finkelstein, May 4, 1927, collection of Gertrude Finkelstein, M.D.

11.   Although he refused interviews with Ellen Schrecker and with Stephen Leberstein, biographer of Finkelstein's City College colleague Morris Schappes, he did speak with Victor S. Navasky and Alfred Friendly, see Victor S. Navasky, *Naming Names*, 3rd ed., (New York: Penguin, 1991), 58; cf. Michael J. Birkner, *McCormick of Rutgers* (Westport, Conn.: Greenwood Press, 2001), 88; Watson, "Man from Syracuse," 132–33. On how other academics dealt with their own pasts, see Alain Boureau, *Kantorowicz: Stories of a Historian*, translated by Stephen G. Nichols and Gabrielle M. Spiegel (Baltimore: Johns Hopkins University Press, 1990); and Landon Storrs, "Red Scare Politics and the Suppression of Popular Front Feminism: The Loyalty Investigation of Mary Dublin Keyserling," *Journal of American History* 90 (2003): 491–524.

12.   M. I. Finley, "Un-American Activities," *New Statesman* 77, February 28, 1969, 296.

13.   Pierre Vidal-Naquet, *Mémoires 2: le trouble et la lumière, 1955–1998* (Paris: Éditions du Seuil, La Découverte,1998), 171–73, 200–201; idem, *La democratie grecque vue d'ailleurs* (Paris: Flammarion, 1990), 271–73.

14. Personal communication, Sylvia Goldfrank, May 11, 2005.

15. Three short letters survive from 1932 and 1933 to the social and economic historian Fritz Heichelheim, who was still in Germany at the time. Heichelheim was forced into exile by the Nazis in 1933, spending the rest of the 1930s and the war years in England, and ending up after the war as a professor of ancient history at the University of Toronto, where his papers have been preserved. Brent Shaw published these three letters and excerpts from later correspondence in "The Early Development of M. I. Finley's Thought: the Heichelheim Dossier," *Athenaeum* 81 (1993): 177–99.

16. Gardner Jackson, *Oral History, 1920–1955*. Individual Interview, Columbia University Oral History Microfiche Collection.

17. See Jackson's letter to Boas, March 6, 1939. The film, *Juarez* starring Paul Muni, merits a separate discussion, so rich is it in motifs of the Popular Front of the 1930s: initially conceived as a costume drama about the Emperor Maximilian and his wife Carlotta, it became a celebration of Juarez, who has Maximilian executed—but not before Maximilian himself explains to an aide that his execution shows that Juarez cares more for "the peace of Mexico" than the "plaudits of the world." Juarez himself dresses like Lincoln, had photographs of Lincoln on his walls, and even receives a supportive letter from him during a retreat. Juarez's fierce condemnation of colonialism was excised from the 1954 reissue of the film. See Harry M. Benshell and Sean Griffin, *America on Film: Representing Race, Class, Gender and Sexuality in the Movies* (Oxford: Blackwell, 2004), 141; Richard Maltby, *Hollywood Cinema*, 2nd ed. (Oxford: Blackwell, 2003), 447–48; Colin Schindler, *Hollywood in Crisis: Cinema and American Society, 1929–1939* (London: Routledge, 1996), 205, among many other discussions.

18. There appears no good reason to contradict Finley's assertion both before the McCarran Committee and, three decades later, to author James Barros, that he was not acquainted with the Asian historian and future Canadian diplomat Herbert Norman, who was at Columbia in 1938 and 1939. Karl August Wittfogel had claimed before the McCarran Committee that Norman was part of a Marxist study group organized by Finley. Dogged by allegations that he was a Soviet spy, Norman committed suicide in Cairo in 1957. The subsequent controversy helped bring about the defeat of the incumbent Liberal government in the Canadian elections later that year. James Barros, *No Sense of Evil: Espionage, the Case of Herbert Norman* (Toronto: Deneau, 1986), accepted the allegations against Norman, while Peyton V. Lyon, "The Loyalties of E. Herbert Norman," *Labour/Le Travail* 28 (1991): 219–59 (a report prepared for the Canadian government), exonerated Norman. United States Congress, Senate, Committee on the Judiciary, *Institute of Pacific Relations: Hearings before the Subcommittee to Investigate the Administration of the Internal Security Act and Other Internal Security Laws of the Committee on the Judiciary* (henceforth, *IPR*), 14 parts (Washington: U.S. Government Printing Office, 1951–1952), 1:318 (Wittfogel testimony); 12:4154–55 (Finley testimony).

19. Moses Finkelstein to Franz Boas, August 3, 1938, Boas Professional Papers, housed at the American Philosophical Society in Philadelphia.

All of the correspondence between Finkelstein and Boas discussed in this essay is preserved in this collection.

20. *Times Literary Supplement*, January 21, 1977, 67.

21. Finley mentioned Boas quite respectfully in passing in a 1972 lecture at Cambridge, published as "Anthropology and the Classics," in *The Use and Abuse of History* (New York: Viking Press, 1975), 102–19, esp. 108. Finley's student Richard Saller reports the surprise in Cambridge upon the mention of Boas in the *Times Literary Supplement* (personal communication, January 2005).

22. For Boas's position on laws and "mental life" see Ruth Benedict, "Franz Boas as an Ethnologist," *American Anthropologist* n.s. 45.3, part 2 (1943): 33. For Finley's opposition to "law-like" generalizations, cf. the introduction of Brent D. Shaw and Richard P. Saller to Finley, *Economy and Society*, xxiv.

23. Boas, "Some Recent Criticisms of Physical Anthropology," *American Anthropologist* n.s. 1 (1899): 98–106; cf. M. I. Finley, *The Ancient Economy* (Berkeley: University of California Press, 1973), 17–34, 71.

24. On Schiller's career, see Peter Stein's obituary reprinted in Roger S. Bagnall and William V. Harris, *Studies in Roman Law in Memory of A. Arthur Schiller* (Leiden: Brill, 1986), xv–xviii.

25. Letter from Finkelstein to Fritz Heichelheim, August 30, 1932, as printed in Shaw, "Heichelheim Dossier," 180, 195. The subject of the dissertation would change to "Land and Credit in Ancient Athens" and would not be completed until 1951.

26. Jacques Barzun, "Reminiscences of the Columbia History Department: 1923–1975," *Columbia Magazine: The Alumni Magazine of Columbia University* (Winter 2000): 24–34.

27. W. L. Westermann, *"Sklaverei," Real-Encyclopädie*, Suppl. 6 (Stuttgart: J. B. Metzler, 1935), coll. 894–1068; Finkelstein's review appeared in the *Zeitschrift für Sozialforschung* 5 (1936): 442; Finley, *Ancient Slavery*, 52–55.

28. Wolfgang G. Haase and Irving Louis Horowitz, "In Memoriam Meyer Reinhold (1909–2002)," *International Journal of the Classical Tradition* 9 (2002): 3–7, esp. 4; cf. Reinhold's review of the papers from a 1987 conference on the German ancient historian Eduard Meyer organized by William M. Calder III and Alexander Demandt, *Eduard Meyer: Leben und Leistung eines Universalhistorikers. Mnemosyne* suppl. 112 (Leiden: Brill, 1990), in *Bryn Mawr Classical Review* 1991; http://ccat.sas.upenn.edu/bmcr/1991/02.05.05.html, accessed May 4, 2005, esp. n. 5.

29. Sandra B. Hammond and C. Edward Scebold, *Survey of Foreign Language Enrollments in Public Secondary Schools, Fall 1978* (New York: American Council on the Teaching of Foreign Languages, 1980), 11; cf. Richard A. LaFleur, "The Study of Latin in American Schools: Success and Crisis," in *The Teaching of Latin in American Schools: A Profession in Crisis* ([Decatur, Ga.]: Scholars Press, 1987), 1–15.

30. Sidney Hook, *Out of Step: An Unquiet Life in the 20th Century* (New York: Harper & Row, 1987), 18–19.

31. Kevin B. Sheets, "Antiquity Bound: The Loeb Classical Library as Middlebrow Culture in the Early Twentieth Century," *Journal of the Gilded Age and Progressive Era* 4 (2005): 149–71.

32. Erskine's 1913 address at Amherst College, "The Moral Obligation to Be Intelligent," is reckoned the starting point for the "Great Books" movement; see Robert A. McCaughey, *Stand, Columbia: A History of Columbia University in the City of New York, 1754–2004* (New York: Columbia University Press, 2003), 288–93.

33. Judah J. Shapiro, *The Friendly Society: A History of the Workmen's Circle* (New York: Media Judaica, 1970).

34. Joseph Dorman, *Arguing the World: The New York Intellectuals in Their Own Words* (New York: Free Press, 2000), 25–40, esp. 33, 35; cf. Wald, *Intellectuals*, 27–45.

35. Whittaker, "Finley," 45–60, goes against family testimony in asserting that Finkelstein trained for the rabbinate. Gertrude Finkelstein's voluminous collection of family papers and news clippings from the 1920s contains no reference to rabbinical training. Both Gertrude Finkelstein and Sylvia Goldfrank, a friend from 1935, confirm that Moses and Mary Finkelstein were quite secular in the 1930s; personal communications, May 11–14, 2005.

36. *The New York Times* from August 24–30, 1927, reported riots in Mexico, Brazil, Paris, Cherbourg, Hamburg, Brussels, Warsaw, Geneva, Sydney, Copenhagen, Johannesberg, Leipzig, and many other cities.

37. See Murray Kempton, "The Dry Bones," in *Part of Our Time* (New York: Simon & Schuster, 1955), 45–52; Stephen Koch, *Double Lives*, 2nd ed. (New York: Enigma Press, 2004), 39–48.

38. When referring to the general philosophy of a society sharing ownership of the means of economic production, the term *communist* will be used without capitalization. When the term is used to refer to an organized political movement, such as the government of the Soviet Union or the Communist Party of the United States of America, *Communist* will be capitalized.

39. Finley, *Ancient Slavery*, 40–41.

40. Eric Hobsbawn, *On History* (New York: The New Press, 1997), 141–70.

41. Harvey Klehr, *The Heyday of American Communism* (New York: Basic Books, 1984).

42. Klehr, *American Communism*, 75–76.

43. Wald, *Intellectuals*, 102.

44. Saller and Shaw devote much of their introduction to Finley's *Economy and Society*, xi–xviii, to a careful review of Finkelstein's work at the institute at this formative stage in his career, including a succinct survey of the reviews Finkelstein wrote for the institute's journal, *Zeitschrift für Sozialforschung* (renamed in its final year as *Studies in Philosophy and Social Science*).

45. Otto Kirchheimer and Georg Rusche, *Punishment and Social Structure* (New York: Columbia University Press, 1939); Max Horkheimer, "Art and Mass Culture," *Studies in Philosophy and Social Science* 9 (1941): 290–304. Finley revealed his involvement in these works in 1972 to Martin Jay while Jay was writing *The Dialectical Imagination: A History of the Frankfurt School and the Institute of Social Research, 1923–1950* (Boston: Little, Brown, 1973); personal communication with Martin Jay, January 2005; cf. MIF statement to Rutgers deans, 1951; Shaw, "Heichelheim," 196–97.

46.   Lazarsfeld: February 24, 1948; Horkheimer: May 28, 1947. Letters in Lewis Webster Jones Papers, Rutgers University.

47.   See Finley, *Economy and Society*, 97–115; Max Horkheimer, "The Authoritarian State," in *The Essential Frankfurt School Reader*, edited by Andrew Arato and Eike Gebhardt (New York: Urizen Books, 1978), 95–117. The "Acknowledgments" section of the *Reader*, 559, states that the English version discussed here appeared in *Telos* 15 (1972) translated by The People's Translation Service, Berkeley.

48.   Finley's later distancing of himself from Marxian categories for precapitalist societies in *The Ancient Economy* (1973) is well known.

49.   "Spectrum": 98; Marx: 111; Kant and Durkheim: 112, Nietzsche: 113.

50.   See below, n. 52.

51.   Helmut Dubiel, *Theory and Politics: Studies in the Development of Critical Theory*, translated by Benjamin Gregg (Cambridge, Mass.: MIT Press, 1985), 16–17; on Massing and Neumann, see "Alexander Vassiliev's Notes on Anatoly Gorsky's December 1948 Memo" with notes by Soviet scholar John Earl Haynes; http://www.johnearlhaynes.org/page44.html [accessed June 29, 2005].

52.   M. I. Finley, "Introduction: Desperately Foreign," *Aspects of Antiquity: Discoveries and Controversies* (New York: Viking Press, 1969), 1–6.

53.   Finley told Martin Jay that Trinkaus and Nelson were his closest friends in graduate school; personal communication with Martin Jay, January 2005.

54.   See David Merian [pseudonym of Meyer Schapiro], "The Nerve of Sidney Hook," *Partisan Review* 10.2 (1943): 248–57, and Andrew Hemingway, "Meyer Schapiro and Marxism in the 1930s," *Oxford Art Journal* 17.1 (1994): 13–29, esp. 25. I am indebted to Patricia Hills for reference to the suite of articles on Schapiro in this issue.

55.   Alan M. Wald, *The New York Intellectuals* (Chapel Hill: University of North Carolina Press, 1987), 33–37, 75–97, 210–17; cf. "Doherty Says Reds Smirch Columbia," *The New York Times*, July 27, 1938, 1, 3.

56.   S. Willis Rudy, *The College of the City of New York: A History, 1847–1947* (New York: City College Press, 1949), 397.

57.   Dorman, *Arguing*, 41–56.

58.   Rudy, *College*, 429.

59.   "The Reminiscences of Moe Foner," Session #3, February 21, 1985, Oral History Research Office, Columbia University; http://www.columbia.edu/cu/lweb/indiv/oral/foner/transcript03.html [accessed May 2, 2005].

60.   Canning claimed to have left the Communist Party "[i]n the latter part of 1938" at which time he was presumably no longer coming over to the Finkelstein home; see Canning's testimony in *IPR*, 2:470, 482.

61.   Schrecker, *No Ivory Tower*, 79, 172–77; "To Aid Colleges Inquiry: Three Fact-Finders Named to Study Subversion in City," *The New York Times*, September 10, 1953, 4.

62.   Walbank, "Finley," 620; Watson, "Man from Syracuse," 136–37.

63.   *IPR*, 11:3962–63 (Thorner's testimony); 12:4153 (Finley).

64.   Brent Shaw, personal communication, January 2005.

65.   Consider the exchange between two physicists admiring Einstein's work, then referring to it as *jüdische Spitzfindigkeit* (Jewish hairsplitting)

when they fear they have been overheard, Bertolt Brecht, *Furcht und Elend des Dritten Reiches* (Berlin: Suhrkamp, 1957), 58.

66. On Stark and "Aryan Physics," see Alan D. Beyerchen, *Scientists under Hitler: Politics and the Physics Community in the Third Reich* (New Haven: Yale University Press, 1977); for a good, brief summary of Stark's 1938 *Nature* article with comments on Stark's career, see A. Loewenstein, "Pragmatic and Dogmatic Physics: Presentation and Response in Nature, 1938"; http://www.technion.ac.il/technion/chemistry/staff/loewenstein/nature.pdf [accessed May 2, 2005]. At Harvard, the young sociologist Robert Merton, "Science and the Social Order," *Philosophy of Science* 5 (1938): 321–23, was reaching similar conclusions about Stark's work. Merton and Finley would travel in linked circles but there is no evidence of their having met.

67. Announcement, "University Federation for Democracy and Intellectual Freedom," filed in Boas Professional Papers at "end of 1939." Peter Kuznick, *Beyond the Laboratory: Scientists as Political Activists in 1930s America* (Chicago: University of Chicago Press, 1987), 184–87; Elazar Barkan, *The Retreat of Scientific Racism* (Cambridge: Cambridge University Press, 1992), 336–40; and more briefly, Hamilton Cravens, *The Triumph of Evolution* (Baltimore: Johns Hopkins University Press, 1988), 189–90.

68. Statement to Dean Herbert P. Woodward, Newark College of Arts and Sciences, Rutgers University, September 5, 1951. Lewis Webster Jones Papers, Rutgers University.

69. G. L. Ulmen, *The Science of Society: Toward an Understanding of the Life and Work of Karl August Wittfogel* (The Hague: Mouton, 1978), esp. 19–20, 361–62; Jay, *Dialectical Imagination*, 15–16; Karl August Wittfogel, *Wirtschaft und Gesellschaft Chinas: Versuch der wissenschaftlichen Analyse einer grossen asiatischen Agrargesellschaft* (Leipzig: C. L. Hirschfeld, 1931).

70. This is not the place to review the full range of scholarship on "hydraulic despotism," which Wittfogel most fully elaborated in his book *Oriental Despotism* (New Haven: Yale University Press, 1957), but cf. Edmund Leach, "Hydraulic Society in Ceylon," *Past and Present* 15 (1959): 2–26.

71. Ulmen, *Science of Society*, 157–219.

72. Daniel Bell reports this; personal communication, February 17, 2005.

73. In general, "bureaucracy" was an explosive term in late-1930s discussions about the Soviet Union; Ulmen, *Science of Society*, 209. Others challenge 1938 as the date of Wittfogel's apostasy from the Communist Party. According to Pierre Vidal-Naquet, Finley in 1968 reported that Wittfogel still admired Stalin in 1945, *Democratie grecque*, 271, 401 nn. 14–15. Exactly what that meant remains unclear.

74. Robert P. Newman, *Owen Lattimore and the "Loss" of China* (Berkeley: University of California Press, 1992), 335. By 1954 the FBI was losing faith in Wittfogel as a witness; report of special agent, Newark, to the Director, February 15, 1954, in Finley FBI file.

75. IPR, 1:312 (Wittfogel); 2:482–83 (Canning).

76. IPR, 11:3962 (Thorner); 12:4153 (Finley).

77.   Cf. Jay, *Dialectical Imagination*, 143–72; Dubiel, *Theory and Politics*, 74–75; Moshe Postone and Barbara Brick, "Critical Theory and Political Economy," in *On Max Horkheimer: New Perspectives*, edited by Seyla Benhabib, Wolfgang Bonss, and John McCole (Cambridge, Mass.: MIT Press, 1993), 236–37. A close study of the activities at the institute shows how far off Sidney Hook was in calling it "fellow-traveling," Hook, *Out of Step*, 594.

78.   Ulmen, *Science of Society*, 218; Vidal-Naquet reports the denunciation, "Karl Wittfogel et la Notion de Mode de Production Asiatique," *Democratie grecque*, 272–73; cf. Alisa Giardinelli, "Olga Lang (1898–1992)," *Swarthmore College Bulletin* 100.3 (2002): 39–40. To date, I have been unable to find any evidence of this denunciation in any source, including the various Senate and House hearings where Wittfogel testified. Hede Massing, ex-Communist and ex-wife of former Institute of Social Research member Paul Massing, did mention Olga Lang in testimony before the McCarran Committee, *IPR*, 1:269.

79.   See Ulmen, *Science of Society*, 324–31, on the chronological confusions resulting from Wittfogel's 1951 testimony.

80.   "Theory of Nazis on 'Aryanism' is False, Anthropologists Hold," *The New York Times*, December 30, 1938, 8; Barkan, *Retreat*, 340; Kuznick, *Beyond the Laboratory*, 184–87.

81.   "Boas Joins Union Held Led by Reds," *The New York Times*, December 31, 1938, 17.

82.   Celia Lewis Zitron, *The New York City Teachers Union, 1916–1964* (New York: Humanities Press, 1968), 22–35.

83.   Boas says as much in letters to Walter Rautenstrauch, February 21, 1939, and to Finkelstein, July 16, 1941; cf. Boas's refusal to attend a party-sponsored luncheon in 1936 ("While I agree with the aims of the Party, I cannot agree with their methods.") and his refusal to support a party-inspired broadside in July 1939 ("[In Russia] free expression of opinion is ruthlessly suppressed. . . .") quoted in Kuznick, *Beyond the Laboratory*, 210, 216.

84.   This is revealed by Finkelstein's note to Boas on August 16, 1939, about joint projects with the union, his exchange of letters with the leader of the Teachers Guild, Abraham Lefkowitz, October 21, 1939, and his explanatory note to Boas on October 4, 1939.

85.   "Scientists to Open Drive for Freedom," *The New York Times*, January 24, 1939, 21; cf. "Dictators Accused of Stifling Science," *The New York Times*, February 12, 1939, 34; Kuznick, *Beyond the Laboratory*, 189–94.

86.   Kuznick, *Beyond the Laboratory*, 196.

87.   Kuznick, *Beyond the Laboratory*, 198–99.

88.   Kuznick, *Beyond the Laboratory*, 201–2.

89.   "Immigration Curb Is Urged in Survey," *The New York Times*, June 8, 1939, 9.

90.   It would not have helped that Laughlin's appendix condemned the "moral turpitude" of a Jew who had smuggled money out of Germany and criticized former U.S. Attorney General Homer Cummings for admitting him to the United States.

91.   E.g., "Aliens Defended in 'Race' Dispute," *The New York Times*, July 23, 1939, 5.

92.   Kuznick, *Beyond the Laboratory*, 211–15.

93.   Finley to Boas, August 9, 1939.

94.   John Dewey, et al., *The Case of Leon Trotsky: Report of Hearings on the Charges Made Against Him in the Moscow Trials* (New York: Harper & Brothers, 1937).

95.   Kuznick, *Beyond the Laboratory*, 196.

96.   "New Group Fights Any Freedom Curb," *The New York Times*, May 15, 1939, 13; ibid., May 17, 1939, 22.

97.   Hook Papers, Hoover Institution Archives, Stanford University.

98.   Boas to Harry Schneiderman, May 15, 1939.

99.   In his autobiography, Hook later contended that "Franz Boas was not a political innocent" and that Boas "went along with the shifting political line of the American Communist Party in the late thirties and early forties," *Out of Step*, 257–59.

100. Sidney Hook to Frank Trager, June 7, 1939. Hook Papers, Hoover Institution Archives, Stanford University.

101. Cf. Sidney Hook, "The Fifth Amendment: A Moral Issue," *New York Times Sunday Magazine*, November 1, 1953, 9, 57–66.

102. The "fit to teach" theme runs through the various Rutgers documents, including the Trustees' report to the President, October 14, 1952, and the statement by the Faculty Emergency Committee, December 12, 1952. Finley's statement to Rutgers trustees recounted by Gertrude Finkelstein; personal communication, May 13, 2005.

103. See *The Daily Worker*, August 14, 1939; *Soviet Russia Today* 8.5 (1939), 24–25, 28; *The Nation*, August 26, 1939.

104. Watson, "Man from Syracuse," 132; my emphasis.

105. Watson's errors include comments about Finkelstein's "humble" upbringing; his "rabbinical training"; and the confusion of the ACDIF with the American League Against War and Fascism, a leftist organization formed in 1933 and which changed its name in 1937 to the American League for Peace and Democracy.

106. Maurice Isserman, *Which Side Were You On? The American Communist Party during the Second World War* (Urbana: University of Illinois Press, 1993), 31–43.

107. "Report on Schools Scored as 'Fascist,'" *The New York Times*, October 3, 1939, 30; Waldemar Kaempffert, "Science in the News," *The New York Times,* October 8, 1939, 60; see also Kuznick, *Beyond the Laboratory*, 202–8.

108. "Dissolve": see above, n. 5.

109. Kuznick, *Beyond the Laboratory*, 217.

110. Benjamin Stolberg, "Innocent Front: Catspaws of Communism," *Washington Post*, December 2, 1939, 11.

111. See Hook's account of the failed negotiations with *Science and Society* and his ongoing assaults on that journal in the 1939 correspondence with Dewey, summarized in his essay "Communists, McCarthy and American Universities," review of Schrecker's *No Ivory Tower* in *Minerva* 25 (1987): 331–48, esp. 340. Finkelstein never wrote for *Science and Society*, though his friend Meyer Reinhold did. Finkelstein and Stern had worked together at the *Encyclopedia of the Social Sciences* from 1930 to 1934 and doubtless knew each other; beyond that, however, we

know nothing at this time that would further connect the two men in 1939.

112. FBI Director J. Edgar Hoover to the U.S. Attorney General, December 12, 1941. Franz Boas FBI File, Franz Boas Papers, American Philosophical Society.

113. Kuznick, *Beyond the Laboratory*, 337 n. 62. On growing anti-Communism in the ACLU in this period, see Navasky, *Naming Names*, 49–50; Michael J. Ybarra, *Washington Gone Crazy: Senator Pat McCarran and the Great American Communist Hunt* (Hanover, N.H.: Steerforth Press, 2004), 242.

114. Harrison Salisbury, "The Strange Correspondence of Morris Ernst and John Edgar Hoover, 1939–1964," *The Nation*, vol. 239, no. 18, December 1, 1984, 575–89.

115. Ybarra, *Washington Gone Crazy*, 241–42.

116. The charges against Phil and Jack Foner are available in the Henry Foner Collection, Tamiment Library, Robert F. Wagner Labor Archives, New York University, Box 10. Benjamin Paskoff's account of his hearing can be found in the files of the American Committee for Democracy and Intellectual Freedom, Boas Professional Papers, American Philosophical Society. Finley's letter to Dean Herbert P. Woodward, September 5, 1951, is found in a packet submitted to Rutgers administrators by Dean Woodward March 27, 1952. Special Collections and University Archives, Rutgers University Libraries.

117. Stephen Leberstein, "Purging the Profs: The Rapp Coudert Committee in New York, 1940–1942," in *New Studies in the Politics and Culture of U.S. Communism*, edited by Michael E. Brown, et al. (New York: Monthly Review Press, 1993), 91–122, esp. 116–17; Bella V. Dodd, *School of Darkness* (New York: Devin-Adair, 1954), 128–30; cf. Rudy, *College*, 451.

118. Schrecker, *No Ivory Tower*, 182–83, 249, 293–94.

119. Haase and Horowitz, "Meyer Reinhold."

120. Robert M. Lichtman and Ronald D. Cohen, *Deadly Farce: Harvey Matuso and the Informer System in the McCarthy Era* (Urbana: University of Illinois Press, 2004), 143. Budenz's use of his "400 concealed Communists" to generate book sales is discussed by Robert Lichtman, "Louis Budenz, the FBI, and the 'list of 400 concealed Communists': an extended tale of McCarthy-era informing," *American Communist History* 3.1 (2004): 25–54. Stewart Alsop accused Budenz of fabricating testimony in the Owen Lattimore case; see Ybarra, *Washington Gone Crazy*, 586–92.

121. Office memorandum to J. Edgar Hoover from special agent in charge, New York, July 14, 1950: "Budenz describes a concealed Communist as one who does not hold himself out as a Communist and who would deny membership in the Party."

122. See special agent, Newark, reports to the director from February 20, 1953 through February 15, 1954.

123. Charles Grutzner, "1,500 U.S. Teachers Red, Dr. Dodd Says," *The New York Times*, September 9, 1952, 1, 9.

124. "40 Reds in City College Staff, Teaching 'Slanted,' Witness Says," *The New York Times*, March 7, 1941, 1, 12. It is important to add that a

more careful analysis of evidence and the dynamics of the hearings of the Rapp-Coudert Committee requires a trip to the New York State Archives in Albany, which I have not yet made.

125. *American Association of University Professors Bulletin* 25 (1939): 550–55.

126. Cf. Hook, "Not Mindful Enough," *Journal of Philosophy* 49.4 (1952): 112–21 and "Communists, McCarthy, and American Universities," *Minerva* 25 (1987): 331–48.

127. Sidney Hook, "The AAUP and Academic Integrity," *The New Leader*, May 21, 1956, 19–21; see also Schrecker, *No Ivory Tower*, 94.

128. Adam Bernstein, "Melvin J. Lasky, 84; Outspoken Anti-Communist," *Washington Post*, May 27, 2004, B7; Hook, *Out of Step*, 432–44.

129. Malcolm Waters, "Daniel Bell," in *The Blackwell Companion to Major Contemporary Social Theorists*, edited by George Ritzer (Oxford: Blackwell, 2003), 164.

130. Gerald J. Blidstein, "Rabbinic Judaism and General Culture," in *Judaism's Encounter with Other Cultures: Rejection or Integration?*, edited by Jacob J. Schacter (Northvale, N.J.: Jason Aronson, 1997), 1–56.

131. Two chapters in David Hollinger's *Science, Secular Culture and the Jews* (Princeton: Princeton University Press, 1996) bear on this topic: "Two NYUs and 'The Obligation of Universities to the Social Order,'" (60–79), and "The Defense of Democracy and Robert K. Merton's Formulation of the Scientific Ethos," (80–96).

132. M. I. Finley, "Greek to Him," *New York Review of Books* 7.2 (1966); idem, "Name Calling," *New York Review of Books* 7.4 (1966).

133. Max Weber, quoted in John Gerard Ruggie, *Constructing the World Polity: Essays on International Institutionalization* (New York: Routledge, 1998), 31.

134. Saller's essay appears in *The Ancient Economy*, edited by Walter Scheidel and Sitta von Reden (New York: Routledge, 2002), 251–69, esp. 253. For an interesting effort to locate "peasantry" in today's world, see Henry Bernstein, "Farewells to the Peasantry," *Transformation* 52 (2003): 1–19.

135. Robert Morris, *No Wonder We Are Losing*, 10th ed. (Plano, Tex.: University of Plano Press, 1975).

Chapter 8

1. Richard Ned Lebow, *The Tragic Vision of Politics* (Cambridge: Cambridge University Press, 2003), esp. 26, 230–31.

2. Robert Gilpin, *War and Change in World Politics* (Cambridge: Cambridge University Press, 1981), 227.

3. Cited in W. Robert Connor, *Thucydides* (Princeton: Princeton University Press, 1984), 3. Cf. Lawrence Resner, "Marshall Warns 'Indifferent' U.S.," *The New York Times*, February 23, 1977, 1, 32.

4. All stand-alone numeric references are to book, chapter and verse numbers in the text of Thucydides.

5. Hans Morgenthau, *Politics Among Nations*, 2nd ed. (New York: Knopf, 1954), 8. The first edition, published in 1948, lacked the quotation of Thucydides. In the later editions, Morgenthau did not provide a footnote for the quotation, which suggests he intended it more as a supplementary reference rather than one of fundamental importance.

6. William H. McNeill, *America, Britain and Russia: Their Cooperation and Conflict, 1941–1946* (London: Oxford University Press, 1953), 432.

7. Donald Kagan, *The Outbreak of the Peloponnesian War* (Ithaca: Cornell University Press, 1969), 112–13. This proposal for a Hellenic congress in 449 B.C. does not appear in Thucydides but is found in Plutarch's *Life of Pericles* 17.

8. Cited in Michael W. Doyle, *Ways of War and Peace: Realism, Liberalism and Socialism* (New York: W. W. Norton, 1997), 50–51.

9. The 1952 essay was reprinted as the appendix to Louis J. Halle, *Civilization and Foreign Policy* (New York: Harper, 1955), 261–77, esp. 262.

10. Connor, *Thucydides*, 3.

11. Peter J. Fliess, *Thucydides and the Politics of Bipolarity* (Baton Rouge: Louisiana State University Press, 1966).

12. Thucydides, *History of the Peloponnesian War* (Oxford: H. Milford/ Oxford University Press, 1943).

13. Louis E. Lord, *Thucydides and the World War*, Martin Classical Lectures 12 (Cambridge, Mass.: for Oberlin College by Harvard University Press, 1945), 232–33.

14. Kagan, *Outbreak*, 205, 236–37.

15. Gilpin, *War and Change*, 38, 191; on the role of the Persians in the conflict, see Donald Kagan, *The Peloponnesian War* (New York: Viking Press, 2003), 334.

16. Cited in John Tosh, ed., *Historians on History* (Harlow, England: Longman, 2000), 300, originally in Arthur Marwick, "Two Approaches to Historical Study: the Metaphysical (Including 'Postmodernism') and the Historical," *Journal of Contemporary History* 30 (1995): 5–35, esp. 12. The idea that there are "lessons" in the past is the sort of thing that laymen and social scientists imagine. Full discussion is impossible, but cf. Edward H. Carr, *What Is History?* (London: Macmillan, 1961), 84–86, who supports the idea, and *contra*, e.g., Arthur Marwick, *The Nature of History* (New York: Knopf, 1971), 123–31.

17. See, e.g., Lebow, *Tragic Vision*, 66, who cites numerous authors who have accepted this reading, including Doyle, *Ways*, 33, 51–52, 83; and Gilpin, *War and Change*, 93, 191.

18. Richard Crawley's 1874 translation was widely available in America during the Cold War, having been published in paperback editions in the Everyman's Library, Modern Library, and Great Books of the Western World series. Rex Warner's translation for Penguin Books first appeared in 1954. Unfortunately, Steven Lattimore's 1998 translation also uses the word "inevitable" in this passage.

19. Leo Strauss, *The City and Man* (Chicago: Rand McNally, 1964), 182–83; cf. Simon Hornblower, *A Historical Commentary on Thucydides*, vol. 1, *Books 1–3* (Oxford: Clarendon Press, 1991), 66.

20. Kagan, *Outbreak*, 357–74, esp. 355–56 and n. 34; cf. F. E. Adcock in *Cambridge Ancient History*, vol. 5 (Cambridge: Cambridge University Press, 1940), 182; idem, *Thucydides and His History* (Cambridge: Cambridge University Press, 1963), 7.

21. Cf. Peter J. Rhodes, "Thucydides on the Causes of the Peloponnesian War," *Hermes* 115 (1987): 154–65, who notes that Thucydides took "pleasure in showing that he knows better than popular opinion."

22.   Enthusiasm for war among the Greeks may in part be explained by cultural attitudes that saw war as a way of life, that success in war was the clearest expression of manly excellence; in other words, war brought out the best in man. See Eric A. Havelock, "War as a Way of Life in Classical Culture," in *Valeurs antiques et temps modernes / Classical Values and the Modern World,* edited by Étienne Gareau (Ottawa: Éditions de l'Université d'Ottawa, 1972), 19–52; cf. 6.24 on the enthusiasm in Athens for the Sicilian expedition, which ended in disaster.

23.   Cf. 1.122.3, 1.124.3 (Corinth on Athens, echoed by Pericles in 2.63.2, Cleon in 3.37.2). For argument that the Spartan drive to "free" the Greeks was only propaganda see Geoffrey de Ste. Croix, *The Origins of the Peloponnesian War* (London: Duckworth, 1972), 154–58, a position challenged by David Lewis, *Sparta and Persia* (Leiden: Brill, 1977), 108–9; Kurt A. Raaflaub, *The Discovery of Freedom in Ancient Greece* (Chicago: University of Chicago Press, 2004), 197–202.

24.   Cf. 1.78.1 (unnamed Athenians at Sparta), and other passages cited in A. J. Gomme, *A Historical Commentary on Thucydides,* vol. 1, *Introduction and Commentary on Book 1* (Oxford: Clarendon Press, 1956), 2, 13.

25.   John Herz, "Idealist Internationalism and the Security Dilemma," *World Politics* 2 (1950): 157–80; see also Gilpin, *War and Change,* 94 and John Mearsheimer, *The Tragedy of Great Power Politics* (New York: Norton, 2001), passim, for more recent treatment.

26.   For discussion see Mearsheimer, *Tragedy,* 3, 32, who notes the problems of the lack of mediation and arbitration in the international political arena. While his focus is the modern day political scene, there can be little doubt that the same factors influenced great powers such as Athens and Sparta, as well as the less great such as Corinth.

27.   My thanks to Kurt Raaflaub for reminding me of this.

28.   Aristophanes, *Peace* 195–219. The play dates to c. 421, the eve of the Peace of Nicias, which temporarily ended the Peloponnesian War.

29.   Thucydides reports these embassies as: 1) the "curse" embassy (1.139.1); 2) the "Potidean and Megarian" embassy of Polyalces (1.139.1); 3) the "autonomy" embassy of Ramphias, Melesippus, and Agesandrus (1.139.3); and 4) the "last ditch" embassy of Melesippus (2.12.1–3). The chronology of the embassies is uncertain, but the Theban attack on Plataea at the beginning of spring, probably about February/March 431 helps. The last embassy dates to late fall or early winter 432, with the first two falling between spring 432 and early fall 432, i.e., after the Spartans voted that the Athenians had broken the Thirty Years Peace in its fourteenth year. Melesippus's last ditch effort came after the attack on Plataea, perhaps in March 431.

30.   Interpreting 1.126.1, see K. J. Dover in *A Historical Commentary on Thucydides,* edited by A. J. Gomme, A. Andrewes, and K. J. Dover, vol. 4 (Oxford: Clarendon Press, 1970), 394.

31.   Gomme-Andrewes-Dover, *Commentary,* vol. 4, p. 394, in an aside commenting on 7.18.2, argued that the Spartan embassies were designed to provoke refusal. This interpretation seems overly cynical. See my own discussion below, and cf. Ernst Badian, *From Plataea to Potidaea* (Baltimore: The Johns Hopkins University Press, 1993), 125–62, esp. 143–

44, who argued that Thucydides misrepresents Spartan "plotting and deviousness."

32.   The Peloponnesian War would not be the last conflict started by one generation and ended by another. Cf. the Hundred Years' War between the English and French; and the Thirty Years' War that devastated Central Europe in the seventeenth century.

33.   Peloponnesian neighbors Argos and Sparta were enemies from the sixth century B.C., when Sparta's Peloponnesian League began expanding at Argos's expense. Around the year 494, the Spartan king Cleomenes I destroyed an Argive army at Sepeia (Herodotus 6.76–80). Argos was so weakened that it played no part in the Persian Wars, and the city remained relatively impoverished into the later years of the fifth century.

34.   Even in the sophisticated Athenian democracy of the fourth century, domestic arbitration was hardly foolproof. Judgments of arbitrators were only final if both parties accepted them and either party could appeal. This suggests that inter-state arbitration at an earlier time was even likelier to fail. See Pseudo-Aristotle, *Constitution of Athens* 53.2, with Peter J. Rhodes, *A Commentary on the Aristotelian Athenaion Politeia* (Oxford: Clarendon Press, 1981), 589–90.

35.   Archidamus (1.84.3) says that the Spartans are wise because they are not educated to despise the law, a clear jibe at the Athenians. In his famous Funeral Oration, Thucydides' Pericles (2.40.2) refers to Athenian daring in taking on bold, though calculated ventures and danger. See also Kurt A. Raaflaub, "Democracy, Power and Imperialism in Fifth-Century Athens," in *Athenian Political Thought and the Reconstruction of American Democracy*, edited by J. P. Euben, J. R. Wallach and J. Ober (Ithaca: Cornell University Press, 1994), 103–46, esp. 105–6.

36.   Raaflaub, "Democracy," 130; on Athens' "modernity" see, e.g., Gilpin, *War and Change*, 96, and Lebow, *Tragic Vision*, 303, 373.

37.   See Kurt A. Raaflaub, "The Transformation of Athens in the Fifth-Century," in *Democracy, Empire and the Arts in Fifth-Century Athens*, edited by Deborah Boedeker and Kurt A. Raaflaub (Cambridge, Mass.: Harvard University Press, 1998), 15–41, for discussion of Athens' rise to "world power" and its development of political institutions and active participation of its citizens in political and military activities. This is essentially state-building of a modern type; cf. Raaflaub, "Democracy," 113–18, 130–31.

38.   On the Greek Enlightenment see A. Geoffrey Woodhead, *Thucydides on the Nature of Power* (Cambridge: Cambridge University Press, 1970), 3–6; Friedrich Solmsen, *Intellectual Experiments on the Greek Enlightenment* (Princeton: Princeton University Press, 1975), 116–22; and Jacqueline de Romilly, *The Great Sophists in Periclean Athens* (Oxford: Clarendon Press, 1992), 135–37.

39.   Havelock, "War," 75.

40.   Kagan, *Outbreak*, 334, argued that Pericles proposed a "defensive" war, but one involving Athenian incursions into the Peloponnesus to hurt Sparta and her allies. Not only were such operations offensive in nature, they also served as counterstrokes to the Spartan led invasions of Attica; cf. Raaflaub, "Democracy," 130–46, on power, citizens' and leaders' motives.

41.　Mearsheimer, *Tragedy*, 367–68; cf. Doyle, *Ways*, 76–80. Classicist Maurice Bowra, *The Greek Experience* (Cleveland: World Publishing, 1957), 76, noted this long before: "Athens provides a signal refutation of the optimistic delusion that democracies are not bellicose or avid of empire."

42.　Jason Warren, "Beyond Emotion: The Epidamnan Affair and Corinthian Policy, 480–421 BC," *Ancient History Bulletin* 17 (2004): 181–94, collects the evidence for the extent of this Corinthian empire in northwest Greece; see also John B. Salmon, *Wealthy Corinth: A History of the City to 338 BC* (Oxford: Clarendon Press, 1984), 270–80.

43.　Mearsheimer, *Tragedy*, 156–59.

44.　Badian, *Plataea*, 125, suggested that Thucydides wrote his history in the context of a *Kriegsschuldfrage*, such as that occupying Europe in the 1920s. While beyond the scope of the present essay, Thucydides's work might be placed in a similar context of a "just war" debate.

45.　R. Harrison Wagner, "What Was Bipolarity?" *International Organization* 47 (1993): 77–106.

46.　Robert Gilpin, "Peloponnesian War and Cold War," in *Hegemonic Rivalry: from Thucydides to the Nuclear Age*, edited by Richard Ned Lebow and Barry S. Strauss (Boulder: Westview Press, 1991), 31–50.

47.　Gilpin, "Peloponnesian War," 48.

48.　Gilpin, *War and Change*, 199.

49.　Gilpin, "Peloponnesian War," 46–48.

50.　Connor, *Thucydides*, 7.

51.　W. R. Connor, "Polarization in Thucydides," in Lebow and Strauss, *Hegemonic Rivalry*, 53–69.

52.　Cf. Lowell S. Gustafson, ed., *Thucydides' Theory of International Relations* (Baton Rouge: Louisiana State University Press, 2000); David McCann and Barry S. Strauss, eds., *War and Democracy: A Comparative Study of the Korean War and the Peloponnesian War* (Armonk, N.Y.: M. E. Sharpe, 2001).

53.　Lebow, *Tragic Vision*, 16–17.

54.　See e.g., 3.10, 8.48, and discussion in de Ste. Croix, *Origins*, 36.

55.　6.72.1 refers to the Syracusans calling an assembly; 6.73.1 records the election of generals, a mirror image of the process in democratic Athens. For further discussion, see also A. Geoffrey Woodhead's article on Syracuse (slightly revised by Roger J. A. Wilson) in the *Oxford Classical Dictionary*, 3rd ed. (Oxford: Oxford University Press, 2003), 1463–64.

56.　Hans J. Morgenthau, *Vietnam and the United States* (Washington: Public Affairs Press, 1965); cf. Lebow, *Tragic Vision*, 49–50, 283. A. Geoffrey Woodhead, in his 1968 Martin Lectures at Oberlin College, drew comparisons between U.S. involvement in Vietnam and the Athenian destruction of Melos; see his *Thucydides and the Nature of Power* (Cambridge, Mass.: for Oberlin College by Harvard University Press, 1970), 23, 155–56. It is also worth noting that academics during the Vietnam War might have been more inclined to discuss such parallels in class rather than in publication, in light of then prevailing attitudes on drawing such comparisons.

57.   Henry Kissinger, "The Viet Nam Negotiations," *Foreign Affairs* 47 (1969): 211–34; cf. "Schlesinger Warns of Danger of 'Americanization' of War," *The New York Times*, July 25, 1966, 3.

58.   Lawrence A. Tritle, *From Melos to My Lai: War and Survival* (London: Routledge, 2000).

Chapter 9

1.   George Stephanopoulos, *All Too Human: A Political Education* (Boston: Little, Brown, 1999), 127.

2.   Robert C. Byrd, *The Senate, 1789–1989: Addresses on the History of the United States Senate*, 4 vols. (Washington: U.S. Government Printing Office: 1988–1994), 2:541, 547–49; "Byrd, Robert Carlyle," *Biographical Directory of the United States Congress*; http://bioguide.congress.gov.

3.   *Raleigh Register,* April 11, 1946.

4.   Byrd, *The Senate: 1789–1989*, 2:542.

5.   Byrd, *The Senate: 1789–1989*, 2:544–45, 551–55.

6.   See Gilbert C. Fite, Richard B. Russell, Jr., *Senator from Georgia* (Chapel Hill: University of North Carolina Press, 1991), esp. 325, 496.

7.   John A. Goldsmith, *Colleagues: Richard B. Russell and his Apprentice, Lyndon B. Johnson* (Washington: Seven Locks Press, 1993), 181.

8.   Byrd, *The Senate: 1789–1989*, 2:559, 567; Fite, *Russell*, 491; Goldsmith, *Colleagues*, 175.

9.   "Byrd," *Biographical Directory*.

10.   See the introduction to Calvin McLeod Logue and Dwight L. Freshley, *Voice of Georgia: Speeches of Richard B. Russell, 1928–1969* (Macon, Ga.: Mercer University Press, 1997).

11.   Neil A. Lewis, "Byrd Keeps Tradition in Senate Aloft," *Charleston Gazette*, November 29, 1997, A1; cf. Byrd's own comments about himself on the floor of the Senate on March 26, 1993, *Congressional Record*, 103rd Congress, First Session, vol. 139, no. 40, p. 3827.

12.   Enid Nemy, "Chronicle," *The New York Times*, August 16, 1993, B7.

13.   Byrd, *The Senate: 1789–1989*, 2:550.

14.   "A Biography of Senator Byrd"; http://www.senate.gov/~byrd/bio.htm.

15.   "Dole, Robert Joseph," *Biographical Dictionary*; http://bioguide.congress.gov.

16.   Barbara Sinclair, "Individualism, Partisanship, and Cooperation in the Senate," in *Esteemed Colleagues: Civility and Deliberation in the U. S. Senate*, edited by Burdett A. Loomis (Washington: Brookings Institution Press, 2000), 59–77, esp. 64; cf. eadem, "The Senate Leadership Dilemma: Passing Bills and Pursuing Partisan Advantage in a Nonmajoritarian Chamber," in *The Contentious Senate*, edited by Colton C. Campbell and Nicol C. Rae (Lanham, Md.: Rowman & Littlefield, 2001), 65–89.

17.   "President Loses Veto Power Plea," *The New York Times*, March 6, 1938, 10.

18.   Louis Fisher, *The Politics of Shared Power: Congress and the Executive*, 4th ed. (College Station: Texas A&M Press, 1998), 83–85, 242–50; cf. Arthur M. Schlesinger, Jr., *The Imperial Presidency* (Boston: Houghton Mifflin, 1973), 235–46.

19. Adam Pertman, "Clinton Favors Authority to Veto Budget Line Items," *Boston Globe*, February 3, 1992, 6.
20. 102nd Congress, H.R. 2164; passed October 3, 1992.
21. 103rd Congress, H.R. 1578; passed April 29, 1993.
22. 102nd Congress, S.Amdt. 1698, rejected February 27, 1992.
23. The speeches were published separately in book form by the U.S. Government Printing Office as Robert C. Byrd, *The Senate of the Roman Republic: Addresses on the History of Roman Constitutionalism* (Washington: U.S. Government Printing Office, 1995); see also "The Veto Fight," April 9, 1996; http://www.pbs.org/newshour/bb/congress/line_item.
24. Byrd, *Roman Republic*, 90.
25. Cicero, *Orator* 34.120; quoted by Byrd, *Roman Republic*, 6.
26. Byrd, *Roman Republic*, 7–8.
27. Byrd, *Roman Republic*, 20; the example of Servius Tullius is somewhat problematic from a constitutional standpoint, for Roman tradition indicated that this king did not seek immediate approval for his accession from the popular assembly until sometime after he had already gained control of the government, Cicero, *Republic* 2.21.37–38; Livy 1.41.6, 1.46.1; James E. G. Zetzel, ed., *Cicero, De Re Publica, Selections* (Cambridge: Cambridge University Press, 1995), 192–94.
28. Byrd, *Roman Republic*, 112; H. H. Scullard, *From the Gracchi to Nero*, 3rd ed. (London: Methuen, 1970), 63.
29. Byrd, *Roman Republic*, 58–60.
30. Byrd, *Roman Republic*, 90.
31. Byrd, *Roman Republic*, 96–97; Cicero, *Republic* 2.33.57.
32. Byrd, *Roman Republic*, 98–101.
33. Byrd, *Roman Republic*, 161–63.
34. Byrd, *Roman Republic*, 164.
35. Byrd, however, has "airplanes" in place of "helicopters," *Roman Republic*, 171–72; cf. an obituary story on Lyndon Johnson, "The Man and His Humor Are Recalled," *The New York Times*, January 26, 1973, 14.
36. See Scot J. Zentner, "Caesarism and the American Presidency," *Southeastern Political Review* 24 (1996): 629–53. This theme is at the core of Schlesinger's *Imperial Presidency*, though Schlesinger did not connect the theme to the ideological concept of Caesarism.
37. Byrd, *Roman Republic*, 169, 172.
38. Byrd, *Roman Republic*, 187.
39. Byrd, *Roman Republic*, 187–88.
40. E.g., Karl Vick, "Many Words, Few Understood," *St. Petersburg Times*, June 27, 1993, F3; Debra J. Saunders, "Tax Dollars at Work—B.C.," *San Francisco Chronicle*, December 31, 1993, A30; cf. Ernie Freda, "Washington in Brief," *Atlanta Journal and Constitution*, November 3, 1993, A9, who noted that fellow Democratic Senator Harry Reid of Nevada, who has reckoned Byrd a mentor, videotaped the C-SPAN broadcasts of all of Byrd's Roman history speeches. Reid then required his younger children to watch.
41. *Congressional Record*, 103rd Congress, Second Session, vol. 140, no. 143, p. 1211, October 5, 1994.
42. Public Law 104-30, 110 Stat. 1200.

43.   "The Supreme Court and the Line Item Veto"; http://www.senate.gov/byrd; "Capital Questions"; http://www.c-span.org/questions/weekly43.
44.   *Clinton v. The City of New York*, 985 F. Supp. 168, decided June 25, 1998.
45.   Helen Dewar and Joan Biskupic, "Line-Item Veto Struck Down; Backers Push for Alternatives," *Washington Post*, June 27, 1998, A1.
46.   E.g., Paul Kennedy, *The Rise and Fall of the Great Powers* (New York: Random House, 1987); Samuel P. Huntington, *The Clash of Civilizations and the Remaking of the World Order* (New York: Simon & Schuster, 1996).

Chapter 10

1.   E.g., James Atlas, "Leo-Cons: A Classicist's Legacy, Empire Builders," *The New York Times*, May 4, 2003, section 4, 1, 4; Seymour M. Hersh, "Selective Intelligence: Donald Rumsfeld Has His Own Special Sources. Are They Reliable?" *The New Yorker*, May 12, 2003, 44–51. In the writing of this chapter I have been indebted to the suggestions and advice of Daniel Brandeis, Jean Coleno, Mark Henrie, and Simon Kow.
2.   "A Giving of Accounts: Jacob Klein and Leo Strauss," in Leo Strauss, *Jewish Philosophy and the Crisis of Modernity*, edited by Kenneth Hart Green (Albany: State University of New York Press, 1997), 457–66. The following abbreviations will be used for Strauss's various texts: *CM* = *The City and Man* (Chicago: Rand McNally, 1964); *CR* = *The Rebirth of Classical Political Rationalism* (Chicago: University of Chicago Press, 1989); *NRH* = *Natural Right and History* (Chicago: University of Chicago Press, 1953); *OT* = *On Tyranny* (New York: Free Press, 1991); *PAW* = *Persecution and the Art of Writing* (Glencoe, Ill.: Free Press, 1952); *SPPP* = *Studies in Platonic Political Philosophy* (Chicago: University of Chicago Press, 1983); *WIPP* = *What is Political Philosophy?* (Glencoe, Ill.: Free Press, 1959); *PPH* = *The Political Philosophy of Hobbes* (Chicago: University of Chicago Press, 1952); *PL* = *Philosophy and Law* (Albany: State University of New York Press, 1995); *TM* = *Thoughts on Machiavelli* (Glencoe, Ill.: Free Press, 1958); *SCR* = *Spinoza's Critique of Religion* (New York: Schocken, 1965); *LAM* = *Liberalism, Ancient and Modern* (New York: Basic Books, 1968); *HPP* = *History of Political Philosophy* (Chicago: Rand McNally, 1972); *JP* = *Jewish Philosophy and the Crisis of Modernity*.
3.   Stefan Halper and Jonathan Clarke, *America Alone* (Cambridge: Cambridge University Press, 2004), 139; see also their warning about conspiracy theories, 9. For the use of the term *cabal* in relation to the neo-conservatives, cf. Hersh, "Selective Intelligence," 48–50.
4.   Halper and Clarke, *America Alone*, 4.
5.   Peter Singer, *The President of Good and Evil* (New York: Plume, 2004), 222. The reference to the "gentleman" refers to Strauss's interpretation of Aristotle and the role of the gentleman, who stands above the people and is open to a respect for philosophy, without being himself a philosopher—a kind of intermediary between philosophy and the city (see the discussion below). That George W. Bush is a "gentleman" in the sense intended by Strauss is at least open to doubt.

6.   Shadia Drury, "The Esoteric Philosophy of Leo Strauss," *Political Theory* 13 (1985): 315–37; eadem, *The Political Ideas of Leo Strauss* (New York: St. Martin's, 1988); *Leo Strauss and the American Right* (New York: St. Martin's, 1997). See also Peter Levine, *Nietzsche and the Modern Crisis of the Humanities* (Albany: State University of New York Press, 1995); and Laurence Lampert, *Leo Strauss and Nietzsche* (Chicago: University of Chicago Press, 1996).

7.   Shadia Drury in an interview with Danny Postel, "Noble Lies and Perpetual War," *Open Democracy*, October 16, 2003; http://www.opendemocracy.net/debates/article-5-107-1542.jsp [accessed May 24, 2005].

8.   *LAM*, 24.

9.   That there is a need to distinguish Strauss from the neo-conservatives while recognizing a larger connection is a point made by a number of different commentators. One version of this is that the neo-conservatives are lesser Straussians that have fundamentally betrayed Strauss's teachings; see Anne Norton, *Leo Strauss and the Politics of American Empire* (New Haven: Yale University Press, 2004).

10.   There are two levels here: a hermeneutical level—does understanding Leo Strauss help us in understanding the Bush White House—and a causal level—did Leo Strauss influence the Bush White House. The second level, I cannot really address. Some neo-conservatives were obviously exposed to Strauss's thought to some extent and some even cite Strauss as an influence. But influence is a very difficult issue, even in one's own self-understanding, and I do not subscribe to Strauss's view that our opinions are fundamentally shaped by "great" thinkers. So Strauss's views are no doubt only one element in the mix of what constitutes the neo-conservative "persuasion." This muddying of the causal connection need not muddy the hermeneutical one: powerful thinkers can provide logical illumination of positions they did not directly influence.

11.   See Halpern and Clarke, *America Alone*, 44–47; James Mann, *Rise of the Vulcans* (New York: Viking Press, 2004), 90–91; Jacob Heilbrun "The Neo-Conservative Journey," in *Varieties of Conservatism in America*, edited by Peter Berkowitz (Stanford: Hoover Institution Press, 2004), 110–20.

12.   Irving Kristol, *Reflections of a Neo-Conservative* (New York: Basic Books, 1983), 209–10.

13.   Irving Kristol, "America's 'Exceptional Conservatism,'" in *Conservative Realism*, edited by Kenneth Minogue (London: HarperCollins, 1996), 9–22, esp. 16.

14.   Kristol, *Reflections*, 76.

15.   The intellectual articulation of the liberalism that Kristol and the neo-conservatives opposed is found especially in the thought of John Rawls, *A Theory of Justice* (Cambridge, Mass.: Harvard University Press/Belknap Press, 1971).

16.   See Halper and Clarke, *America Alone*, 157–81.

17.   See Kristol, "America's 'Exceptional Conservatism,'" 12–13.

18.   Kristol, *Reflections*, xiii.

19.   Halper and Clarke, *America Alone*, 77.

20.   The highly charged moral language of post-9/11, was already fully operative in neo-conservative writings before 9/11. See Halper and

Clarke, *America Alone*, 102. The claim is simultaneously that the war on evil "is going to go on forever" and that we bring "an end to evil." The dynamism of the policy requires both moments.

21. See Mann, *Vulcans*, 209–15.

22. Halper and Clarke, *America Alone*, 141–46.

23. See Letter to President Clinton, January 26, 1998, *Project for a New American Century*; http://www.newamericancentury.org/iraqclintonletter.htm [accessed May 25, 2005].

24. In fact, quite the opposite: see Kristol, "Machiavelli and the Profanation of Politics," in idem, *Reflections*, 123–35, for a critique of Machiavelli and his effect on political virtue.

25. *OT*, 212.

26. Most notably Shadia Drury, see above, n. 6.

27. Leo Strauss letter to Karl Löwith, June 23, 1935, printed in "Correspondence: Karl Löwith and Leo Strauss," translated by George Elliot Tucker, *Independent Journal of Philosophy* 5/6 (1988): 177–92, esp. 183.

28. *SPPP*, 33.

29. As I have argued in "Leo Strauss' Platonism," *Animus* 4 (1999); http://www. mun.ca/animus/1999vol4/roberts4.htm [accessed May 24, 2005], the interpretation of Plato that Strauss furnishes is not the historical Plato but a distinctively "Post-modern Plato"—to use Catherine Zuckert's useful phrase. Strauss's Plato is fully in accord with the non-metaphysical phenomenology that was developing in Germany in his youth. This is not to elide Strauss's Plato with Nietzsche or Heidegger: it is a distinctive kind of phenomenology.

30. This claim is explicitly made by Drury, *Political Ideas of Strauss*; but cf. *NRH*, 114–15.

31. *NRH*, 120–21.

32. *NRH*, 81–164. Drury, *Political Ideas of Strauss*, 62–71, claims that the pre-Socratic (i.e., Nietzschean) and the Platonic (i.e., Straussian) accounts of natural right are in fact identical. According to Strauss, what separates Heidegger and Nietzsche, for whom there is a similar indifference to the political, from the pre-Socratics, is the presence of a religiously-inspired transformative will in their philosophical positions; see *SPPP*, 174–91 and *CR*, 27–46.

33. *NRH*, 120–23; *WIPP*, 39–40.

34. *NRH*, 146–64.

35. *WIPP*, 54.

36. *LAM*, 62. Strauss frequently pointed out that Cain and Romulus, depicted as founders of societies, were also fratricides.

37. *TM*, 295; *SPPP*, 238.

38. *WIPP*, 84–85. Strauss saw the reduction of politics to external relations as a characteristic of the break with classical thought; see *WIPP*, 44.

39. Compare *NRH*, 7–8, 123. For Strauss there was a partially intelligible, stable, articulated whole available to a moral and political phenomenology, but whether that whole will cause justice to occur in the relation of its parts remains unknown.

40. *LAM*, 230, 271

41. *JP*, 465.

42. *WIPP*, 91; *OT*, 198.

43.   *OT*, 197–98; *LAM*, 31–32.

44.   *OT*, 204, 209–10; *NRH*, 151–52; *WIPP*, 38–40; *LAM*, 8.

45.   *CR*, 162–64; *CM*, 27; *NRH*, 151–52.

46.   *CM*, 27.

47.   *NRH*, 160.

48.   *NRH*, 162.

49.   Shadia Drury, *Leo Strauss and the American Right*, 7; eadem, "Noble Lies," 2.

50.   *NRH*, 246; *PPH*, 121.

51.   *NRH*, 274. Strauss saw that this role for history is absent in Rousseau himself, who was not so easily reconciled to the "actual."

52.   *WIPP*, 54.

53.   Leo Strauss, "The Three Waves of Modernity," in *Political Philosophy: Six Essays by Leo Strauss*, edited by Hilail Gildin (Indianapolis: Pegasus: 1975), 81–98.

54.   In this sense, Strauss's argument parallels Nietzsche's critique of the ascetic ideal in the third essay of *The Genealogy of Morals*, translated by Walter Kaufmann (New York: Vintage Books, 1967), 97–163.

55.   Strauss nonetheless argues that Nietzsche does not fully escape from a relation to nature. See *SPPP*, 183.

56.   See Kristol, "America's 'Exceptional Conservatism,'" 17. Strauss had a similarly ambiguous relation to religious belief.

57.   The two essays "What is Liberal Education?" and "Liberal Education and Responsibility" in *LAM*, 3–25, are Strauss's clearest expositions of this ambiguity.

58.   Tod Lindberg, "Neo-conservatism's Liberal Legacy," in Berkowitz, *Varieties of Conservatism*, 142–47.

59.   *NRH*, 136–40.

60.   *CM*, 100.

61.   *CM*, 5. This quotation can be nicely juxtaposed with the title of the recent book by David Frum and Richard Perle on the war in Iraq: *An End to Evil* (New York: Random House, 2004).

62.   *CM*, 6.

63.   *CM*, 100, *WIPP*, 84–85. See also Thomas West, "Leo Strauss and American Foreign Policy," *The Claremont Review of Books* 4.3 (2004): 3. The passage from *Republic* 470c–471c seems to contradict Strauss's view that Plato argued for an amoralism in foreign affairs. However, Strauss read the whole of *Republic* book 5 as fully ironic in its suggestions and as providing a critique of all political idealism. See *CM*, 127.

64.   *CM*, 6.

65.   West, "Strauss and Foreign Policy," 3.

66.   The connection between the neo-conservative foreign policy and Sicilian expedition in the Peloponnesian War is nicely developed in Norton, *American Empire*, 181–200.

67.   See also Francis Fukuyama, *The End of History and the Last Man* (New York: Free Press, 1992). Fukuyama is often connected to the neo-conservatives, but he articulates a position closer to Kojève than Strauss.

68.   *CM*, 4.

69.   There is a possible Straussian defense here. This comes in the call for "manliness" by a number of neo-conservatives; e.g., Harvey C. Mansfield, *Manliness* (New Haven: Yale University Press, 2006); or the various books of Victor Davis Hanson. Part of the goal of the new idealism is not so much to make the world safe for democracy, as to retain the virtues that belong to a military nation in face of the elimination of the last really threatening opponent.

Afterword

1.   Garry Wills, "There's Nothing Conservative about the Classics Revival," *The New York Times Sunday Magazine*, February 16, 1997, 38–42.

2.   Richard A. LaFleur, "Latin and Greek in American Schools and Colleges: An Enrollment Update," *Classical Outlook* 77 (2000): 101–3. At the college level, the trend is less clear, though enrollments nationwide do not appear to be dropping in any significant way.

3.   Celia McGee, "The Classics Moment: Signs that B.C. is P.C.," *The New York Times Sunday Magazine*, February 16, 1997, 41.

4.   E.g., Josh Trevino, who later became one of the founders of the Website RedState.org that actively promoted Republican candidates beginning with the 2004 election, originally blogged under the pseudonym Tacitus.

5.   Page DuBois, *Trojan Horses: Saving the Classics from Conservatives* (New York: New York University Press, 2001).

6.   Perhaps the most memorable comment at the session came from the audience, when Harvard classics professor Richard Thomas publicly proclaimed that he was now ashamed that prominent neo-conservative William Kristol had been the best man at his wedding.

7.   The promotion of virtue as a primary goal of education is most strongly associated with former U.S. Secretary of Education William J. Bennett, author of *The De-Valuing of America* (New York: Summit Books, 1992) and *The Book of Virtues* (New York: Simon & Schuster, 1993).

8.   Even when I entered graduate school in the 1980s, the most compelling English-language treatment remained Ronald Syme's *The Roman Revolution* (Oxford: Clarendon Press, 1939), written by a New Zealand-born Oxford scholar with an eye to the rise of fascism in Europe. Cf. David Potter, "Roman History and the American Philological Association 1900–2000," *Transactions of the American Philological Association* 131 (2001): 315–27.

List of Contributors

JOHN MILTON COOPER, JR. is E. Gordon Fox Professor of American Institutions at the University of Wisconsin in Madison, Wisconsin. An expert on the presidency of Woodrow Wilson, Cooper has written several books examining American history in the early twentieth century, most recently *Breaking the Heart of the World: Woodrow Wilson and the Fight for the League of Nations* (Cambridge: Cambridge University Press, 2001).

ROBERT F. MADDOX, who passed away in September 2002, was professor of history at Marshall University in Huntington, West Virginia. An expert in twentieth-century American history and in the history of West Virginia, Maddox was the author of books on industrial cartels during World War II and the career of United States senator Harley M. Kilgore.

MICHAEL MECKLER is a permanent fellow in the Center for Epigraphical and Palaeographical Studies at The Ohio State University in Columbus, Ohio. A scholar of Roman and medieval history, he has also maintained an active journalism career, serving as a CBS Radio reporter and as a newspaper columnist.

CARL J. RICHARD is professor of history at the University of Louisiana in Lafayette, Louisiana. His book *The Founders and the Classics: Greece, Rome and the American Enlightenment* (Cambridge, Mass.: Harvard University Press, 1994) won the 1995 Fraunces Tavern Museum Book Award.

NEIL G. ROBERTSON is associate professor of humanities and social sciences at the University of King's College in Halifax, Nova Scotia, where he also teaches in the affiliated institution Dalhousie University. Robertson has written articles on political philosophy, particularly on Leo Strauss and critiques of modernity.

MICHELE VALERIE RONNICK is associate professor of classics, Greek and Latin at Wayne State University in Detroit, Michigan. She edited *The Autobiography of William Sanders Scarborough: An Amercan Journey from Slavery to Scholarship* (Detroit: Wayne State University Press, 2005) and has written other publications on the classical tradition.

DANIEL P. TOMPKINS is director of the Intellectual Heritage Program and associate professor of classics at Temple University in Philadelphia. An expert on the Greek historian Thucydides, Tompkins has written on a wide variety of topics, including the poetry of Wallace Stevens.

LAWRENCE A. TRITLE is professor of history at Loyola Marymount University in Los Angeles, California. He has written extensively on Greek history, and he drew upon his experiences both as a scholar and as a Vietnam war veteran in his book *From Melos to My Lai: War and Survival* (London: Routledge, 2000).

CAROLINE WINTERER is assistant professor of history at Stanford University in Palo Alto, California. She is the author of the award-winning book *The Culture of Classicism: Greece and Rome in American Intellectual Life, 1780–1910* (Baltimore: The Johns Hopkins University Press, 2002) and is completing a book on American women and classicism for Cornell University Press.

WILLIAM J. ZIOBRO is associate professor of classics at the College of the Holy Cross in Worcester, Massachusetts, where he regularly teaches a course on classical America. He also served as secretary-treasurer of the American Philological Association from 1990 to 1997.

Index